Social Media for Academics

CHANDOS
SOCIAL MEDIA SERIES

Series Editors: Geoff Walton and Woody Evans
(emails: g.l.walton@staffs.ac.uk and kdevans@gmail.com)

This series of books is aimed at practitioners and academics involved in using social media in all its forms and in any context. This includes information professionals, academics, librarians and managers, and leaders in business. Social media can enhance services, build communication channels, and create competitive advantage. The impact of these new media and decisions that surround their use in business can no longer be ignored. The delivery of education, privacy issues, logistics, political activism and research rounds out the series' coverage. As a resource to complement the understanding of issues relating to other areas of information science, teaching and related areas, books in this series respond with practical applications. If you would like a full listing of current and forthcoming titles, please visit our website www.chandospublishing.com or email wp@woodheadpublishing.com or telephone +44 (0) 1223 499140.

New authors: we are always pleased to receive ideas for new titles; if you would like to write a book for Chandos in the area of social media, please contact Jonathan Davis, Commissioning Editor, on jonathan.davis@chandospublishing.com or telephone +44 (0) 1993 848726.

Bulk orders: some organisations buy a number of copies of our books. If you are interested in doing this, we would be pleased to discuss a discount. Please email wp@woodheadpublishing.com or telephone +44 (0) 1223 499140.

Social Media for Academics
A practical guide

EDITED BY
DIANE RASMUSSEN NEAL

Oxford Cambridge New Delhi

Chandos Publishing
Hexagon House
Avenue 4
Station Lane
Witney
Oxford OX28 4BN
UK
Tel: +44 (0) 1993 848726
Email: info@chandospublishing.com
www.chandospublishing.com

Chandos Publishing is an imprint of Woodhead Publishing Limited

Woodhead Publishing Limited
80 High Street
Sawston
Cambridge CB22 3HJ
UK
Tel: +44 (0) 1223 499140
Fax: +44 (0) 1223 832819
www.woodheadpublishing.com

First published in 2012

ISBN: 978-1-84334-681-4 (print)
ISBN: 978-1-78063-319-0 (online)

Chandos Social Media Series ISSN: 2050-6813 (print) and ISSN: 2050-6821 (online)

© The editor and contributors, 2012

British Library Cataloguing-in-Publication Data.
A catalogue record for this book is available from the British Library.

All rights reserved. No part of this publication may be reproduced, stored in or introduced into a retrieval system, or transmitted, in any form, or by any means (electronic, mechanical, photocopying, recording or otherwise) without the prior written permission of the Publishers. This publication may not be lent, resold, hired out or otherwise disposed of by way of trade in any form of binding or cover other than that in which it is published without the prior consent of the Publishers. Any person who does any unauthorised act in relation to this publication may be liable to criminal prosecution and civil claims for damages.

The publishers make no representation, express or implied, with regard to the accuracy of the information contained in this publication and cannot accept any legal responsibility or liability for any errors or omissions.

The material contained in this publication constitutes general guidelines only and does not represent to be advice on any particular matter. No reader or purchaser should act on the basis of material contained in this publication without first taking professional advice appropriate to their particular circumstances. Any screenshots in this publication are the copyright of the website owner(s), unless indicated otherwise.

Typeset by Domex e-Data Pvt. Ltd., India
Printed in the UK and USA.

Contents

List of figures and tables	xi
Acknowledgements	xv
About the editor	xvii
About the contributors	xix
Introduction by Diane Rasmussen Neal	xxiii

PART 1:	**THE NUTS AND BOLTS OF SOCIAL MEDIA FOR ACADEMICS**	**1**
1	**Blogging your academic self: the what, the why and the how long?**	3
	Carolyn Hank	
	Introduction	3
	Scholars in the blogosphere	4
	Motivations and benefits	5
	Blog publishing: getting started ... or getting more	7
	Your blog today? Tomorrow?	13
	Conclusions	17
	Notes	18
	References	18
2	**Non-academic and academic social networking sites for online scholarly communities**	21
	Anatoliy Gruzd	
	Introduction	21
	General public platforms for online scholarly communities	22
	Academic sites for online scholarly communities	28
	Conclusions	35

	Acknowledgements	36
	References	37
3	**Research and teaching in real time: 24/7 collaborative networks**	**39**
	Anabel Quan-Haase	
	Real-time technologies for academics	39
	The concept of real time	41
	Real-time technologies and research	42
	Real-time technologies and teaching	48
	Choosing a real-time technology	49
	Conclusions	53
	Acknowledgements	54
	Notes	54
	References	55
4	**Locating scholarly papers of interest online**	**59**
	Maureen Henninger	
	Introduction	59
	Overview of online scholarly search services	60
	Scholarly communication and social media	61
	Use and purpose of scholarly search services	62
	Impact of the Open Access movement	63
	Search engine functionality	65
	Social media and public scholarly search	79
	Conclusions	79
	Notes	80
	References	81
	Appendix: features of web-based public scholarly search services	82
5	**Tracking references with social media tools: organizing what you've read or want to read**	**85**
	Jackie Krause	
	Introduction	85
	Why use online social bibliographic tools?	87

	A look at top social bibliographic tools: Zotero, Mendeley, CiteULike and Connotea	93
	How these tools can improve your research, writing and collaboration	101
	How to choose the right tool for your needs	101
	Conclusions	103
	References	104
6	**Pragmatics of Twitter use for academics: tweeting in and out of the classroom**	**105**
	Lynne Y. Williams and Jackie Krause	
	What is Twitter? An introduction	105
	How can Twitter be used by academics?	107
	How to get started	108
	Research	110
	Teaching	113
	Professional branding	115
	'In the field': academics using Twitter	116
	Using Twitter to encourage professional engagement, connection and collaboration	118
	Is tweeting for you?	119
	References	120
7	**The academy goes mobile: an overview of mobile applications in higher education**	**123**
	Adam Craig	
	Introduction	123
	Leveraging the backchannel and immediate collaboration	125
	QR codes: creating linkages to online content in physical space	130
	Treading lightly in uncharted territory	136
	References	138

PART 2: PUTTING SOCIAL MEDIA INTO PRACTICE — 139

8 Incorporating web-based engagement and participatory interaction into your courses — 141

Maureen Henninger and Diane Rasmussen Neal

- Online engagement and interaction: what does it mean? — 141
- Choose the right tools for the job — 144
- Social networking services in the classroom: a case study — 149
- Wikis in the classroom — 151
- Tools for virtual conferences: a case study — 155
- Conclusions — 158
- Notes — 158
- References — 158

9 When good research goes viral! Getting your work noticed online — 161

Diane Rasmussen Neal

- Introduction — 161
- Social networking: Facebook, Twitter, LinkedIn, YouTube, and so on — 163
- Google, you and 'the filter bubble' — 167
- Official university pages: viral is not always better — 171
- Conclusions — 172
- References — 173

10 Who is the 'virtual' you and do you know who's watching you? — 175

Lynne Y. Williams

- Awareness of data privacy, digital footprints, maintaining separate work and personal online identities, and other types of identity concerns — 176
- What is an online identity? — 176
- What is privacy? — 177
- Data privacy and the 'virtual' you — 182
- Tracking your digital footprints — 188
- Keeping your work 'you' and your personal 'you' apart — 188

	What should you know in order to adequately protect all of your 'you's?	190
	References	191
11	**Social media for academic libraries**	**193**
	David J. Fiander	
	Introduction	193
	Overview of social media types and sites	194
	Creating a Facebook page	198
	Promoting and managing the library's Facebook page	201
	Social media policies and procedures	204
	Community acceptable behaviour policies	207
	Monitoring and interacting with your users	207
	Users must have persistent identifiers	208
	Identifying and stopping bad behaviour	208
	Conclusions	209
	Note	209
	References	210
12	**Learning social media: student and instructor perspectives**	**211**
	Robert Foster and Diane Rasmussen Neal	
	Introduction	211
	Designing and delivering a class in social media	213
	The students' motivations and expectations for the course	215
	The instructor's expectations	217
	Students' views about the course	218
	Students' take-aways from the course	220
	The instructor's take-aways from the course	222
	Conclusions from the student	224
	Conclusions from the instructor	225
	References	225
Index		**227**

List of figures and tables

Figures

I.1	Facebook status	xxv
2.1	AcademiaMap.com interface	25
2.2	Google+ circles, a feature that allows users to manually organize their contacts into groups	27
2.3	ResearchGate: recommendation page of researchers with similar research	29
2.4	ResearchGate: topic page on Open Source Scientific Software (OSSS)	30
2.5	Academia.edu: profile page	31
2.6	Academia.edu: visitors' statistics dashboard	32
2.7	rDmap for discovering collaborators and potential supervisors	34
3.1	Digital scholarship: be online or be irrelevant	40
3.2	Using hangouts for collaborative writing	44
3.3	Google Docs as a means for team writing, editing and commenting	46
4.1	Timeline of the release of online academic search engines	61
4.2	Web of Science citation report for the paper, As we may think, by Vannevar Bush	63
4.3	Web of Science interactive hyperbolic visualization of the forward and backward citation of a paper by Henry G. Small	64

4.4	Scopus search interface showing searchable metadata fields	66
4.5	Example of a citation analysis in the Google Scholar gadget	69
4.6	Example of a Google Scholar public profile	70
4.7	Display of results of an author search in Academic Search	71
4.8	Academic Search's co-citation, co-author path and citation graph for Henry G. Small	72
4.9	Rich searchable metadata options in Scirus	74
4.10	Scopus bibliometric visualizations: 1) h-index graph of 7 documents with self-citations removed, and 2) the SNIP (contextual citation impact) analysis of four journals	76
4.11	Web of Science options for filtering search results	78
4.12	Results of Web of Science query passed through to Scientific WebPlus	79
5.1	Zotero tag cloud	92
5.2	Zotero's main page	94
5.3	Mendeley's dashboard	96
5.4	CiteULike's portal page	99
5.5	Connotea's library view	100
7.1	Scanning pattern of one-dimensional vs. two-dimensional barcodes	130
7.2	RedLaser QR code scanner in use	134
8.1	Edmodo, a 'social' LMS	149
8.2	Mentoring service for first-year undergraduate students	150
8.3	A new information resource – Wiki: ECM in the cloud	153
8.4	Online presentation and peer evaluation	154
8.5	Elements of a student digital poster in a virtual conference	157
9.1	Search result list for 'Diane Rasmussen Neal' on *google.ca*	169

9.2	Google Scholar results for 'Diane Rasmussen Neal'	170
10.1	Top ten social networking sites by market share, August 2011	185
10.2	Instant personalization	186

Tables

3.1	A comparison of web-based collaborative writing tools	45
8.1	List of elements and tools incorporated into a digital poster presentation at a virtual conference	156

Acknowledgements

Because social media inherently involves connections to people, it amazes me to think about all the communities and individuals who have contributed to my expertise in this area as well as to the daily developments in the industry. I must thank first the people I talked to on Bulletin Board Systems, Usenet and ICQ that I accessed on campus as an undergraduate and with my noisy dial-up modem at home. I also thank the colleagues I worked with at the Central Texas Library System and the Northeast Texas Library System five or six years ago, who gave me numerous opportunities to train library staff on the powers and challenges of implementing social media in libraries. Currently, my colleagues and administrators at the Faculty of Information and Media Studies at The University of Western Ontario provide the perfect balance of professional autonomy and support so that I can teach social media classes with the pedagogical strategies that I choose as well as perform empirical research into this new age of communication. The American Society for Information Science and Technology, my professional home, has been a source of ideas surrounding social media development for many years now. Robert Foster, a Master of Library and Information Science student in my faculty and a student on two of my past courses, supplied encouraging editorial assistance as well as half of this book's final chapter. I must also thank the other authors of this book for their high-quality content. Finally, thanks go out to my friends and family for their loving support, although they do not all understand why I check my social media accounts every day, even on holidays!

About the editor

Diane Rasmussen Neal is an Assistant Professor in the Faculty of Information and Media Studies at The University of Western Ontario, and she holds the permanent title of Visiting Scholar at The University of Sydney in Sydney, Australia. She earned her information science degrees (MS 2001, Ph.D. 2006) from the University of North Texas. Additionally, she has been a systems librarian and a corporate information technology professional. Diane serves as an elected Director-at-Large (2012–14) of the American Society for Information Science and Technology (ASIS&T). Since 2007, she has taught professional workshops and university courses on the use of social media in libraries and other non-profit settings. Her research areas include analysing users' tagging of photographs and music as well as developing engaging, effective online mental health information resources for emerging adults. She has published in many peer-reviewed journals, including the *Journal of the Medical Library Association*, *Library & Information Science Research*, the *Journal of Information Science*, *Knowledge Organization*, and the *Journal of Library Metadata*. Her other new edited volume, *Indexing and Retrieval of Non-text Information*, will be published by DeGruyter Saur in 2012. A lifelong gamer and a haphazard blogger since 2005, she is currently the co-editor of the blog 'tl-dr.ca: where games and information collide'.

About the contributors

Adam Craig is a recent graduate of the Master of Library and Information Science programme at The University of Western Ontario and has a background in philosophy. Currently working as a branch manager in the Essex County Library system, his research interests include teen information literacy and best practices for library marketing and outreach. Adam is an active blogger and performer in the Windsor and Essex County music community.

David J. Fiander is the Web Services Librarian at The University of Western Ontario, where he has worked since 2000. David holds a Bachelor of Maths degree from the University of Waterloo and a Masters of Library and Information Science degree from the University of Western Ontario. At Western, David is responsible for the library's website and for tracking emerging technologies. David was a software developer for over a decade before becoming a librarian. He is active in the open source software development community, and has contributed to both the Evergreen and Koha ILS projects.

Robert Foster is a Master of Library and Information Science student in the Faculty of Information and Media Studies at The University of Western Ontario. He holds a Bachelor of Arts in Political Science degree from McMaster University. Robert's career has included over 20 years as a project management and information technology professional, having achieved a Project Management Professional (PMP) designation. He also has an active interest in politics, having been elected four times as a municipal councillor in the town of Lincoln, Ontario.

Anatoliy Gruzd is Director of the Social Media Lab at Dalhousie University and an Assistant Professor in the School of Information Management in the Faculty of Management and the Faculty of Computer Science where he teaches Information Policy, Information Management Systems, Digital Libraries, Data Mining, User Experience and Beyond Google. Dr Gruzd's current research explores how online social media and other Web 2.0 technologies are changing the ways in which people disseminate knowledge and information. In addition, he is also actively developing and testing new web tools for discovering and visualizing information and online social networks. The broad aim of his research is to provide researchers, managers and other information seekers with additional insights into the behaviours and attitudes of online network members and their relationships to each other. His work has appeared in numerous peer-reviewed journals and at a wide variety of conferences, including the *Journal of Education for Library and Information Science* (JELIS), the American Society for Information Science and Technology (ASIS&T), *Information Processing & Management* (IP&M), the Joint Conference on Digital Libraries (JCDL), the Hawaiian International Conference on System Sciences (HICSS), the International Network for Social Network Analysis (INSNA), GROUP and Networked Learning.

Carolyn Hank is an Assistant Professor in the School of Information Studies at McGill University. Dr Hank holds a Bachelor of Arts degree from the Department of Psychology at Antioch College, a Master in Library and Information Science from Kent State University and her Ph.D. in Information and Library Science from the University of North Carolina at Chapel Hill. Dr Hank's research interests include blog preservation, scholarly communication and new media, and information policy and social networks. In her current research, she examines ways in which our digital production behaviours impact future communications of our scholarly and cultural record, both in terms of informational value and impact and the associated technical and regulatory frameworks in which these activities take place. This perspective is particularly relevant when considering the need to negotiate between a climate of finite resources and the infrastructures required to support lifecycle management of digital content. She teaches in the areas of digital curation, digital preservation, human information interactions and research methods. Dr Hank's work has been presented at a variety of international conferences and in numerous publications.

Maureen Henninger has a Masters degree in Information Science and a Graduate Diploma in Information Management (Librarianship) and is currently a Senior Lecturer in Information and Knowledge Management at the University of Technology, Sydney. She has had extensive academic and professional experience in the storage and retrieval of digital information, particularly database design, and in information design. Maureen consults widely for industry, government and non-government organizations in these areas. She has been invited to speak at many conferences on digital information retrieval on a wide range of topics, including competitive intelligence, biomedical technology and government information. In her current academic position she has developed subjects in information design, investigative research, information architecture, digital libraries and digital curation. She is the coordinator of the undergraduate programme in information and media and is on the education committee of the Australian Library and Information Association. Maureen's research activities include web retrieval processes, digital libraries and data curation. For many years Maureen managed a successful continuing professional education programme at the University of New South Wales. She is the author of books about digital information retrieval, the latest of which is a second edition of *The Hidden Web*. Maureen plays an active role in the education of information professionals and in 2011 led the workplace sub-study for an Australian-wide research grant, 'Re-conceptualising and re-positioning Australian library and information science education for the 21st century'. Her current research interests are in data and information visualization, information design and usability issues.

Jackie Krause has spent over 35 years in the information technology field working for both large and small organizations as a business systems analyst and project manager. When looking to capitalize on sharing of knowledge among those participating in information technology projects, Jackie became fascinated with the notion of knowledge transfer in the workplace. Her dissertation topic included the transfer of knowledge through social media among those working in highly technical fields. Currently, Jackie is an Adjunct Professor in the School of Information Systems and Technology with Kaplan University. Jackie has been an adjunct instructor for over 18 years, teaching both face to face and online. She earned her doctorate in Applied Management and Decision Systems from Walden University (Ph.D., 2010). Her Masters is in Educational Technology from Pepperdine University (OMAET, 2004), where she developed a love for education, andragogy and all areas related to adult learning and development. Jackie volunteers for the Merlot Board (information technology) where she evaluates educational artefacts and enjoys presenting learning webinars for students. She is an avid user of screen casting and web cameras in both synchronous and asynchronous communications and is currently researching adult student engagement in the online classroom. In addition to student engagement, Jackie's research interests revolve around the use of social media in both organizations and student collaborative environments as a means of knowledge transfer. She blogs at *http://jackiekrause.wordpress.com*.

Anabel Quan-Haase is an Associate Professor at the Faculty of Information and Media Studies and the Department of Sociology, The University of Western Ontario. Dr Quan-Haase holds an M.Sc. in Psychology from Humboldt University, Berlin, and a Ph.D. in Information Studies from the University of Toronto. She is interested in the awareness and use of electronic resources by both students and faculty in all areas of the humanities for scholarship, networking and teaching. She is engaged in a project entitled 'The Role of Ebooks in Humanist Scholarship' with Kim Martin, which investigates the adoption of ebooks in the humanities and its impact on scholarship, teaching and reading for pleasure. She is also currently project leader of 'eNETS-H (Electronic Networks of Exchange and Tools for Scholarship in the Humanities)' in collaboration with Juan Luis Suárez and Kim Martin. Her current interests also lie in looking at how electronic resources are changing the nature of scholarship. One key interest focuses on how such factors as serendipity, insight and work routines are changed through technology. Her book, *Techno-Digital Society*, is scheduled to be published in 2012 by Oxford University Press. In 2010, she and Bernie Hogan from the Oxford Internet Institute published a double special issue on 'Social media: persistence and change' in the *Bulletin of Science, Technology, and Society*.

Lynne Y. Williams has more than 20 years' experience in information technology, both academically and professionally. She has worked as a computer graphics designer for Los Alamos National Laboratory, a systems administrative consultant for Butler Contracting, and as an instructional technologist for the Title V Grant programme at the University of New Mexico, Los Alamos. Currently teaching at Kaplan University, Dr Williams also taught at Northern New Mexico Community College and Santa Fe Community College, and still teaches in a part-time capacity for the University of New Mexico, Los Alamos. Dr Williams received her undergraduate degree in fine arts, with an emphasis on painting and printmaking, from New Mexico State University, a Master of Science in Network Architecture and Design from Capella University, and a Doctorate of Philosophy in Information Technology Management, with a security emphasis, from Capella University. Her research interests include cybercrime and cyberlaw, the ethics of personal information aggregation and other topics related to how humans use or are affected by networks.

Introduction

Diane Rasmussen Neal

What is social media?

These days, it seems we cannot escape mentions of the popular online services that comprise social media. Television news anchors tell us to learn more about their stories by following them on Twitter. Our favourite local coffee shop displays a sign at the register, inviting customers to 'Like us on Facebook.' Charlie Sheen tweets that he's #winning, and the world talks about it. We learn that citizens of countries whose governments are in upheaval use social media to organize grassroots political efforts. The song 'Friday', performed by an unknown 13-year-old girl, garnered 167 million views on YouTube, and Ms Black's name was the '#1 fastest rising search on Google in 2011' (Google, 2011, para. 2).

Social media – and its sister term, 'Web 2.0' – are difficult to define, because there is little agreement about what they mean. My view, in the simplest terms possible, is that these phrases refer to the many easy-to-use services that anyone can use to interact with other people online. For example, when you watch and/or comment on a YouTube video, 'Like' a friend's Facebook update and read your colleague's blog, you are using social media. In the pioneer days of the World Wide Web, we had to put content online by writing HyperText Markup Language (HTML) files, which is what is used to display a web page in an Internet browser. (HTML is still necessary for website development, but we don't have to know the code to put our content online.) That old-school approach to creating web pages is known as 'Web 1.0', in which HTML was created and posted for one-way communication: from the website developer to the people reading the site, not the other way around. For example, if the BBC posts a news article online for people to read – and that's it – that is considered Web 1.0 technology. If the BBC allows readers to comment on the story, then that might be considered a Web 2.0 approach to information dissemination. Social media websites such as Facebook, YouTube and Twitter exist based on people's ability to post, share and view one another's thoughts, links to interesting web pages and other online content such as blog posts, videos, photographs, tweets and – yes – even old-fashioned Web 1.0-style pages.

With today's easy-to-use social media tools, creating an online presence is as easy as signing up for a Facebook account, which is a two-minute process. Or, on Twitter, type in a tweet such as 'I am looking forward to grading the 150 papers piled on my desk' – and you've created web content! Your Twitter followers can respond to you just as easily by tweeting back to you, 'No! Don't grade until you've had a glass of wine!' There are, of course, web programmers who create the technologies behind these sites, but the advent of Web 2.0/social media means that the rest of us don't have to know what they know in order to create online content.

Of course, the idea of easily communicating with each other online did not come about just when early social networking sites such as MySpace and Friendster ramped up in the early 2000s. When I was an undergraduate student in the early 1990s, I used technologies such as bulletin board systems, ICQ and Usenet to talk to people daily. (I even dated a few men I met online; the Internet was a young female geek's oyster in those days.) Thanks to the rapid improvements in hardware and web-based information provisions, 'social media' is now in the mainstream. According to the web metrics company alexa.com, the top three sites on the web are Google, Facebook and YouTube, respectively.

When I lecture on social media, I always emphasize that it is ultimately not about the technology itself; it's about *connections between people*. I do not believe that social media isolates us because it glues us to a computer screen or a smartphone; I believe it brings us together in remarkable ways. I've happily found old friends through Facebook, learned that other people do in fact like the same obscure 1980s bands I like via YouTube, and told people I was going to bed ridiculously early on Twitter. These small exchanges are not always necessarily life-changing (which is why sceptics argue that they are a 'waste of time'), but they keep us in touch and they can in fact be extremely meaningful. When my wonderful father died in 2010, the tremendous support I received as a result of sharing the moments leading up to his death with my Facebook friends was invaluable. Even with the physical presence of my family and closest university colleagues around me at that time,

I would have felt so much more alone through that horrible time without my virtual social network surrounding me. Facebook changes its news feed, its privacy policies and its profile pages constantly, and people get angry about it, but they keep coming back and new accounts are added every day. Why? That's where their friends are. Figure I.1 shows my Facebook status on my final day of editing this manuscript:

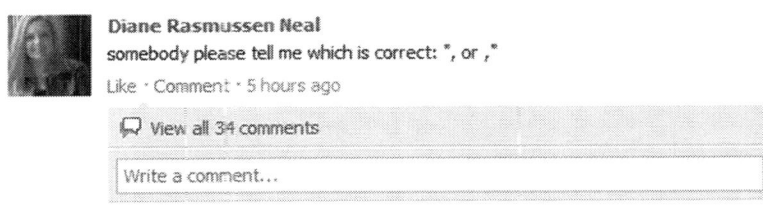

Figure I.1 Facebook status

Wow! – 34 comments on one silly status! (Not all of the comments were from me.) Commenters included people who are contributors to this book, colleagues at various universities who knew about this book and librarians who just enjoy talking about things like citation styles and punctuation quandaries on Sunday mornings.

As another exemplar of social media use, my contributors and I created this book largely using a Google Docs site; instead of emailing endless versions around, it was all on one shared site. Google Docs files live in 'the cloud'. Cloud computing, a term you will see throughout this book, is used to describe all the online services that store your content and make it available on demand. Using the cloud means you don't have to worry about hard drive crashes, USB drives gone missing, or other predicaments that cause traumatic data loss. Your data is perhaps safest in the cloud – in the sense that it's saved on a professionally managed and backed-up server. But, those companies that run the servers – whether it's Google, Facebook, Amazon, or any other cloud-based site – sometimes do things with your data that compromise your privacy; see Chapter 10 of this book for more details. (Hint: a site's privacy policy is, in my words, an anti-privacy policy.)

Social media is emergent; it's exciting; it evolves faster than any of us can imagine. This book will be outdated as soon as I finish this sentence. Even my students and I cannot keep up with the changes, and we don't try to do so. But, the precepts and the abstractions that support the backbone of social media as a phenomenon – and as a societal game-changer – will not go away anytime soon. For this reason, I believe that the concepts presented in this book will remain relevant even if Facebook goes bankrupt while the book is in press!

Why should academics care about social media?

We have so many reasons to care! In the process of educating our students, we need to incorporate social technologies into our classes and our student communications. Students already exist in the social media world – just pay attention to how many of them are attached to Facebook on their laptops as you walk around the student centre – but they do not necessarily know how to use social technologies effectively. I spend a lot of time pondering what my 22-year-old second cousin (an amicable, intelligent undergraduate at the University of Michigan) told me recently, during a fleeting moment when he was not texting: 'Email is for old people.' Additionally, in our research endeavours, we can utilize social media to share our work with our colleagues and work collaboratively in more efficient ways.

The tricks lie in knowing what tools are available, deciding what tools suit your personal needs and personal style, and then using them as your preferences dictate. I edited this book to help you determine these variables in your practice as an academic, regardless of your field. (Our universities have different needs as organizational entities. Those needs are beyond the scope of this volume.) Whether you are a chemistry professor, a linguistics professor, or an engineering professor, this book is for you. Social media can unite us all.

Part 1 of this book, 'The nuts and bolts of social media for academics', explores specific uses and practical tips for getting started with a variety of social technologies. We start with blogs, perhaps a more traditional bread-and-butter form of social media (if there is such a thing), and one which we should not neglect to consider. Next, we provide an overview of social networking websites that can be used to grow and nurture your own scholarly community; networking isn't just for conferences anymore! We also discuss social tools that we can use for collaborative work; once we can learn to move beyond the scores of email that plague our lives, research collaborations become more productive and more pleasant. The next chapter describes how to find scholarly papers online with a variety of advanced search tools and strategies; if this gets too technical for you, see your local librarian for assistance. This is followed by a chapter outlining methods to keep track of your references online using social media tools specially designed for this purpose – yes, there are *many* apps for that! We give special consideration to Twitter with its own chapter, because there are many particulars and peculiarities on Twitter that call for special attention. The last chapter in Part 1 explores a variety of uses for mobile devices in higher education, such as Android-based smartphones and iPads.

Part 2, 'Putting social media into practice', blends these nuts and bolts together into creative packaging. Part 2 opens with a chapter on choosing and implementing Web 2.0 tools for student engagement, whether your students are solely online or traditional students attempting to find their way at university. I then provide a chapter on making your research go 'viral', or wildly popular, on the web. A scary but necessary chapter on online privacy and identity concerns follows. The penultimate chapter is provided just for academic librarians. Finally, the book concludes with a chapter that one of my former students and I co-authored on teaching and learning social media via *only* social media.

All the contributors to this book have significant, relevant knowledge in their respective areas of social media. Some chapters are more academically grounded than others, but all provide useful tips that you can start using *today* in your own daily work. The contributors represent a necessary mix of students, academics who are prolific researchers, and other academics who focus more on teaching. We present a diverse scope of knowledge within information science and information technology, and we all believe in the enormous potential of social media in academic settings.

I hope this book ignites sparks of inspiration and ideas for you. You don't have to be a 'techie' to use Web 2.0 tools; in fact, the opposite is true. It would not be possible to include every social media website, every *type* of social media tool, or social media's every potential academic use within this volume. By the time this book is in print, the social media world will have changed drastically. But it is that energy behind the technology – and, especially, the meaningful connections I foster with the friends and colleagues who use it with me every day – that fuels my enthusiasm for the potential of Web 2.0 (and whatever comes next) each morning without fail. Thank you for reading this book; use it in whatever way is meaningful to you. I'll look for you online, but I might not read your old-fashioned email.

Further reading

O'Reilly, T. (2005) 'What is Web 2.0: design patterns and business models for the next generation of software'. Retrieved from *http://oreilly.com/web2/archive/what-is-web-20.html*.

O'Reilly, T. and Battelle, J. (2009) 'Web squared: Web 2.0 five years on'. Retrieved from *http://www.web2summit.com/web2009/public/schedule/detail/10194*.

References

Google (2011) 'Google zeitgeist 2011'. Retrieved from *http://www.googlezeitgeist.com/en/top-searches/rebecca_black*.

Part 1
The nuts and bolts of social media for academics

Blogging your academic self: the what, the why and the how long?

Carolyn Hank

Abstract: Blogging emerged as a novel channel for communication, but considering the ubiquity of blogs today, the idea of this channel being 'new' seems, well, a bit old. Blogs are everywhere, and the blogs of scholars are no exception. It might be more accurate to think of the form as evolved, since informal modes of communication are a staple of academe. This chapter is intended to benefit those considering personal blogs for communicating their own scholarly works and ideas, highlighting motivations to blog, rewards from blogging and tips for getting started. It is also intended to benefit those in the early majority already blogging, as both a refresher and confirmation of blogging strategies and benefits, as well as a twist – presenting issues and tips in regard to blog access and availability, both now and into the future.

Key words: web blogs, scholarly communication, benefits, preservation, back-up.

Introduction

Many blogging academics report a wide variety of motivations to blog. For many, it is to quickly communicate their ideas and research to wider audiences than might be possible through formal publications, like the peer-reviewed journal article or (conveniently enough) the book chapter. A variety in motivation is coupled by variety in academic bloggers' topical treatments, styles and approaches. And it gets to a bit of the challenge (and a bit of the fun) in discussing the blogs of academics. The blogosphere is immense. Technorati (2011), the largest blog directory in the world, indexes nearly 1.3 million blogs. While there has been much anecdotal reporting on academics' adoption of blogs, available across a range of disciplines, no exhaustive, complete inventory of academic blogs or bloggers exists. The sheer size of the blogosphere does not lead to simply a 'needle in a haystack' scenario. Considering the variety in academic blogs and bloggers and the low barrier of entry for publication, it is more akin to a chameleon in a haystack. Blogs are added, deleted and forgotten on a daily basis. Lifespans vary, from blogs that are active – added to, modified and maintained – for mere days or weeks, to blogs remaining active for years.

Scholars in the blogosphere

Several neologisms have emerged to describe academics in the blogosphere, such as bloggership (Caron, 2006) and the blogademia (Saper, 2006). Consider some of these fairly straightforward titles, taken from a directory of academic blogs: 'Information Processing'; 'Quantum Quandaries'; 'Discursive Philosophical Thought'; and 'Finance and the Public Interest'. Now, how about these: 'Eat the Dogs: On Science, History, and Exploration'; 'Blog Them Out of the Stone Age, Steamboats are Ruining Everything'; and even, 'Another Boring Academic has a Blog'. Following our primary school advice to not judge a book by its cover, we might also want to resist judging an academic's blog by its header.

While no comprehensive inventory exists, there are ways to go about identifying blogging academics. You could simply visit departmental and individual faculty websites and have a look around. However, considering that blogs have diversity in form, styles, topicality and audience, identification as such may depend on navigational and identification clues provided by the blogger or host, or you may have to interpret for yourself whether it merits qualification. There are some tell-tale hallmarks of the medium. Blog posts are typically displayed in reverse chronological order and support a range of object types and formats, including text, images, audio and video. Content published to the blog may be original to the blog or represent work originating elsewhere. Blogs support interactivity, such as through a commenting system and trackback features. They typically also support access controls to further refine interaction scenarios, such as password protection mechanisms.

In seeking out the blogs of academics, there is also a 'birds of a feather' effect. Have a look at an academic blogger's blogroll. More often than not, this will lead to another academic's blog (and another, and another, and so on). However, to take a more systematic approach to understanding the extent of blog publishing by academics, two important sources are academic blog directory listings and networks of scholar blogs. Networks are distinguished as an aggregate of blogs at one location that are typically organized by topical treatment or institutional affiliation, and, also typically, are organizationally-sponsored, such as by a publisher or a university. Just a few examples include the Law Professor Blogs, the Scientific American Blog Network and ScienceBlogs. Blog directory listings provide an index of academic blogs compiled for various reasons, such as topical treatment. For example, the Fourth Annual ABA Journal Blawg 100 is a listing of legal scholarships blogs, or *blawgs*, of merit (McDonough and Randag, 2010).

With all of these blogs, who are these academic bloggers then? The academic bloggers responding to my own study were found across all levels of professional age, real age, faculty rank, tenure status and publication and service history (Hank, 2011). The majority were tenured faculty, employed at the associate professor rank or higher. Nearly all blogged under their real names rather than pseudonymously. So, have a look around, as an academic blogger may very well be your colleague across the hall.

Motivations and benefits

Returning to motivations, two commonly reported are the sharing of professional experiences and ideas with peers and the general public, and to foster and build networks among an audience of readers, both the known and the unknown. Academics' blog posts and topics may not relate exclusively to research, teaching and service. Just as motivations to blog are not mutually exclusive, nor is blog style, as found by White and Winn (2009). Bloggers tend to identify their blogs as both personal and professional.

When considered within the system of scholarly communication, an obvious question is whether a blog is a publication or, worded another way, does it qualify as scholarship? In my own study, eight out of ten scholars felt their blogs were a component of their scholarly records (Hank, 2011). Further, nearly seven out of ten scholars agreed that their blogs satisfied the parameters of scholarship for 'unpublished scholarly outcomes and publications', identified by Braxton et al. (2002) as 'public, subject to critical review, and in a form that allows use and exchange by other members of the scholarly community' (p. 141). Blogs can also be seen to be a link in a chain of scholarship and communication. A majority of respondents to my study reported that their blogs led to invitations to publish, present, provide service and collaborate.

Impact was also felt in other ways. A majority of scholars in my study felt their blogging had a positive impact across different aspects of their scholarly lives, including:

1. their creativity in examining research in new ways;
2. the overall quality of their research;
3. the quality and efficiency of their writing;
4. the quality of their teaching; and
5. their ability to share pre-publication materials with colleagues.

Further, nearly all respondents reported that blogging contributed to their enjoyment of their work as a scholar and improved visibility (Hank, 2011).

The one aspect of scholarly life that respondents did not feel improved as a result of their blogging was opportunities for promotion at their respective institutions. However, their blogs also did not impair these opportunities. Most felt that their blogs had no impact in regard to promotion. Several offered strategies, gained from personal experience as well as the experience of peers, for presenting blogs when up for tenure or review. The first was to emphasize the blog in regard to the requirement for service. The second was to apply Google Analytics, or a similar tool, to demonstrate the audience and reach of your blog (if you think it is demonstrable enough to show favourably on you). And third, it was recommended that one quantify invitations resulting from blogging. While these can be categorized, as mentioned earlier, to publish, present, serve and collaborate, specific examples of these invitations and resulting activities and publications might include:

- *Publishing*: for example, monographs, textbooks and chapters; peer-reviewed journal articles and conference papers; other scholarly papers and essays; commentary and opinion pieces; book reviews.
- *Presenting*: for example, keynotes and plenary sessions; conference panels and paper sessions; workshops and tutorials; guest lectures.
- *Service*: for example, professional association leadership roles and committees; conference committees; editorial boards; peer-review.

- *Collaboration*: for example, research projects, grant monies; count of collaborators, including institutional affiliations and geographic locations, if different from your own.

Blog publishing: getting started ... or getting more

While academics either new to blogging or considering starting a blog might be a bit hesitant joining this late in the game, late is not 'too late'. Blogging isn't going away just yet. Approximately six out of ten scholars blog about the same amount of time or more compared to when they first began to blog (ibid.).

The growth in blogging is attributed to many catalysts, one being the availability of free, easy-to-use blog publishing and hosting services. There are a range of publishing and hosting options, from application- or hosting-only tools and services to application and hosting services, either free or fee-based. Further, blog software programs may be provided as an exclusive application or in addition to a suite of applications. A clear majority of bloggers use a free blog publishing and hosting service, such as Blogger or WordPress.com. Some universities and colleges provide their own institutional blog hosting service. A minority take a homegrown approach, building the application and hosting it on their own servers.

And you may not use just one of these options. Blogger to blog is not necessarily a 1:1 ratio. Blogs may be published to by just one person, or be published to by a group of primary authors, referred to here as co-blogs. Bloggers may also publish to more than one blog, as reported by over four out of ten respondents in my study (ibid.). For example, an academic might publish to a blog for which they are the only author, then also contribute to a co-blog with colleagues from other institutions as well as maintain a teaching blog for communicating with students.

When choosing where and how to blog, think of the features and functions that are essential for you, with some questions below to get you started:

- *Do you want to go it alone, or invite others to join in?* If the latter, blog publishing applications and hosting services typically allow for multiple people to publish to a blog. Make sure whatever application you choose supports this.

- *Do you want to pay for it?* Obviously, your time is a valued resource that you spend on blogging, but consider whether you want to use a free or fee-based service. While blog subscription or hosting costs are typically low, such costs may impact which option you choose.
- *Where do you want to blog from?* Blog applications support a range of options for publishing to your blog, such as directly through a blog editor feature, or through email and your mobile devices. Consider the different ways you may want to publish to your blog and check to make sure the applications you are considering support these.
- *What features are essential to you?* So, are you ready to publish everything to the open web, or do you want to restrict access to your blog, in part or in whole? Do you want to allow commenting on all, some or none of your posts? Blogs support a variety of user interface elements. White and Winn (2009) identified 13 common blog tools, reporting that bloggers use, on average, seven of these tools. The most common are commenting systems, post-archiving by date or category, and built-in syndication. Other common features include search utilities, assigning posts to more than one category, trackbacking, support for video and photos, collaborative authorship, Twitter or other real-time update applications, mobile updating tools, blogrolls and a variety of widgets in support of other functions. What application and the associated features you choose will be informed by what you do – and don't want to do – with your blog.

These features are not exhaustive. There are many other features to consider. Experiment and explore. I selected a particular layout for one of my now-defunct blogs once that did not allow me to remove the commenting system. As I wanted to publish some static pages, such as an 'about page' and a 'disclaimer' page, I didn't just want to turn off the commenting feature, I wanted to make it invisible on those particular pages. After some experimentation and exploration, I ultimately went with another design.

Changing the design and layout of your blog, including adding or deleting features, is a given. And whether you are starting a blog or are a current blogger, whatever service and hosting option you choose may not be the only option you stay with during the lifetime of your blog. Approximately three out of ten scholars reported migrating, or moving, their respective blogs from one host location to another – and for some, more than once (Hank, 2011). For a few others, the migration was done for them by, for example, their service providers, blog network or co-bloggers.

And remember, you are entering into a co-dependent relationship when you blog, whether with a blog publishing application and hosting service provider, a managed blog network, or your institution's own blog publishing service. Read the Terms of Service (TOS) agreements before subscribing to a service or agreeing to participate in a network. Are these terms you can live with? For example, we are aware of copyright issues when submitting our works to traditional publishers. Blogs also present our works, so considerations on what you can do with your content, as well as what you are agreeing to let providers do with it, may impact with whom and how you choose to publish a blog.

And still on the conventions of traditional publishing, we publish by our real names and we cite and credit the work of others that informs our own. Consider how you will incorporate these conventions into your blog writing. Blog publishing allows pseudonymous authorship which, depending on how you manage your online identity, might be more akin to anonymous authorship. However, a clear majority of scholars do identify themselves by their real names, along with other personal identifiers, such as field of study, professional role and place of employment (ibid.). This is typically achieved through a sidebar 'about' statement or a separate 'about' page. Consider publishing such a brief biography to your own blog. Such disclosure may contribute to awareness of your credibility and authority among your blog readers.

Also, give credit where credit is due. Blogs allow us to easily borrow or reuse content originating somewhere else. While formal citations crediting such use are not the norm in blogs, there should, at minimum, be an acknowledgment of the originating source. This is not just good academic practice, it is good blogging practice. Tim O'Reilly (2007) initiated the drafting of a 'Blogger's code of conduct'. You may want to check to see if your home institution or service provider has its own blogging code of conduct or other regulation or guidance documents, in addition to what is found in any TOS agreements.

Whatever codes of conduct you choose to follow or TOS agreements you agree to, listed below are a few suggestions on policies or other statements you may want to incorporate into your academic blog to help your readers, whether regular or occasional, make use of your blog. Such statements may be explicit (e.g., a distinct 'policies' or similarly named page) or implicit (e.g., included in a broad description of a blog's overall scope and intent, as typically found in an 'about' page).

- *Who can do what with what?* A copyright statement is a common feature of most blogs, typically appearing in the footer. While you may want to claim copyright to the content posted to your blog, it limits others' ability to make use of what is on your blog. So, consider incorporating a Creative Commons licence. And consider making this applicable not only to original content you post to the blog, but also to contributions your readers might make, typically via commenting. See the Digital Curation blog (*http://digitalcuration.blogspot.com/*) for one such example.

- *How to, and who can, comment?* In addition to addressing comments and use rights, you may also want to consider the inclusion of a commenting policy to inform commenters of how you plan to manage any comments, as well as set the tone for what is – and what is not – acceptable, and how unacceptable comments will be treated. Such a policy might address issues related to your moderation (i.e., reviewing, editing, deleting), eligibility (i.e., whether anonymous comments are allowed or not) and tone and language (i.e., no cursing, no name-calling, no spam).

- *Who is responsible for the blog's content?* This may seem an obvious answer; that is, you. But, is your institution responsible as well, if you've made your affiliation known to your readers? Or, say you are a blogging legal scholar, does your content represent legal advice? From a reading of a handful of disclaimer-style statements posted to legal scholarship 'blawgs', the answer is no. Consider including such a disclaimer-style statement on your own blog, regardless of your topical treatment. It might include a statement to the effect that the opinions expressed in your posts are your own and do not represent those of others. Those 'others' may include your employers, home institution, funders, blog network or other sponsoring organization and, as found on one blog, even the blogger's own previously held opinions. Statements might make clear that the blog content does not constitute advice, whether medical, legal, investment, or otherwise. There are several examples of disclaimer-style language for content, whether original to you or linked or taken from other sources. For example, the blogger (and co-bloggers, if applicable) are not responsible for content, do not guarantee it is correct, and may not even necessarily agree with it. One blog disclaimer statement I reviewed addressed issues of confidentiality, stating that there was no guarantee communications made with the blogger would remain confidential, and another blogger addressed issues of privacy, stating that person(s)

described on the blog represented composites of people, unless specifically identified.
- *There today, gone (or modified) tomorrow.* Blogs are constantly changing. Not only are new posts published, but previously published posts might be modified or even deleted. A statement addressing such editing might be appropriate, though this is not a policy-style statement typical to most blogs. Such a statement might describe conditions under which posts may be edited with – or without – acknowledgement of such change. For example, one blog's editing policy is that no acknowledgement is made if edits are presentation-related (i.e., spelling errors or other style-related edits), but if a post is determined to be 'too misleading to leave posted', or, 'if we change our minds about something, we will fess up or just move on, but we won't be sneaky about it'. Otherwise, posts will remain posted, even if 'we later regret it' (The Conglomerate, n.d., para. 2). A blog editing statement might also describe how such edits or modifications will be made known to readers. For example, as related at one blog, any change to a previously published post is listed at the bottom of that respective post, with a short description of why and when such change was made.

Getting noticed

There are lots of ways to bring attention to your blog (and, working in the reverse, these can be ways to avoid if you are not seeking to draw attention). Readers find their way to your blog through many paths. Think of the variety of ways you have found blogs (e.g., mentions in articles, interviews, or in other blog posts; blogrolls; institutional faculty pages or personal websites; business cards; faculty biographies posted to conference programmes or in publications, etc.) Consider these experiences as opportunities for yourself.

And there are things you can do to keep readers aware of your blog postings and other doings, with syndication services, such as Really Simple Syndication (RSS), a primary method. RSS allows automatic syndication. It benefits you as a blog author, allowing you to draw attention to your blog by making the content available in XML format through a variety of feed, or aggregator, services. Basically, you can deliver content to your readers, such as through email, rather than requiring them to directly visit your blog's website. And as a blog reader, RSS allows you to subscribe to other bloggers' feeds to stay aware of new content published to the blog without having to visit each respective blog site. There are several RSS or feed services you can consider using, both in your blog publishing and blog reading activities. Google Reader (*http://www.google.com/reader*) is one example of a popular feed subscription service. Also, be aware of Atom (*http://www.atomenabled.org*) as well. Atom is another syndication format, developed as an alternative to RSS, though RSS is more commonly used. And, if you do tweet (or plan to tweet), you can syndicate your Twitter account with your blog to draw more traffic. See Chapter 6 for more about Twitter.

To raise your blog's exposure, seek out blog indexing and search services, such as Technorati.com, or academic blog directories. A simple Google search will lead you to different indexes and directories where you can request that your blog be listed. Maybe you cross-publish posts between different blogs you publish to, and something found on one leads to regular reading of the other. Being listed or mentioned in others' blogs, whether through a blogroll or from a mention in other bloggers' posts, with trackbacks to your own, may lead to new readers discovering your blog. The opportunities for exposure are many. Simply summarized, promote your blog – using a number of channels and avenues available to you – if you want to draw readers. And, if you don't, well, you can take some action to reduce traffic, such as asking to be de-listed in whatever directories or indexes your blog is found. There are, of course, limits to how much control one has over how your blog is linked and indexed on the web. However, enabling access controls at your blog, such as through password-protection mechanisms, can at least serve to prevent your blog from being read, even if found.

Getting over it

While blogging may capture your attention now, what about in the future? While disruptions of service may take you out of the blogging game briefly (as was the recent experience of those subscribing to Blogger), what of disruptions to our own lives? Our schedules change, our priorities change, our interests change. There may come a point in your blogging life where you want to take a break. It is recommended that you communicate such starts and stops, whether for now or forever, to your readers. If a short-term break, a simple 'I'll be back' message, à la the Terminator, would suffice, though more information, such as an approximation of when, may be helpful to your readers. There might come a point, as well, when you want that break to be a permanent one.

As academics, we don't typically end an article, book, or conference presentation halfway through, leaving our readers and audiences hanging; nor do we have to with our blogs. Lawrence Lessig provides a great example of a last post, letting his readers know about the discontinuation, or in his words, 'hibernation', of his blog (Lessig, 2009). And, if you are stopping your blog, you may want to consider whether you will leave it up, letting your inactive blog fend for itself in a sort of blogosphere purgatory, or if you want to delete it. Keep in mind that even if you stop publishing to a blog, it doesn't mean others, like blog spam bots, won't try to. The blog you leave behind today, with all of its insightful posts and informational content, might look like a giant advertisement for things both savoury and unsavoury in the future.

Your blog today? Tomorrow?

Whatever reasons motivate you to blog, whether personal, professional, or a little bit of both, or whatever your thoughts on the legitimacy, value and impact of blogs within the system of scholarly communication, the form itself presents its own set of challenges when considering that a hallmark characteristic of the scholarly record is that it be cumulative. Borgman (2007) succinctly comments on the emergence of informal digital communications, such as blogs, noting, 'they can be captured because digital communications leave a trace' (p. 99).

These communications may leave a trace, but when considering the nature of the blog form as well as the technical, regulatory and social frameworks in which blogging takes place, for how long? Without either deliberate personal and/or programmatic approaches to the long-term stewardship of these digital communications, the scholar blogs of today may be unavailable in the future. And not only in the future, but even today. We have probably all experienced losing a work-in-progress or some other digital document (e.g., a spreadsheet, or lecture slides from a couple of years back). With our blogs, potential for loss is further complicated due to their co-produced form.

While we might think of 'blogging as one's personal printing press', as aptly described by an interviewee in my study, the 'personal' element does not imply an independent printing press. Blogs are most definitely a co-dependent form, representing a mix of code, content and co-creators, the latter including – to name a few – bloggers, both the known and anonymous, blog commentators and service providers. This multiplicity of co-creators complicates blog preservation actions and raises a number of questions, not just in regard to issues as to what elements of blogs should be preserved, but, also, what elements can actually be preserved when considering the technical and regulatory landscape in which blogging takes place?

Bloggers in general, as Viegas (2005) reported, assume the persistency of their blogs unless deliberate action is taken by bloggers to remove their respective blog. Even if no longer maintained, it is assumed the blog will still be available via search engine caches. This assumes no other influences impacting service. We might not think Google will go dark one day, forever, taking Blogger with it, or that the Internet Archive's Wayback Machine,[1] with its vast collection of blogs being just one of the content types presented, will just disappear. I am not so 'Henny Penny, the world is ending'. I can't imagine the web without Google or the Internet Archive (and nor do I want to). But isn't a proactive approach to your blog content better than leaving things to chance? Garrett and Waters (1996), in a seminal report on digital preservation, identified content creators as the first line of defence. So, consider what you are doing, or might do, from the front line in respect to your blog.

Before going further, I think it is important to point out a distinction in terminology between 'back-up' and preservation, as well as those other related terms we might hear, including web archiving and digital archiving. Simply, back-up is used here to imply keeping content available and safe in the immediate use environment (the now) as well as into the short-term future. Preservation, however, implies access and use in the indefinite future, which might be a mighty, mighty long time. The goals of digital preservation have been succinctly described by Caplan (2008) as to get, describe, interpret, secure, authenticate, access and perform. These goals, respectively, necessitate a consideration of a triage of actions and approaches, when treated in the aggregate, to facilitate long-term preservation. A fuller treatment of these issues is beyond the scope of this chapter, but it does merit mentioning that many projects are currently ongoing to develop web archiving solutions.

So, depending on your preference – to keep or not to keep; in the short-term future or the long – I'd advise you to have a look around, as someone may very well already being doing it for you. Namely, the Internet Archive, through its Wayback Machine, which has been collecting blogs as part of a broader web archiving programme begun in 1996. Another example of an active, dedicated 'blawg' archiving programme is the Library of Congress' Legal Blawgs Web Archive, begun in 2007. You don't have to go it alone. You may want to look into whether there is a service or programme already available to you, maybe locally, through your home institution, such as a digital repository or archiving programme. Or through a national cultural heritage institution, such as the Library of Congress in the United States. Or, also, through a third-party provider blog back-up or archiving service. And remember the earlier reference to Creative Commons licences.[2] The application of such licences to your blogs may help in sending the message to services, and their crawlers, working in support of archiving, as to what use they are permitted to make of your blog.

Whether you are more inclined to take personal action to preserve your blog or to let someone else take some action for you (or a combination of both approaches), there is no single best strategy, regardless if intent is for back-up or preservation. There's an aptly named digital preservation initiative and open-source software application that provides some fundamental advice for those interested in the sustainability of their digital content, in whatever form it takes: LOCKSS, or Lots Of Copies Keeps Stuff Safe (*http://www.lockss.org*). The approach has been described as preservation by proliferation. A combination of strategies, for those inclined to keep their blogs of today available into tomorrow, is recommended. Further, you may want to consider what elements of your blog are most important for you to keep. While the default may be the entire blog, go back and have a look at your TOS agreements. Issues of copyright are much too grand – and challenging – to address here. But just be aware that while you may hold copyright to the content you post to your blog, it is a co-produced medium. What about the actual application and code itself? And again, what about the content originating elsewhere or posted to your blog by others? Intellectual property rights is a giant, thorny beast, but as any attempt to back-up or preserve your blog entails the basic act of copying, it is one we should be mindful of, though to what extent is debatable, particularly from a personal preservation perspective. Back-up of your blog does not necessarily mean you want to keep it all. Maybe you are only interested in the content of your posts, or maybe only select posts rather than all posts. Maybe you want to keep all the comments associated with the posts, or only some of them, or even none. The point is, we may not want to keep it all. Consider what you think will be useful into the future, both for your own access and use as well as for whomever else you think might benefit from such access and use. We could probably all agree that we live in an era of a surplus of recorded information. Managing all of the content we have available to us now is challenging. Considerations on what to keep and what not to keep, while they won't alleviate these challenges into the future, may at least provide some relief, however mild, from seeking out the good and useful from the not so useful (or not at all useful) in the future.

From my work on the back-up and preservation preferences and practices of bloggers, a variety of approaches have been identified. You may want to consider how you might incorporate one or more of these into your regular blog maintenance activities.

- *Subscribe to a web or blog archiving or back-up service.* And 'subscribe' is used loosely here. For example, maybe your blog is not listed on the Internet Archive's Wayback Machine but you would like it to be. You can take action to enable its web crawler to pick up your blog. There are also free and fee-based blog back-up services, such as Backupify, BlogBackupr and BackupMyBlog.

- *Use export tools provided by your blog service provider.* Most blog publishing and hosting services offer an export tool for your blog. That way, you can make and maintain your own back-ups whenever you want.

- *Do your own personal back-ups.* You can also do your own personal back-ups using a variety of techniques, such as a blog back-up utility,[3] database dump or other manual back-up. You can store these back-ups to a variety of locations, such as a personal server, institutional server, your workstation, removable storage media, out on the cloud[4] or a number of other local or remote storage locations. And, depending on your personal preference, you may very well want to back-up the back-up to another location as well. Again, lots of copies keeps stuff safe.

- *Use back-up services provided at your institution.* These back-up services can take many forms. Check with your institutional IT departments as well as your library or archive to see what services might be available to you. This may simply be daily back-ups to a remote host location, such as Iron Mountain, or a deposit to your institution's digital repository.

- *Save and back-up 'traces' of your blog content.* Again, maybe you are only interested in the content of your posts. Some bloggers report composing their posts in their email editor or a word processing program, or receiving their posts immediately following publication via their provider's email notification system. And then, subsequently, saving and maintaining these 'traces' of their blogs as back-up. Also, others report capturing and saving the content that is syndicated as XML, such as through their blog's respective RSS feed.

- *Mirror your blog, in part or in whole.* Bloggers publishing to more than one blog may choose to cross-publish certain posts. This, in some way, contributes to the posts being available in more than one location, and hence serves somewhat as a form of back-up. Some bloggers even report mirroring their blogs in their entirety to another website. This, likewise, is seen to be reflective of a back-up by proliferation approach. This does introduce issues of version control, but simply noting that the blog is duplicated from another site, and possibly even a note as to the 'official' version – if you have so identified one as official – would be helpful for your readers.

- *Leave a paper trail.* Some bloggers report that they print out their blog and file away these hardcopy surrogates of their digital form. While that impacts future users' performance of the blog (you can't exactly click a link printed to paper), it does provide an accurate copy of the informational content and layout of the blog. And further, paper, under ideal circumstances, is more stable than code.

If your blog is collaboratively authored, you may want to have some conversations with your co-bloggers in regard to back-up and preservation preferences and strategies, and then coordinate your approach among your blog's primary authors. Co-authorship also introduces another conversation thread: are you interested in backing-up just your content, or the blog as a whole, representing the content of your co-bloggers? That will further inform your approach. And for those bloggers affiliated with a managed blog network, consider what back-up and preservation features are supported by your network. In interviews I conducted with some network-affiliated bloggers, none reported any awareness of their network's back-up and preservation strategies.

Conclusions

Whether you are a blogging novice or a blogging pro, it is hoped that this chapter provides some useful information to either get you going, to keep you going or, even, to get you out. Blogging is not for everyone, me included. I am a sporadic and occasional blogger. However, I am a pretty prolific blog reader. Presented here are some suggestions on elements to consider including in your blog, such as policy statements and the like, to assist readers like me in knowing bloggers like you a little better (and, in turn, to better know your content). And further, while the barrier to beginning a blog is low, with plenty of free service options to choose from, it can still be seen as a costly endeavour when considering the time and resources needed to maintain it. Maintaining and sustaining a blog, and an audience, over the course of a week or a month may very well take as much time as the journal article you submitted last month. Blogging, depending on how integral it is in your life, is a potentially substantial investment of your time and resources. Hopefully, some of the back-up and preservation strategies provided here will serve you in protecting this potentially valuable asset, both for your own use into the future, as well as for the use of others.

Notes

1. The Internet Archive posts information on how to enable crawling and capture to its website.
2. Creative Commons (CC) licences fall into different licence categories according to the following conditions: attribution, noncommercial, no derivative works, and share alike.
3. Blogger Backup is an example of a blog back-up utility.
4. Dropbox and Joyent Public Cloud Hosting are two examples of cloud storage and service providers.

References

Borgman, C.L. (2007) *Scholarship in the Digital Age: Information, Infrastructure and the Internet*. Cambridge, MA: MIT Press.

Braxton, J.M., Luckey, W. and Helland, P. (2002) *Institutionalizing a Broader View of Scholarship Through Boyer's Four Domains: ASHE-ERIC Higher Education Report*. San Francisco, CA: Jossey-Bass.

Caplan, P. (2008) The preservation of digital materials, *Library Technology Reports*, 44(2): 5–38.

Caron, P.L. (2006) Are scholars better bloggers? Bloggership: how blogs are transforming legal scholarship, *Washington University Law Review*, 84(5): 1025–42.

The Conglomerate (n.d.) A non-exclusive list of blog policies & disclaimers. Retrieved from *http://www.theconglomerate.org/disclaimers.html*.

Garrett, J. and Waters, D. (1996) *Preserving Digital Information: Report of the Task Force on Archiving of Digital Information* [CLIR Publication No. 63]. Retrieved from *http://www.clir.org/pubs/reports/pub63watersgarrett.pdf*.

Hank, C. (2011) Scholars and their blogs: characteristics, preferences and perceptions impacting digital preservation (Doctoral dissertation). Retrieved from ProQuest Dissertations and Theses database (UMI No. 3456270).

Kessler, E. (2011, 13 May) Blogger is back [blog post]. Retrieved from *http://buzz.blogger.com/2011/05/blogger-is-back.html#!/2011/05/blogger-is-back.html*.

Lessig, L. (2009, 20 August) Announcing the hibernation of lessig.org/blog (from the blogs-deserve-a-sabbatical-too department). Retrieved from *http://lessig.org/blog/2009/08/announcing_the_hibernation_of.html*.

McDonough, M. and Randag, M. (2010, 1 December) The 4th annual ABA Journal blawg 100 [blog post]. Retrieved from *http://www.abajournal.com/magazine/article/the_2010_aba_journal_blawg_100/*.

O'Reilly, T. (2007, 8 April) Draft blogger's code of conduct [blog post]. Retrieved from *http://radar.oreilly.com/archives/2007/04/draft-bloggers-1.html*.

Saper, C. (2006) Blogademia, *Reconstruction*, 6(4). Retrieved from *http://reconstruction.eserver.org/064/contents.shtml*.

Technorati (2011) Technorati blog directory. Retrieved from *http://technorati.com/blogs/directory/*.

Viegas, F.B. (2005) Bloggers' expectations of privacy and accountability: an initial survey, *Journal of Computer-Mediated Communication*, 10(3). Retrieved from *http://jcmc.indiana.edu/vol10/issue3/viegas.html*.

White, D. and Winn, P. (2009) State of the blogosphere: 2008. Technorati. Retrieved from *http://technorati.com/blogging/feature/state-of-the-blogosphere-2008/*.

Non-academic and academic social networking sites for online scholarly communities

Anatoliy Gruzd

Abstract: This chapter discusses various social networking sites and tools that can be used to support and advance a variety of scholarly activities. It is divided into two main sections: (1) popular non-academic social networking sites; and (2) popular and emerging academic social networking sites for online scholarly communities. Each section includes analysis and discussion about the relative strengths and weaknesses of different social networking platforms, their target audience and community norms. The chapter concludes with a discussion on how to decide what social networking sites (academic or non-academic) are the best for academics and for what purposes. After working through the chapter, readers will understand the purpose and functionality of various social media and social networking sites and tools, as well as how they can be used to create and support online scholarly communities.

Key words: online communities, scholarly practices, social networking sites.

Introduction

Since the start of the Internet, communities of scholars have relied on more traditional computer-mediated communication (CMC) tools such as email and mailing lists to communicate and facilitate collaboration. With the recent advent of social media and social networking sites, scholars are now making the transition to these more versatile and interactive platforms to support their scholarly activities (CIBER, 2010; Gruzd, Staves and Wilk, 2011; Procter et al., 2010). In addition to being able to participate in informal peer-review processes, other frequently cited benefits associated with the scholarly use of social media and networking sites include their ability to:

1. help scholars find and establish new connections;
2. strengthen and maintain existing connections;
3. keep up to date with the latest research in their research community; and
4. promote one's work among peers and the public at large.

This chapter will focus on these and other benefits with a special focus on how social media and networking sites can help to foster and strengthen online scholarly communities. The chapter will discuss some popular and up-and-coming general social networking sites that are being adopted by scholars for professional purposes, explore social networking sites and collaboration tools specifically geared towards academics, and conclude with a comparison between both types.

General public platforms for online scholarly communities

With the popularity of online social networking skyrocketing in early 2000 and the lack of sites designed specifically for academic communities, some scholars have turned to mainstream sites such as Facebook and Twitter to connect professionally and personally with their colleagues from around the globe. For example, a recent online survey conducted by Gruzd, Goertzen and Mai (2011) showed that 85 per cent ($n=367$) of respondents, mainly North American and European researchers in social sciences, use non-academic social networking sites monthly or more frequently, versus 51 per cent who use academic social networking sites. The two most frequently used non-academic social networking sites that scholars use are Facebook and Twitter.

Facebook

Facebook (*http://facebook.com*) is currently the leading social networking site in the world with 800 million active users as of October 2011 (Facebook, 2011). As a result, it is not surprising that there are some scholars mixed in among the avid users of Facebook. However, some of the scholars who do use Facebook for professional purposes find it extremely difficult to separate their personal and professional lives and are wary about what they perceive as a loss of personal privacy; see Chapter 10 in this volume for more about privacy concerns. The inability to separate and control various information silos on Facebook has forced some scholarly users to create multiple profiles on Facebook in order to regain a semblance of control over their various online identities (e.g., professional versus informal). And in a few extreme cases, some have even made the decision to withdraw from Facebook completely (see Gruzd, Staves and Wilk, 2011; Mendez et al., 2009). Nevertheless, the majority of academics who are using social networking sites still rely on Facebook to support their scholarly communication.

Twitter

Twitter (*http://twitter.com*), a microblogging site for exchanging messages under 140 characters long, is another example of a general purpose social networking site that some scholars have embraced as a medium to establish and maintain their professional online communities. For instance, in a survey of 61 Semantic Web scholars (primary European), 92 per cent of respondents had a Twitter account that they used for academic purposes (Letierce et al., 2010). Twitter's simple interface, real-time connections and its ability to form one-way connections (in which one person can subscribe to another user's updates) creates an effective environment for dissemination of scholarly news and updates. It also creates an informal atmosphere in which two strangers who work in similar areas are now able to easily find and connect to each other via this site. Twitter is commonly used during academic conferences as a service to elicit instant feedback and chat among conference attendees (Young, 2009). But the question still remains: can a semi-anonymous social networking site for exchanging short messages such as Twitter foster and sustain a scholarly online community? Interestingly, early evidence indicates that it might.

A recent study by Gruzd, Wellman and Takhteyev (2011) attempted to answer this very question of whether Twitter can be used by scholars to create a sense of community, a key factor in establishing a successful online community. The study examined the use of Twitter by a networked researcher and scholar, Barry Wellman, who also happens to be a very active Twitter user with a relatively large follower base. The study examined the following three theoretical constructs that have proven to be necessary to support a lively online community, namely Anderson's Imagined Communities, Jones' Virtual Settlement, and McMillan and Chavis' Sense of Community theories. The study confirmed that Twitter is capable of sustaining and fostering various interconnecting communities of scholars. Specifically, it found that Twitter is a common public place where scholars can meet and interact with one another, maintain the awareness of other community members through others' messages, and experience the feelings of belonging and influence over one's online community by forwarding others' messages, and getting help with questions from other online users. One of the key discoveries of this work is that while there was indeed a core group of more closely connected users within Barry Wellman's Twitter network who held the community together, it was still possible and relatively easy for newcomers to feel welcome and to create connections to members in the core.

One of the challenges of being on Twitter and other social media sites lies in handling an endless stream of information that comes from a multitude of sources. This often leads to information overload and eventually a desire to tune out. This is especially challenging on Twitter where many users follow on average anywhere from 100 people to 400 people (if those with over 500 followers are included) (Takhteyev et al., 2012). As social networking sites such as Twitter gain more acceptance among scholarly users, there are a lot of concerns over how users can deal with the inevitable information overload and how to differentiate conversations among various online communities. Chapter 6 of this book discusses many aspects of Twitter in greater detail. Here, I present one tool that addresses the above concerns of scholars, called AcademiaMap.com, which is in development at the Social Media Lab of Dalhousie University.

AcademiaMap

AcademiaMap (*http://AcademiaMap.com*) is an online Geographic Information Visualization (GIV) system that tracks Twitter conversations (in real time) and visualizes communication connections between scholarly users of Twitter from across the globe. The main interface of the system is shown in Figure 2.1. The tool is designed to help scholars filter the noise from their Twitter stream and allow more popular and potentially more relevant conversations within their scholarly community to be brought to the forefront. The infrastructure of AcademiaMap is

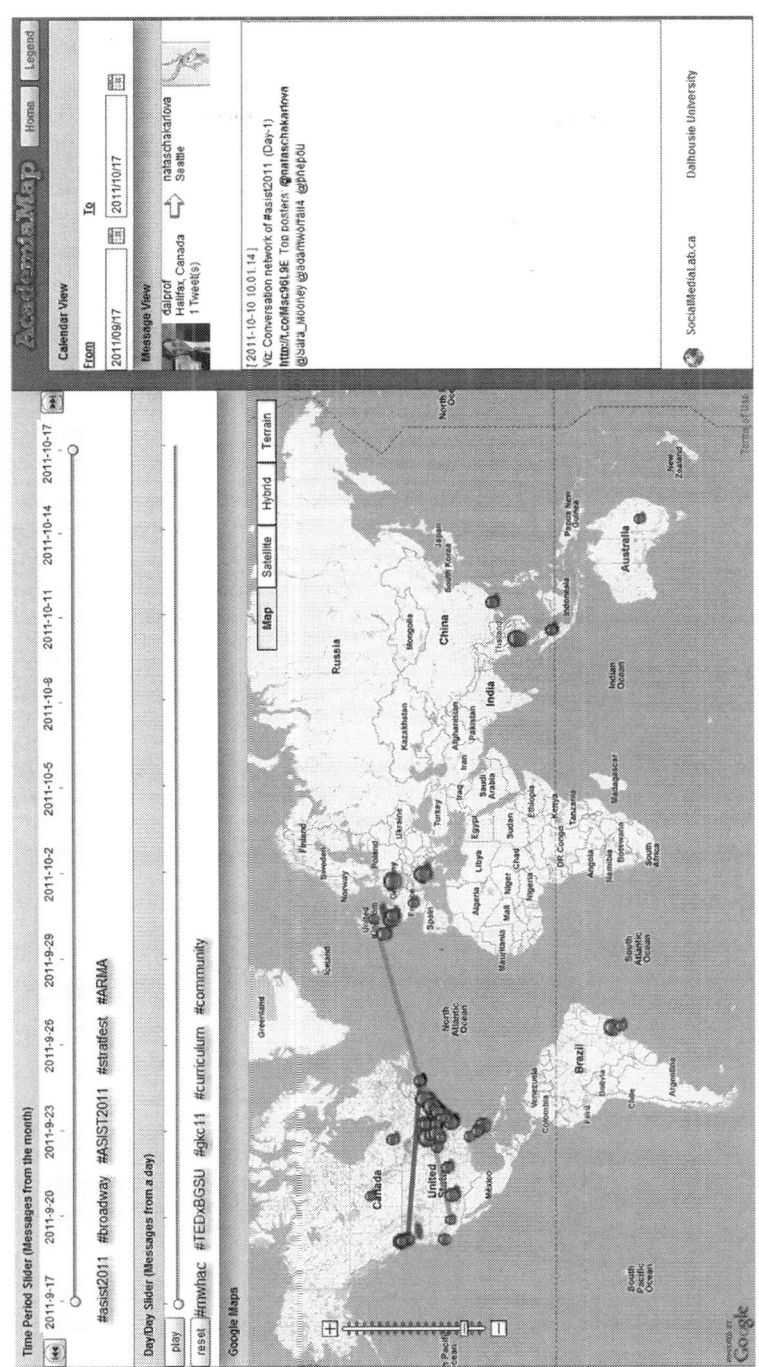

Figure 2.1 AcademiaMap.com interface

designed to track the conversations of any scholarly community found within Twitter. The current beta version of AcademiaMap only tracks the public tweets of scholars who have been followed by the Twitter account @asist2011, which belongs to the American Society for Information Science and Technology (ASIS&T).

The interface is divided into three main areas: (1) the map, which shows where community members come from geographically; (2) the two sliders that control the date range for Twitter messages; and (3) the conversation pane to the right that shows profile information and messages posted by a selected individual or between any two people in the community. For a selected date period, the interface also displays the top five most popular topics (hashtags) posted by the community members. Clicking on any of these hashtags will bring up a list of messages in the conversation pane that mentioned this hashtag. In addition to showing topics that are popular in this community, the tool also shows its most engaged members and how these members are connected to other members of this scholarly community. For example, if one person mentioned another person in his or her message, there will be a line connecting these two individuals. Clicking on this line will show only the messages posted from the original user that mentioned the connecting user. Because of the way this tool is designed, it allows scholars to identify popular topics and voices among their Twitter peer group during a specific time period of their choice. It can also help its users increase their awareness of the community conversations without necessarily having to read the hundreds of messages posted daily. Finally, it can help its users identify new contacts within this community to pursue potential collaborative projects with colleagues in the future, or to follow their messages on Twitter.

Google+

The final social networking site for the general public that will be discussed in this chapter is Google+ (*http://plus.google.com*). Released in summer 2011, the site has already captured the attention of over 40 million users, according to one estimate (Allen, 2011). Not surprisingly, many researchers are found among this group of early adopters of Google+. Many of the scholars seem to be interested in exploring the possibility of using the site for their professional purposes. Just anecdotally, out of about 70 people who initially found and added me to their Google+ profiles, all of them are professional, academic contacts (students, collaborators and colleagues in the same or related research areas). As a result, conversations that appear in my profile on Google+ are primarily academic. Depending on how Google chooses to develop Google+, it has the potential to address many of the concerns over privacy that some scholars have expressed with regards to Facebook and might eventually become a hub for scholarly communities. One of the selling points of Google+ for academics is that the site incorporates many of the useful features found in both Facebook and Twitter. For example, like Twitter, Google+ supports asymmetric relationships where one user can follow another but the second user does not have to follow the first one back. As in the case with Twitter, such asymmetric relationships make it easier for one researcher to initiate contact with another researcher without having shared any previous work history together. This is because there is no expectation that the person whom you decide to follow has to also follow you back. At the same time, similar to Facebook, Google+ allows its users to organize people in their personal networks into groups, or what Google calls 'circles' (see Figure 2.2), which makes it easier to share information with, and receive information from, only relevant groups of online followers (e.g., friends, family or colleagues). But what might give Google+ an edge over competing general purpose social networking sites such as Facebook is the fact that Google already offers an entire suite of free, web-based collaborative productivity tools that are well suited for scholarly work such as Google Docs for research

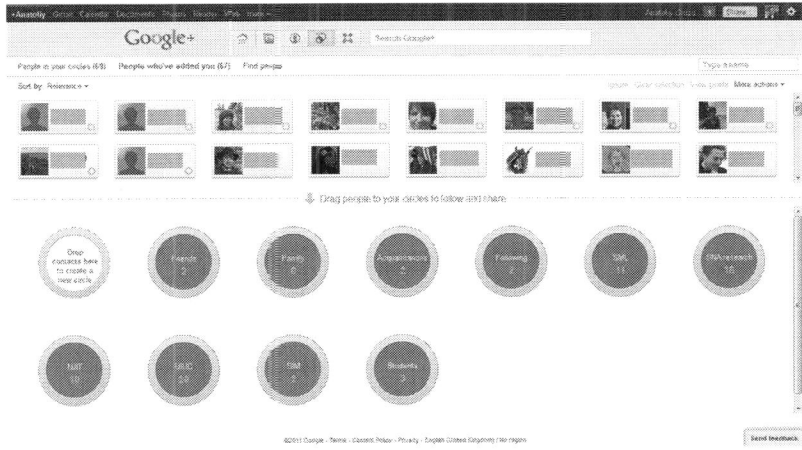

Figure 2.2 Google+ circles, a feature that allows users to manually organize their contacts into groups

collaboration, and Google Chat for synchronous communication among remotely distributed teams; see Chapter 3 for more about technologies that facilitate collaboration. It is likely that over time, Google+ will also offer an even tighter integration among all of its various online properties, making Google+ the default social networking site for scholars. However, as at the time of this writing, it is still too early to declare Google+ a winner or even a contender in the general social networking space or as a niche scholarly social networking space.

Academic sites for online scholarly communities

The previous section outlined some of the popular and trending social networking sites for the general public that have been adopted by scholars for professional uses. However, as noted earlier, these sites raise some privacy concerns and do not have all of the features that make them ideal for use in a scholarly and professional setting. For example, Facebook makes it very easy for its users to share photos with friends; this is a very popular activity, especially among younger users. However, scholars are more likely to be interested in sharing articles and comments about articles than photos. But Facebook does not offer features that would enable sharing of peer-reviewed articles (including the full citation data such as article title, authors, year of publication, journal title, etc.) with other users. Due to these hindering concerns and limitations associated with the mainstream sites, over the last few years a few niche social networking sites specifically aimed at scholars have been launched. In this chapter, only the two fastest growing scholarly sites, ResearchGate. net and Academia.edu, will be discussed. Sites such as Mendeley and Zotero, which have social networking features but primarily focus on the collection and dissemination of bibliographic records, are discussed in Chapter 5.

ResearchGate.net

Launched in 2008, ResearchGate (*http://ResearchGate.net*) had over 1 million users as of 1 December 2011. Most of its current users are researchers from medicine and biology (over 200,000 members in each discipline), followed by researchers in engineering, chemistry, computer

Non-academic and academic SNSs for online scholarly communities

science and agricultural science (with ~70,000–98,000 members each). Users from other disciplines are also present on the site, but they are few and far between.

From a user interface perspective, ResearchGate includes many of the popular features and functionalities that are now common among current social networking sites such as creating unique user profiles, posting public and private messages, sharing information, and finding other users with similar interests. However, since this site is designed with academics in mind, it contains many features that allow and encourage its user base to connect and converse around research interests and publications. The registration process is easy: once registered, users are required to: (1) enter their research interests in the form of keywords; (2) select one or more research fields; and (3) add publications. Publications can be added by uploading from popular reference managers such as EndNote, by searching publications in databases such as PubMed, IEEE or CiteSeer, or by adding them manually.

One of the useful features of the site is that it can recommend relevant articles and other researchers in the same area just based on the research interests that a user entered (see Figure 2.3). The recommended articles can also be rated and shared with others.

ResearchGate also has a built-in blogging feature that enables users to write a 'microarticle' (a short review of a published peer-reviewed paper)

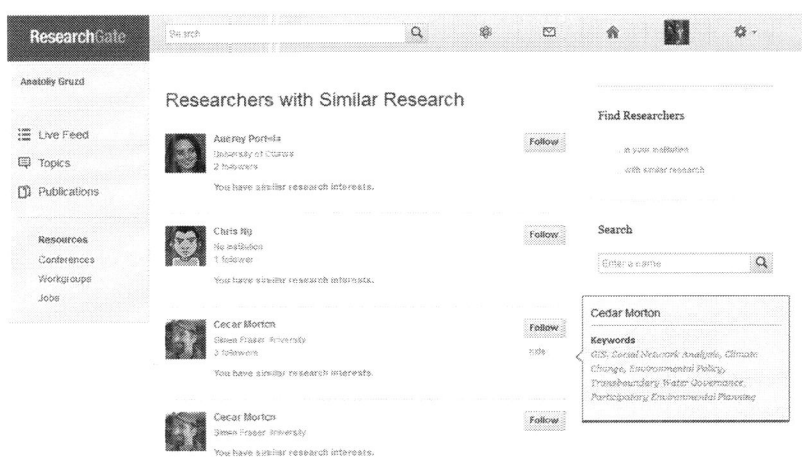

Figure 2.3 ResearchGate: recommendation page of researchers with similar research

or a 'post' on a general topic, such as a recent conference trip. Users can also submit their blog posts to be featured on ResearchGate's main blog where the post will likely get a larger audience. This is a useful and easy-to-use feature. Unfortunately, ResearchGate does not currently offer an automated way for users who already maintain their own blogs elsewhere to cross-post from their external blogs.

In addition to being able to follow other users, ResearchGate also allows its users to follow research topics. For example, Figure 2.4 shows a page about Open Source Scientific Software (OSSS). The stated purpose of this page is to help users 'discover useful OSSS such as OpenFOAM, R, Maxima, Salome, ParaView, and learn how to use it' (Velten, 2011, para. 1). As of November 2011, it had 834 followers. What makes this page interesting and useful to its users is the fact that it is set up like an online forum where users can post and reply to each other's questions. Some other features worth mentioning here are the ability to create a 'workgroup' as well as an invitation-only space to collaborate with colleagues, create polls and share files.

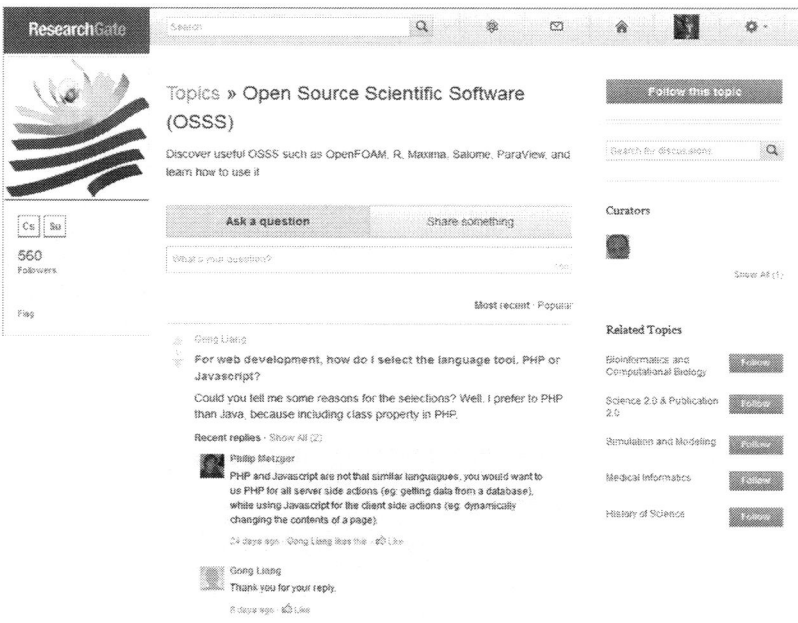

Figure 2.4 ResearchGate: topic page on Open Source Scientific Software (OSSS)

Academia.edu

Another popular academic social networking site, also launched in 2008, is Academia.edu. It has over 800,000 members, primarily in the social sciences. Academia.edu has many of the features found in ResearchGate such as maintaining a list of one's publications, following topics or researchers with similar research interests and publishing blog posts (see Figure 2.5). However, Academia.edu also has a set of unique features that distinguish it from other scholarly social networking sites. First, the

Figure 2.5 Academia.edu: profile page

site allows its users to add sections to their profiles such as a CV, teaching documents and talks. The site also has the ability to automatically re-post updates to Facebook, a useful feature for academics who maintain their presence on more than one social networking site. Another unique feature of Academia.edu is that it provides its users with information on how many people visited their profile, from what countries and what they found interesting on the user profile (see Figure 2.6). Such analytics offer valuable insights to scholars about the popularity of their research and its geographic reach. They can give users a rough indication as to what papers might get more citations in the future, which in turn may inspire a scholar to pursue and expand a certain line of research.

Other academic social networking sites

Some other (more niche) academic-oriented social networking sites that the reader might find interesting include:

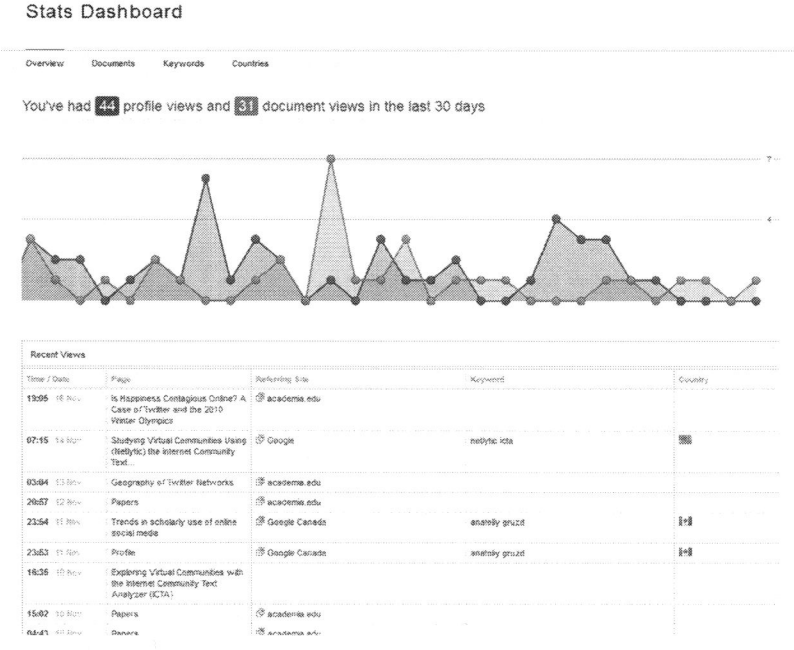

Figure 2.6 Academia.edu: visitors' statistics dashboard

- MethodSpace.com, which focuses on methods for qualitative, quantitative and mixed methods research, run by the publisher, Sage.
- ScienceFeed.com, a microblogging platform for scientists
- InSciences.org, a site for experts in science fields.

The review of these and other social networking solutions for scholars can be found on the Social Media Lab blog at *http://SocialMediaLab.ca*.

The sites listed above are all public sites and are accessible by any researcher in the world. But sometimes a research group or an institution needs to set up a private social networking solution just for its members. Such solutions can be a simple blog for a research group using an open source platform like WordPress, or a wiki using the popular MediaWiki software. But it can also include a more complex solution for social networking and collaboration such as HUBzero *(https://hubzero.org)*, developed in conjunction with the Network for Computational Nanotechnology or VIVO *(http://vivoweb.org)*. The first solution, based on a blogging or a wiki platform, is especially useful for smaller research labs and can be effectively used to coordinate the lab's work as well as build a sense of community among lab members. The last two solutions, HUBzero and VIVO, are especially useful for the discovery of experts and potential collaborators based on users' research interests within a larger unit such as an academic department or a university.

Other similar platforms in this area include KnowledgeNetwork, being developed at the University of British Columbia *(http://knowledgenetwork.ubc.ca)*, and the rDmap (Research Discovery Map) application, currently being developed at the Social Media Lab at Dalhousie University. Both applications attempt to visualize existing and potential research connections among university researchers. For example, rDmap connects faculty members to their research topics and their peers within their university. This helps faculty members to quickly and easily identify potential collaborators, while allowing students to find potential supervisors for their thesis work or reading courses (see Figure 2.7). A sample installation of rDmap for Dalhousie University Faculty of Management is available at *http://iresearch.management.dal.ca/fommap*.

The primary advantage of such custom solutions is that an institution is in control of the content and customization of the site, but the limitation is that it requires the installation and maintenance of special software.

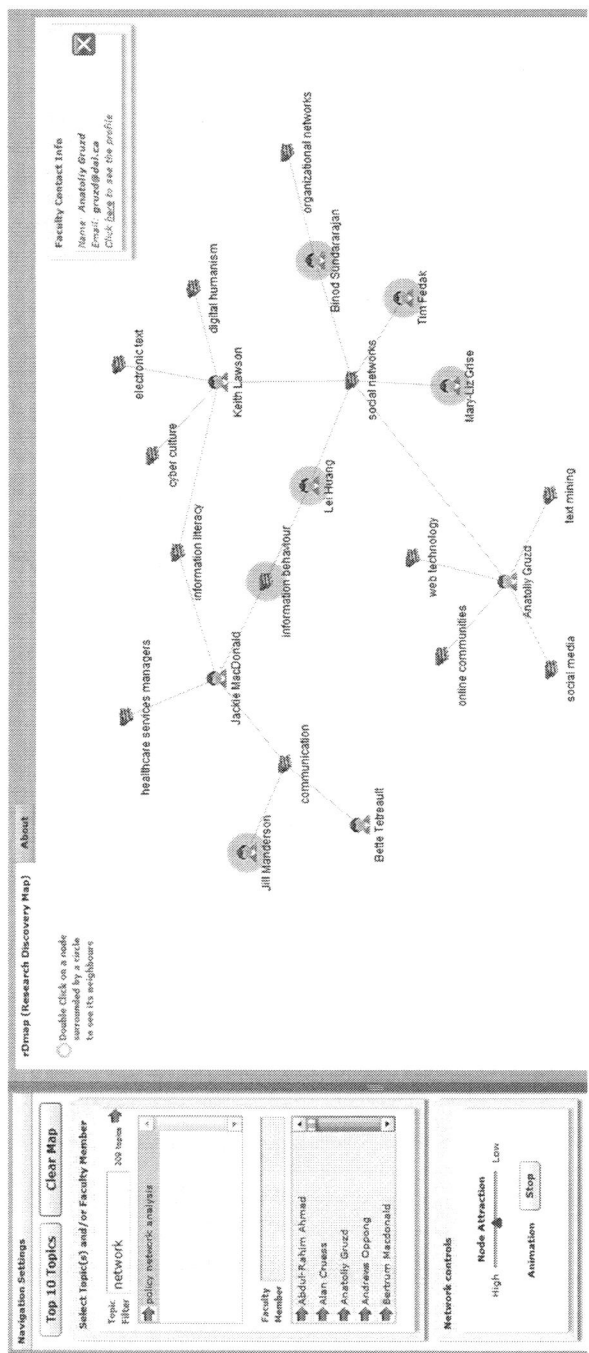

Figure 2.7 rDmap for discovering collaborators and potential supervisors

Conclusions

With so many different social networking sites available to network and share information with peers, which one should you choose? Should you go with a general purpose non-academic site or maybe start a profile on an academic-specific site? One way to answer this question is to ask your local and distant peers in your field what social networking site(s) they are using and then create the profile(s) accordingly. This is because your offline peers will likely be your online 'followers' as well. However, be aware that by going down this route, you might be unknowingly excluding some other groups of researchers and professionals in other fields who might also be interested in your work since they may be using a different social networking site. So we are back to the initial question: what site do you choose if you are new to online social networking?

Both non-academic and academic social networking sites discussed in this chapter offer many similar features and benefits to their users such as the ability to: make new research contacts; promote current research; follow other researchers' work; and keep up-to-date with current topics in your field. However, there are also some clear differences between them. The positive side of non-academic platforms is that they potentially have a larger user base due to their early start and general appeal. But because of their general appeal, it might be difficult for a scholarly user to separate personal from professional contacts and avoid potentially embarrassing and sometimes career-ending situations. As one participant from the study discussed in Gruzd, Staves and Wilk (2011) stated, 'Managing and negotiating the always changing privacy settings of Facebook is an ongoing task for me.' On the other hand, academic-specific platforms such as ResearchGate.net and Academia.edu are free of these types of worries, since their users are less likely to find their personal contacts on those sites. But the drawback is that they do not have nearly as many users as Facebook, Twitter or Google+. As a result, many researchers still doubt whether spending time building a professional online identity on academic-only sites will pay off professionally in the long run.

One possible solution to the conundrum outlined above is to maintain multiple accounts on both academic and non-academic social networking sites. The drawback is obvious; it is already time-consuming to manage one online account, not to mention two or three. But the advantage is that it will be easier to reach various overlapping and non-overlapping online communities of scholars and professionals. If you do decide to follow this advice, instead of simply duplicating material on multiple sites, try to identify who follows you on different sites and then customize your messages and content to match different online communities (e.g., scholars in your field, scholars in other fields, professionals, students, media, etc.) Also, try to write goals that you might want to achieve via different networking sites. For example, I reserve Facebook for communication with friends and close collaborators in academia (socializing and awareness maintenance purposes), and Twitter for gathering and disseminating research-related news, publications and events to academic peers and other professionals. I use Academia.edu to maintain an up-to-date list of my publications, which makes it easier for other researchers to discover and cite them, and also to find related others' papers. And finally, I use LinkedIn, a social networking website for career-related networking, to stay in touch with current and former students and to maintain contacts with industry partners. Furthermore, to help manage these multiple profiles, I often rely on software tools such as TweetDeck (*http://www.tweetdeck.com*) and Hootsuite (*http://hootsuite.com*) to follow and cross-post messages to multiple online social networks at once (when it is appropriate).

In summary, there is currently no *one-stop* solution that will satisfy all of the social networking needs of scholars, and it looks like it might take some time for a clear leader to emerge, if at all. In the meantime, to be an effective online networker in the age of social media, scholars will, for the time being, need to maintain multiple social networking accounts. This can be very daunting for any scholar, since doing so will require a certain level of time commitment. But this effort does often have very tangible pay-offs in the form of new professional and media contacts as well as an increase in the visibility and reach of one's research initiatives. As one scholar in the Gruzd, Staves and Wilk (ibid.) study noted, it is also time-consuming to go to conferences, but we still do it.

Acknowledgements

This work was supported by the Social Sciences and Humanities Research Council (SSHRC) and NCE Graphics, Animation and New meDia (GRAND) grants. I would like to thank Philip Mai and Kathleen Staves, members of the Social Media Lab at Dalhousie University, for their help and feedback during the preparation of this chapter.

References

Allen, P. (2011, 22 September) Google+ is really taking off! Millions joining daily [Google+ public post]. Retrieved from *https://plus.google.com/117388252776312694644/posts/K9Qf1UVNyGy*.

CIBER (2010) Social media and research workflow [report]. Retrieved from *http://www.ucl.ac.uk/infostudies/research/ciber/social-media-report.pdf*.

Facebook (2011) Statistics. Retrieved from *http://facebook.com/press/info.php?statistics*.

Gruzd, A., Goertzen, M. and Mai, P. (2011) Survey results highlights: trends in scholarly communication and knowledge dissemination in the age of social media [report]. Retrieved from *http://socialmedialab.ca/?p=4308*.

Gruzd, A., Staves, K. and Wilk, A. (2011) 'Tenure and promotion in the age of online social media', in A. Grove (ed.). *Proceedings of the ASIS&T 2011 Annual Meeting*. Silver Spring, MD: American Society for Information Science and Technology.

Gruzd, A., Wellman, B. and Takhteyev, Y. (2011) Imagining Twitter as an imagined community. *American Behavioral Scientist*, 55(10): 1294–1318. DOI: 10.1177/0002764211409378.

Letierce, J., Passant, A., Breslin, J.G. and Decker, S. (2010) 'Using Twitter during an academic conference: the #iswc2009 use-case', in M.A. Hearst, W. Cohen and S. Gosling (eds). *Proceedings of the Fourth International AAAI Conference on Weblogs and Social Media* (pp. 279–82). Galway: National University of Ireland.

Mendez, J.P., Curry, J., Mwavita, M., Kennedy, K., Weinland, K. et al. (2009) To friend or not to friend: academic interaction on Facebook. *International Journal of Instructional Technology and Distance Learning*, 6(9). Retrieved from *http://www.itdl.org/Journal/Sep_09/article03.htm*.

Procter, R., Williams, R., James, S., Poschen, M., Snee, H. et al. (2010) Adoption and use of Web 2.0 in scholarly communications. *Philosophical Transactions of the Royal Society A: Mathematical, Physical and Engineering Sciences*, 368(1926): 4039–56.

Takhteyev, Y., Gruzd, A. and Wellman, B. (2012) Geography of Twitter networks. *Social Networks*. Special Issue on Space and Networks, 34(1): 73–81. DOI:10.1016/j.socnet.2011.05.006.

Velten, K. (2011) Open Source Scientific Software (OSSS). Retrieved from *http://www.researchgate.net/topic/Open_Source_Scientific_Software_OSSS/*.

Young, J. (2009) 10 high fliers on Twitter. *The Chronicle of Higher Education*, 55: A10.

Research and teaching in real time: 24/7 collaborative networks

Anabel Quan-Haase

Abstract: The work of academics has radically changed since the introduction of social media tools. One area that has received considerable attention is that of real-time technologies for communication and collaboration. Academics can use tools such as Google Docs, Skype and Dropbox to facilitate the exchange of information, the dissemination of research findings and the creation of new knowledge in real time. The present chapter examines the concepts, theories and key study findings in the area of real-time technologies to show how these tools are being used in the academic setting. Despite the many advantages of using real-time tools for both collocated and dispersed collaborative work, some concerns have been raised about the potential negative effects on productivity and scholarship. I discuss both the advantages and problems associated with the use of real-time collaborative tools and outline strategies for effective implementation.

Key words: real-time collaboration, social networks, Internet studies, instant messaging, collaboration, social media, digital tools, academics, digital humanities.

Real-time technologies for academics

Communication has always been an essential part of academic work – both for research and teaching – because it represents an important means of sharing ideas, collaborating, consulting with colleagues and disseminating research findings. With the diffusion of social media amongst faculty and students, we have witnessed major changes in how academics communicate and collaborate (Bonetta, 2007; Quan-Haase and Young, 2010). While not all academics are equally enthusiastic about the move toward digital communication, a large proportion is finding creative ways of connecting with collaborators and students, discussing important topics, obtaining feedback and disseminating their research findings. Not only that, in a widely cited blog, Dave Parry has stated that the more scholars associate themselves with social media, the more benefits they will derive '[n]ot because social media is the only way to do digital scholarship, but because I think social media is the only way to do scholarship period' (Parry, 2010, para. 14). There is a clear sense that social media is not just a buzzword, but rather is a phenomenon that is here to stay and will fundamentally impact the work of academics.

A number of different tools are aggregated under the rubric of social media, including microblogging, blogs, social networking sites and video sharing and streaming websites (Hogan and Quan-Haase, 2010). Nonetheless, not all social media support the same kind of functionality, with each type providing diverse features and thereby fulfilling different scholarly needs.

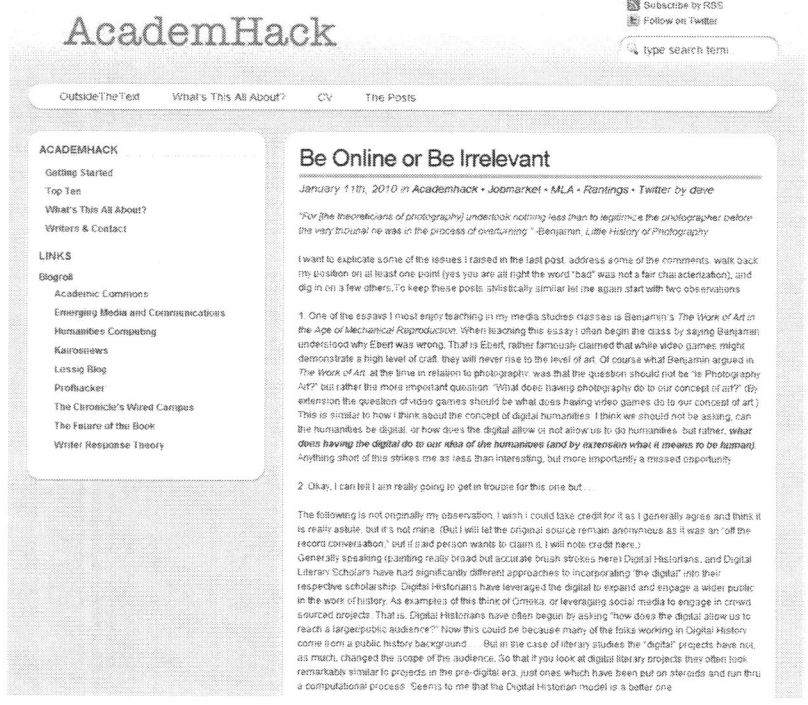

Figure 3.1 Digital scholarship: be online or be irrelevant

Digital tools that fall under the designation of real-time technologies have become widely used among scholars because they facilitate communication and collaboration by allowing for the rapid exchange of messages, the emulation of in-person conversations, the reaching of large and diverse audiences, the simultaneous co-editing of text and other data and real-time access to ideas and feedback. Real-time communication and collaboration has indeed become a large part of the daily work of many academics and has the potential to lead toward innovation.

Three current trends make real-time technologies increasingly relevant for academics in terms of teaching and scholarship. The first is the move from localized collaborative clusters to large-scale, networked partnerships spanning regionally, nationally and internationally. This has further pressed the need for real-time digital tools to aid with communication, coordination and collaboration. The second trend is the quick growth of distance education in most universities, which calls for the integration of innovative tools to maintain a high level of student engagement and collaboration (Haythornthwaite and Andrews, 2011). Beldarrain (2006) has stressed the importance of integrating real-time technologies into education, seeing the value in particular for distance courses and degrees that take place only online with little to no physical contact with students. The third trend is the increasing reliance of college and university students on social media tools to accomplish school-related tasks, necessitating a better understanding of how 'to motivate, cultivate, and meet the needs of the 21st-century learner' (ibid., p. 140).

In this chapter, an overview of real-time technologies for communication and collaboration in academic settings is provided by focusing on the two core areas of research and teaching. The aim of this chapter is not only to present the advantages, but also to investigate some of the problems and detrimental effects related to the reliance on these tools. In the final discussion, the chapter compares various real-time technologies and shows what strategies the literature has identified for users to effectively integrate these technologies into their work practices.

The concept of real time

Real-time technologies can be defined as those tools that allow for instant communication and collaboration with multiple individuals located nearby or far away via data exchange of voice, text and image (Quan-Haase, 2010). What constitutes real time has been closely tied to the limitations of the technology itself. In the past, delays of as much as

10–15 seconds were considered acceptable. However, recent technological developments have changed our understanding of what constitutes real time, with programs such as Google Docs allowing for immediate updates with basically zero delay (Berlind, 2010).[1] From a collaboration point of view, this creates a sense of high levels of work integration among project members.

Real-time technologies are distinguished between those that support communication and those that support collaborative work. It is important to make this distinction as the first type facilitates conversations via voice, video and text, while the second type primarily facilitates exchanging, editing and visualizing data (e.g., text, sound and image). Skype is a good example of a real-time communication technology, while Google Docs is a prototype of a real-time collaborative tool. Some platforms integrate both communication and collaboration features allowing participants to work jointly on data and communicate through the same interface about their work (see Table 3.1 on p. 45); the communication in this case represents a meta-level of work (Quan-Haase, 2009).[2]

Key features that distinguish real-time digital tools from other tools include the immediacy of messages and updates and the inclusion of tracking tools (Quan-Haase et al. 2005). Another central feature of real-time digital tools is that they signal the presence and availability of other users by displaying notification regarding whether a contact has logged in or logged out. For instance, Facebook provides information about a user's current login status by displaying in the chat window a green dot next to those users who are logged into the site. This information is necessary to identify potential communication partners. In Google Docs, information is provided about who else is viewing a document through a display of active collaborator names (see Figure 3.3 on p. 46). These unique features of real-time digital tools facilitate both distance and collocated collaboration and communication in digital environments.

Real-time technologies and research

Research projects are moving from localized collaborative clusters to large-scale, networked partnerships with collaborators from other regions. As projects are distributed, these necessitate means for team members to come together virtually to discuss project goals, procedures and milestones. For these distributed teams it is also important to engage in brainstorming sessions and to be able to prototype at a distance. The speed of interaction, display of availability information and support for multiple conversations has made real-time technologies an appealing tool for supporting the work of distributed teams. In a study of how students on campus use real-time technologies, it was found that they often coordinated tasks and helped each other with writing assignments by chatting and exchanging files via instant messenger applications (Quan-Haase and Collins, 2008). Chat provides an informal, spontaneous means of communication that allows collaborators to ask quick questions and obtain prompt clarifications, and coordinate and schedule meetings (Nardi et al., 2000). Further advantages include the ability to negotiate social accessibility, conduct intermittent conversations and maintain a sense of connection with others in the project, even without necessarily communicating (ibid.; Quan-Haase and Collins, 2008).

Skype is the most commonly used real-time technology for one-to-one and group meetings because it is free, easily accessible from any computer/mobile device and supports text, audio-only and video chat. Another useful feature of Skype for collaborative purposes is the possibility of desktop sharing. This allows communication partners to see each other's desktops in real time and manipulate data at a distance. Skype desktop sharing can be useful for various tasks, such as computer support and maintenance, design work and collaborative writing and editing (Kendrick, 2009). Skype Premium offers group video-calling, allowing two or more people to converse, with the key advantage of the premium edition being that each individual can see all the other parties on a single screen.[3] A recent partnership with Facebook has now also integrated videostreaming into Facebook, allowing users to connect in real time on yet another platform.

Skype has also become an important research tool because scholars frequently use it for interviewing purposes. When it is difficult to interview participants face-to-face because of scheduling conflicts or pricey travel, it can be convenient to use Skype as a means to reach them. Because of the video feature, participants' nonverbal cues are not missed as would be the case in a telephone interview, and additionally it has no long-distance charges. A major deterrent to using Skype has been the inconsistent sound and video quality, making it difficult to predict how useful Skype will be as a reliable tool for hosting collaborative meetings and for data collection purposes.

The recent addition of Google+ provides the option of creating a virtual 'hangout', where users can be online on videostream. Hangouts can either be public or private. Public hangouts are announced at *http://gphangouts.com/*, where detailed information is provided about when the hangout will start, the topic and who can participate. These provide open forums of communication for anyone who is interested in a topic to join. Public hangouts also provide new venues for researchers to disseminate their research findings to the larger community, while allowing for input and feedback from the participants. Private hangouts require participants to be added to the hangout and can be used for team meetings. A useful feature in hangouts is the possibility to share, look at and edit documents. Figure 3.2 shows how the SocioDigital Lab (*http:// sociodigital.info*) is sharing and editing a document in real time on the main screen while simultaneously engaging in a discussion. One limitation is that no more than 10 people can join a hangout at any point in time, drastically restricting the number of individuals who can actively participate (see the discussion on scalability below).

Being able to co-write and co-edit documents (text, spreadsheets, presentations, drawings, etc.) in real time has become an important part of many projects. Even though collaborative projects are much more prevalent in the sciences, they are also becoming increasingly common in the social sciences and humanities. A wide range of open source, free software is available on the web to support collaborative writing, analysis and drawing. The most commonly used and developed tools are collaborative writing tools, which allow users to see the same text, edit it and import/export it from the screen. Table 3.1 shows several writing tools and compares their features.

One of the most widely used collaborative writing tools is Google Docs, which is an application that can be accessed via a Google account

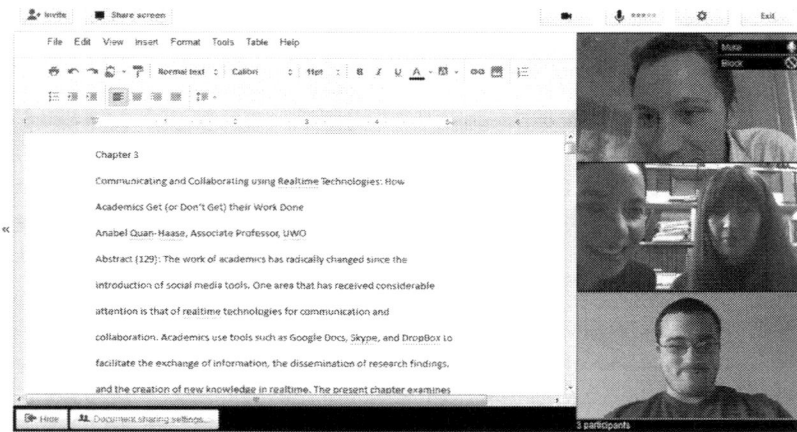

Figure 3.2 Using hangouts for collaborative writing

Table 3.1 A comparison of web-based collaborative writing tools

Tool	Editing capability	Tracking capability	Communication possibilities	Presence information
Docs.Google.com	Fairly good, no delay	Excellent version control, flexible comments	Excellent: integrated with real-time chat	Excellent
Hangouts	Fairly good, no delay	Integrated with Google Docs	Excellent, including videostreaming	Excellent
Piratepad.net	Limited, no delay	Very good version control	Good integration of chat	Available
Etherpad.org	Limited, no delay	Very good version control	Good integration of chat	Available
PrimaryPad.com	Limited, the updating is with a short delay	Very good version control	Limited integration of chat	Available
http://willyou.typewith.me	Limited, no delay	Very good version control	Limited integration of chat. The Pad could not be shared	Available

Note: the various tools were tested on 23 November 2011.

and allows users to create documents, spreadsheets, drawings and presentations online at no cost. One of the most widely used Google Docs applications provides basic word processing functions, including composition, editing, formatting and printing. Also useful for scholars is the 'Google forms' feature (accessible via Google Docs), which allows the design of online surveys and provides a means to collect participant responses. Files created with Google Docs are located in the cloud and, as a result, can be accessed from anywhere. One key advantage of the Google Docs platform is that it allows for multiple editors to work on a single document simultaneously with near up-to-the-second responsiveness (see Table 3.1 above and Figure 3.3).

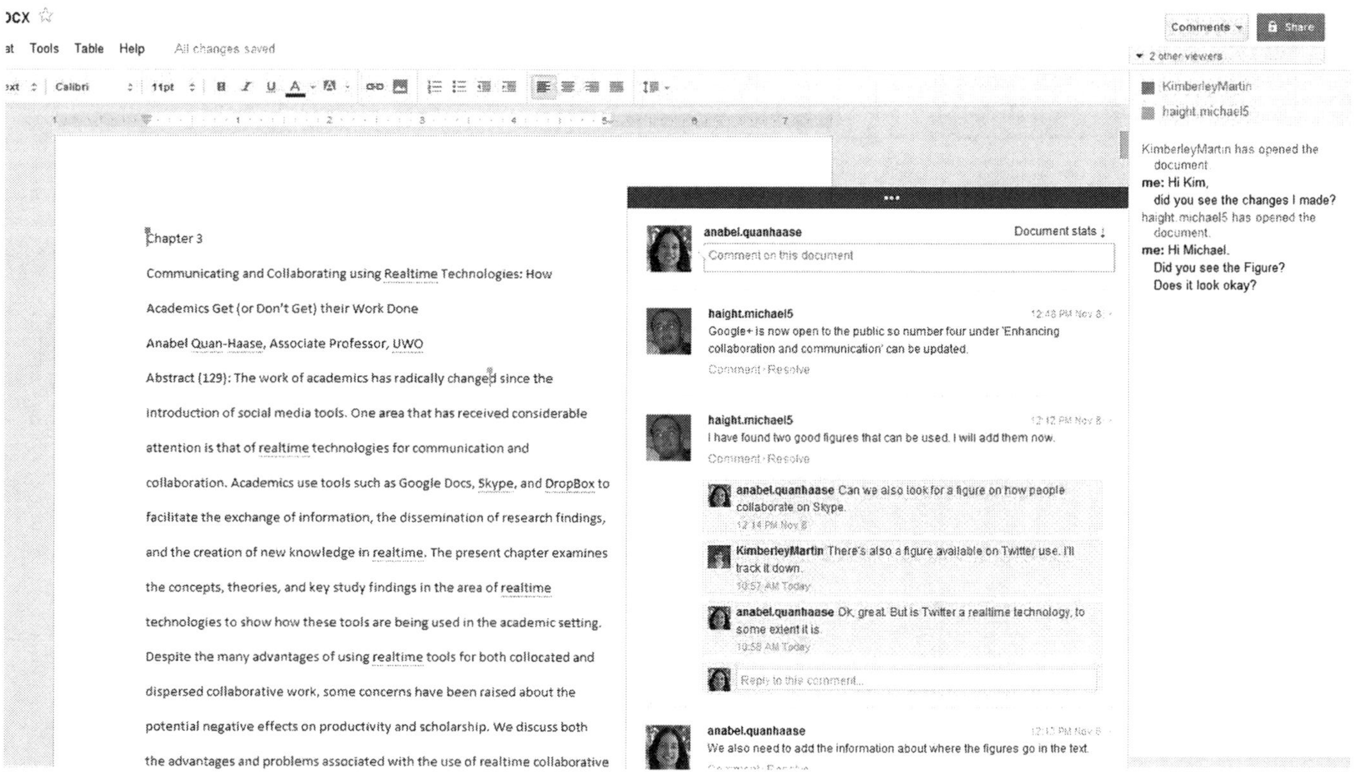

Figure 3.3 Google Docs as a means for team writing, editing and commenting

Revision control or version control is the term used to describe the problems that arise from keeping track of changes made to a document by multiple authors. To prevent such problems, various new digital tools provide safeguards to control and coordinate updates (see Table 3.1 above). For instance, SketchPad.com has a feature that allows the reviewing of the history of the document. Through this feature, the system shows users a true visualization of how the document has evolved. This is a useful way of keeping track of changes, but can also be overwhelming when many versions of a single document exist. The introduction of the real-time feature called 'presence' in Google Docs, which shows the location of other collaborators' cursors (in different colours) has been a useful tool for dealing with revision control and for being able to monitor changes collaborators make to a file in real time (Berlind, 2010). The feature allows for multiple parties to work simultaneously on a document without interfering with collaborators' writing and editing.

Data in these collaborative writing systems are located in the cloud and, as a result, a number of privacy concerns have emerged. While data in the majority of systems cannot be accessed by others without access privileges, it is nonetheless located on servers in the US or in undisclosed locations. As data fall under the laws of the country where the servers are being hosted this can cause major problems and conflicts in terms of data protection and data privacy (see Chapter 10, this volume). These concerns are of particular relevance to projects that collect, manage and analyse data from participants, and to those projects that include patents, proprietary data or confidential information. Most ethics review boards will not allow for participant data to be collected in the cloud unless the necessary precautions have been put in place (e.g., guaranteed anonymity of responses).

New tools are also emerging that allow for collaboration across projects. At the 2011 Open Science Summit a number of new forms of collaboration were introduced.[4] One of these was Science Exchange, which *Nature* has described as the eBay of Science because it allows project members to post research problems on a site and then other academics, institutions and organizations can bid on these entries to aid with identifying a solution.[5] This helps academics with particular research needs to connect with other research clusters and seek help specific to their projects in real time.

Real-time technologies and teaching

Adding real-time technologies as another form of student engagement provides more options for out-of-class communication and interaction with faculty. Not surprisingly, some of the top American schools have moved towards real-time applications such as Google Docs. Sixty-one of the top 100 US universities in 2011 used Google Apps to facilitate communication and collaboration among students and faculty (Google Enterprise Blog, 2011).[6] While many of the privacy concerns that arise from this move toward cloud computing have not been addressed sufficiently, the reliance on these apps in educational settings seems to be increasing. What often motivates the move toward real-time technologies is educators' aspiration to increase student–faculty interaction and student engagement (Dobransky and Bainbridge Frymier, 2004), therefore providing communication and collaboration alternatives that are flexible and suit students' needs.

Several attempts have been made to integrate real-time communication tools into the learning environment. Balayeva and Quan-Haase (2009) used MSN Messenger as a means to hold weekly office hours with the aim of increasing student–faculty interaction. These virtual office hours were offered in addition to in-person office hours. While the study showed an increase in interaction, respondents reported some apprehension with using only chat for communicating with their instructors because conversations progressed slower than those taking place in person and did not allow for the discussion of complex questions and topics. These characteristics of chat can lead to misunderstandings that are difficult to disambiguate. Therefore, the authors have argued that chat can supplement (not replace) email and its key advantage is to fill communication gaps between face-to-face communication. Research by Roper and Kindred (2005), also on the use of chat for out-of-class communication, shows that the 'tone of the messages was friendly and polite, much like how one would act if stopping by the office or calling on the phone' (Roper and Kindred, 2005, discussion section, para. 3). This suggests that real-time technologies could be useful to support some aspects of student–faculty interaction and collaboration.

The rapid growth in distance education has created a need to better support students who rely only, or primarily, on virtual communication. The majority of online course management tools integrate real-time tools, allowing students to communicate with one another as well as with the instructor. The most commonly used tool is chat but some course management tools also allow for video- and voice-streaming. These real-time tools can assist in increasing the frequency, and perhaps quality, of in-class and out-of-class communication.

Choosing a real-time technology

In addition to the broad categorization of real-time tools into those supporting communication and those supporting collaboration, several dimensions have emerged as central when making decisions about which tools are best suited for a project or course. Next, I will discuss in more detail four key dimensions:

1. network type
2. scalability
3. data type
4. push versus pull.

Network type. Digital tools that are geared towards closed network structures support communication and collaboration among a small group of scholars who share a common affiliation or are clustered together in a meaningful way (e.g., a research cluster, the members of a lab, or students taking a course). Skype and Google Docs are two tools that best support closed network structures, as only those interlocutors who are in a user's contact list can communicate with one another. In comparison, open network structures are those that support communication and collaboration between people who may or may not know each other or at least are not formally associated. One example of this type of real-time technology is Google+ Hangout, where any user can join a hangout, as long as they have a Google account, a webcam and a microphone. In general, real-time digital tools tend to support closed network structures because even a minimal level of acquaintance is needed for two individuals to feel comfortable contacting each other spontaneously in real time (Quan-Haase et al., 2005).

Scalability. Scalability[7] refers to the extent to which a tool is designed to effectively support the work of a larger group of users. Tools may be limited in their ability to scale out to larger groups. These limitations may result from technological constraints or from the affordance of the tool. Some tools have been developed to facilitate contact between small groups ranging from two to five individuals. Even though Google Chat has no limit to the number of people that can be added, it is best suited for conversations among two to five individuals; once more than five individuals are added to the chat, it is difficult to keep track of who is conversing, and making sense of a conversation that includes more than six people is almost impossible (i.e., unless some users are not participating). In general, asynchronous forms of communication are better suited to scale out (i.e., adding more users to the system) because it is easier to track who is leaving a message and also follow the evolution of a conversation. Herring (1999) found in her analysis of text-only computer-mediated communication (e.g., Internet Relay Chat) that the negative effect of incoherence was offset by the availability of a persistent textual record that could help communication partners make sense of messages. This is also true of chat, where conversation partners can scroll up to see text previously typed to help them make sense of the conversation, but has its limitations once the conversation moves too quickly and consists of too many interlocutors.

Data type. Real-time technologies support the exchange of different types of data, including voice, image, text and multimedia. While some tools are geared toward transmitting and sharing a single type of data, others allow for multi-modal exchanges. For example, Google Docs primarily supports collaboration in a textual environment. By contrast, Skype is multi-modal in nature: providing visual and auditory information on the interlocutors, and having a window for simultaneous text, file and image sharing.

Push vs. pull. Push technology displays information without any action being required from the user, whereas pull technology necessitates users to seek out updates. Instant messaging is a push technology because presence information about other users is automatically transmitted without the user needing to request the information. In push technology, users can also choose to display availability through the use of status settings (e.g., busy or away), or they can leave messages to others about their social accessibility by way of customizable messages (Baron et al., 2005; Quan-Haase and Collins, 2008). Therefore, chat provides a variety of ways in which to display a user's presence and availability in a flexible manner over time. In pull technology, users are required to seek out information about other users. In Google Docs, for instance, users need to select the 'revision history' to see the changes made to a document by collaborators. These updates are not automatically presented to the user. It is clear from this distinction that it is useful to have both push and pull technology in place to more effectively manage information overload (Baron, 2008; Quan-Haase, 2010).

Challenges using real-time technologies

As students and faculty adopt real-time technologies, it is becoming evident that these also have potential negative consequences. These detriments are often summarized under the term productivity paradox, which is defined as 'a phenomenon in which investments in the use of information technology have not resulted in productivity improvements' (Hannula and Lönnqvist, 2002, p. 83). In this section, six potential negative consequences are discussed that have been identified in the literature.

Losses in productivity. The concerns raised in the literature are primarily linked to losses in productivity that can result from multitasking (Gonzalez and Mark, 2004; Su and Mark, 2008), workflow interruptions, shifts in attention and loss of focus (Cutrell et al., 2001; Quan-Haase, 2010). Quan-Haase and Collins (2008) argue that the social norms of real-time technologies lead users to reply quickly because others know they are available for communication, even when it may be disruptive. When people are 'always on, always available', it makes it difficult to keep focused on a task (Quan-Haase et al., 2005).

Information overload. Similar to concerns considered in other learning infrastructures, the increased volume of communication caused by real-time technologies requires management (Oua and Davison, 2011). When used to engage with students for out-of-class communication, these tools can add considerable effort to a faculty member's workload (Balayeva and Quan-Haase, 2009). For e-learning initiatives this increased volume of messages between faculty and students may be a desired outcome. In large traditional classrooms with over 100 students, an increase in volume may represent an unnecessary burden for the instructor, particularly if no teaching assistants have been assigned to the course. This shows that practical implications need to be taken into consideration prior to adoption. The use of real-time technologies to communicate with collaborators may, on the other hand, be an effective way to exchange messages without adding considerably to the regular workload when used effectively.

Lack of nonverbal cues. Karpova et al. (2008) identify numerous challenges associated with virtual collaborations. The authors see some disadvantages because 'the inability to use nonverbal language in virtual communication made the interaction more challenging' (p. 49) and can lead to misunderstandings and slow down progress. This common reoccurring theme throughout the research in this area shows that text-only learning environments may constrain the kinds of interactions that are possible (Finegold and Cooke, 2006). Nonetheless, the widespread adoption of Twitter among academics – which is not only a text-based tool, but restricts posts to 140 characters – suggests that the lack of nonverbal cues can be beneficial for certain scholarly communities and scholarly purposes.[8]

Awareness of responsibilities. Another significant hurdle faced by virtual teams is the absence of clear team-based working processes (Karpova et al., 2008; Leinonen et al., 2005). Teamwork involves the collaboration of a number of individuals who all participate in the process of creation. However, it is essential that all members of the team are aware of the other members' responsibilities. Previous research shows that the role of awareness in virtual collaboration is an important issue, the lack of which certainly can inhibit productive and creative teamwork (ibid.).

Loss of privacy and control over data. Even though many users express concerns about how real-time technologies represent an invasion of privacy, this does not usually deter them from using them (Young and Quan-Haase, 2009). The attitude expressed by most users is that as long as they have not had any negative experiences themselves, they do not see a need to proactively protect their data. There are two kinds of potential threats to privacy in the use of real-time technologies, one is social and the other is institutional (Raynes-Goldie, 2010). Social privacy refers to the risks associated with friends, colleagues or acquaintances finding out personal information that users may not want to disseminate. Institutional privacy describes the loss of privacy on a more structural scale; for instance, companies who provide online services potentially sharing data with third parties or aggregating data from various sources. Both kinds of loss of privacy represent a major problem as data are not locally stored but are rather on the cloud[9] and therefore they fall under different jurisdictions.[10]

Relationship type. The use of real-time technologies is most appropriate for supporting interactions among close-knit networks (Quan-Haase et al., 2005). For collaborative and teaching purposes, trusting relationships are an important factor for real-time technologies to work efficiently. Wymer, in her study, made herself available for consultation to students via virtual office hours using chat and her experience made her 'question the extent to which our students want us to reach out to them in those new ways' (2006, pp. 37–8). Part of the problem is that students use social media to 'express themselves and their individuality' (ibid.) and might not feel comfortable letting faculty into their personal world. Balayeva and Quan-Haase (2009), in a similar study, asked students how comfortable they were communicating with instructors via chat. The results showed that 10 per cent of students felt uncomfortable communicating with faculty via chat because of the type of formal relationship they have with them. While students may not feel comfortable adding faculty to their personal Facebook pages, they may welcome opportunities to talk to them in real time when supported by a formal system (such as edmodo.com). Therefore, it is important to obtain a better understanding of the unique features of various real-time tools and how to design them so that they will better serve student and faculty needs. These options are further explored in Chapter 8.

Conclusions

An important question when examining different types of real-time technologies is the appropriateness of different tools for various types of collaborative networks and class settings. The duration of projects, the amount of interaction needed and the interdependence of tasks are all important considerations when making choices about which real-time tools are most suitable. Also, different classroom settings, ranging from smaller classrooms or seminars with about 20–30 students to large classrooms, may necessitate different approaches. In smaller classrooms, where the faculty know all of their students, real-time communication may enhance interaction and engagement with the material. In large classrooms, the number of real-time interactions may become so large that it becomes a burden for faculty. Future research needs to compare the use of various real-time technologies in different kinds of settings.

As Generation Y (also known as the Millennial generation) continues to move into academic settings, it will become critical for faculty to obtain a grasp on how this cohort uses real-time technologies and the social and productivity implications this use will have on their work habits and scholarship. A study by the Pew Internet & American Life

Project found that Generation Y is more likely to rely on the Internet for communicative, creative and social uses; for example, showing significantly more social media usage than other generations (Lenhart et al., 2010; Madden and Smith, 2010).

Real-time technologies offer many benefits to academics. However, the resulting work environment of 'always on, always available' also represents a number of challenges. On the one hand, the advantages of real-time technologies to academics lie in the timeliness of information available and the possibility to connect with colleagues at a distance. The social web continually provides a stream of up-to-date information on relevant topics as well as on developments occurring in the field. The importance of being connected to the field can be of great relevance. On the other hand, a central problem in real-time communication is the disruptive nature of the technology. Various strategies can help users deal more effectively with multitasking, management of virtualization and distractions. This area of study becomes increasingly relevant because today's work practices are undergoing changes due to the ongoing development of social media (Rennecker and Godwin, 2003). While concerns remain as to the consequences of real-time technologies, the need for adoption to collaborate, disseminate research findings and reach a larger, diverse audience is inherently evident.

Acknowledgements

This work was supported by funding from an Academic Development Fund from the University of Western Ontario and GRAND, a Canada Network of Centres of Excellence grant. The manuscript has greatly benefited from the input of Michael Haight and Kim Martin, students in the SocioDigital Lab at the University of Western Ontario.

Notes

1. Google Documents or Google Docs is owned and managed by Google. Even though the term Google Docs may suggest that it refers only to word processing files, it is actually used more broadly including spreadsheets, presentations, tables, and drawings.
2. The term meta-level of work refers to a conversation about the work that is taking place in the real-time collaborative environment as it unfolds.
3. In October 2011, the price for Skype Premium was USD$4.49/month.

4. The Open Science Summit is a conference dedicated to using distributed innovation to address pressing needs in academia.
5. See the article at: *http://www.nature.com/news/2011/110819/full/news.2011.492.html*.
6. The Google Enterprise Blog is located at: *http://googleenterprise.blogspot.com/2011/09/tradition-meets-technology-top.html*.
7. Scalability is defined as 'the ability of a system, network, or process, to handle growing amounts of work in a graceful manner or its ability to be enlarged to accommodate that growth' (Wikipedia, 2011, para. 1).
8. See Chapter 2 of this volume on scholarly communities.
9. This is an inherent benefit of cloud computing as the data can be retrieved from any location.
10. See Chapter 10 in this volume.

References

Balayeva, J and Quan-Haase, A. (2009) Virtual office hours as cyberinfrastructure: the case study of instant messaging. *Learning Inquiry*, 3(3): 115–30.

Baron, N.S. (2008) *Always On: Language in an Online and Mobile World*. New York: Oxford University Press.

Baron, N.S., Squires, L., Tench, S. and Thompson, M. (2005) 'Tethered or mobile? Use of away messages in instant messaging by American college students', in R.R. Ling and P.E. Pedersen (eds). *Mobile Communications: Re-negotiation of the Social Sphere* (pp. 293–311). New York: Springer-Verlag.

Beldarrain, Y. (2006) Distance education trends: integrating new technologies to foster student interaction and collaboration. *Distance Education*, 27(2): 139–53.

Berlind, D. (2010). First look: Google docs gets realtime collaboration. *InformationWeek*, 15 April. Retrieved from *http://www.informationweek.com/news/software/productivity_apps/224400349*.

Bonetta, L. (2007) Scientists enter the blogosphere. *Cell*, 129(3): 443–5.

Cutrell, E., Czerwinski, M. and Horvitz, E. (2001) Notification, disruption, and memory: effects of messaging interruptions on memory and performance. In *Proceedings of the Human-Computer Interaction Conference (Interact '01)*. Retrieved from *http://research.microsoft.com/en-us/um/people/cutrell/interact2001messaging.pdf*.

Dobransky, N.D. and Bainbridge Frymier, A. (2004) Developing teacher-student relationships through out-of-class communication. *Communication Quarterly*, 52(3), 211–23.

Finegold, A.R.D. and Cooke, L. (2006) Exploring the attitudes, experiences and dynamics of interaction in online groups. *Internet and Higher Education*, 9: 201–15.

Gonzalez, V. and Mark, G. (2004) '"Constant, constant, multi-tasking craziness": managing multiple working spheres', in E. Dykstra-Erickson and M. Tscheligi (eds). *Proceedings of the ACM CHI 2004 Conference on Human Factors in*

Computing Systems (pp. 113–20). New York: ACM. DOI:10.1145/985692.9 85707.

Hannula, M. and Lönnqvist, A. (2002) How the Internet affects productivity. *International Business & Economics Research Journal*, 1(2): 83–91.

Haythornthwaite, C. and Andrews, R. (2011) *E-learning Theory and Practice*. London: Sage.

Herring, S.C. (1999) Interactional coherence in CMC. *Journal of Computer-Mediated Communication*, 4(4): 1–27.

Hogan, B. and Quan-Haase, A. (2010) Persistence and change in social media: a framework of social practice. *Bulletin of Science, Technology and Society*, 30(5): 309–15. Retrieved from *http://bst.sagepub.com/content/30/5/309.full.pdf+html*.

Karpova, E., Correia, A.-P. and Baran, E. (2008) Learn to use and use to learn: technology in virtual collaboration experience. *Internet and Higher Education*, 12: 45–52.

Kendrick, J. (2009) Collaboration with Skype desktop sharing: the best free method? *Gigaom*. Retrieved from *http://gigaom.com/mobile/collaboration-with-skype-desktop-sharing-the-best-free-method/*.

Leinonen, P., Järvelä, S. and Häkkinen, P. (2005) Conceptualizing the awareness of collaboration: a qualitative study of a global virtual team. *Computer Supported Cooperative Work* 14: 301–22.

Lenhart, A., Purcell, K., Smith, A. and Zickuhr, K. (2010) Social media and young adults. *The Pew Internet and American Life Project*. Retrieved from: *http://www.pewinternet.org/Reports/2010/Social-Media-and-Young-Adults.aspx*.

Madden, M. and Smith, A. (2010) Reputation management and social media. *The PEW Internet and American Life Project*. Retrieved from *http://www.pewinternet.org/Reports/2010/Reputation-Management.aspx*.

Nardi, B.A., Whittaker, S. and Bradner, E. (2000) Interaction and outeraction: instant messaging in action. In *Proceedings of the Conference on Computer Supported Cooperative Work (CSCW)* (pp. 79–88). New York: ACM. DOI:10.1145/358916.358975.

Oua, C.X.J. and Davison, R.M. (2011) Interactive or interruptive? Instant messaging at work. *Decision Support Systems*, 52(1): 61–72.

Parry, D. (2010) Be online or be irrelevant [blog post]. Retrieved from *http://academhack.outsidethetext.com/home/2010/be-online-or-be-irrelevant/*.

Quan-Haase, A. (2009) *Information Brokering in the High-tech Industry: Online Social Networks at Work*. Berlin: LAP Publishing.

Quan-Haase, A. (2010) Self-regulation in instant messaging (IM): failures, strategies, and negative consequences. *International Journal of e-Collaboration*, 6(3): 22–42.

Quan-Haase, A. and Collins, J.L. (2008) 'I'm there, but I might not want to talk to you': university students' social accessibility in instant messaging. *Information, Communication & Society*, 11(4): 526–43.

Quan-Haase, A., Cothrel, J. and Wellman, B. (2005) Instant messaging for collaboration: a case study of a high-tech firm. *Journal of Computer-Mediated Communication*, 10(4). Retrieved from *http://jcmc.indiana.edu/vol10/issue4/quan-haase.html*.

Quan-Haase, A. and Young, A.L. (2010) Uses and gratifications of social media: a comparison of Facebook and instant messaging. *Bulletin of Science, Technology and Society.* 30(5): 350–61. Retrieved from *http://bst.sagepub.com/content/30/5/350.abstract*.

Raynes-Goldie, K. (2010) Aliases, creeping, and wall cleaning: understanding privacy in the age of Facebook. *First Monday*, 15(1). Retrieved from *http://firstmonday.org/htbin/cgiwrap/bin/ojs/index.php/fm/article/viewArticle/2775*.

Rennecker, J. and Godwin, L. (2003) Theorizing the unintended consequences of instant messaging productivity. *Sprouts: Working papers on Information Environments, Systems and Organizations*, 3(3): 137–68.

Roper, S.L. and Kindred, J. (2005) 'IM here.' Reflections on virtual office hours. *First Monday*, 10(11). Retrieved from *http://www.ischool.utexas.edu/~i385q/readings/firstmonday_im.htm*.

Su, N.M. and Mark, G. (2008) 'Communication chains and multitasking', in M. Czerwinski, L. Arnie and T. Desney (eds). *Proceedings of the ACM CHI 2008 Conference on Human Factors in Computing Systems* (pp. 83–92). Florence, Italy: ACM.

Wikipedia (2011) Scalability. Retrieved from *http://en.wikipedia.org/wiki/Scalability*.

Wymer, K. (2006) The professor as instant messenger. *The Chronicle of Higher Education*, 7. Retrieved from *http://chronicle.com/article/The-Professor-as-Instant/46916*.

Young, A.L. and Quan-Haase, A. (2009) 'Information revelation and internet privacy concerns on social network sites: a case study of Facebook', in J.M. Carrol (ed.). *Proceedings of the Fourth International Conference on Communities and Technologies* (pp. 265–74). Dordrecht: Springer Verlag.

4

Locating scholarly papers of interest online

Maureen Henninger

Abstract: Discovering the existence of scholarly papers in an online environment has been possible since the middle of the last century and the retrieval of their full text reliably possible only in the last quarter of the century. Since then several public web-based scholarly search engines have become available and directly compete with the older proprietary database search services to aid scholars and researchers. This chapter compares three public services, Google Scholar, Academic Search and Scirus, with two proprietary services, Web of Science and Scopus, in their effectiveness as tools for communicating and raising awareness of scholarship. It examines the three main functions required at different times by scholars – the discovery and retrieval of scholarly literature, the analysis of journals for publishing decisions and citation analysis for mapping collaborative scholarly networks and communities.

Key words: search engines, scholarly communication, bibliometrics, information visualization.

Introduction

It is obvious that academics and researchers have always needed to find literature, particularly research literature, to alert them to new developments in their discipline(s), to further their own research and to pass this on to students through research-based teaching. Once upon a time the 'literature' was knowledge which was passed on by oral communication, and possibly messenger services, to one's personal and scholarly 'networks'. We have now come full circle – the passing on of scholarly knowledge through social media technologies. Along the way we have cycled through a number of innovative services and technologies. The digital environment has brought 'qualitative and quantitative changes in the ways that scholars communicate with each other for informal conversations, for collaborating locally and over distances, for publishing and disseminating their work, and for constructing links between their work and that of others' (Borgman and Furner, 2002, p. 4). It is within this context that this chapter examines the tools of such academic literature finders, as well as their use for bibliometric analysis and mapping.

This chapter concentrates on three public search systems – two general, multi-disciplinary ones: Google Scholar and Microsoft's Academic Search (beta); and one specialized or vertical one: Scirus (science). For comparison, I measure two proprietary, fee-based subscription systems: Elsevier's Scopus and Thomson's Web of Science.

Overview of online scholarly search services

The rapid growth of the Internet began with three not quite concurrent events: the development of the World Wide Web in 1989; the lifting of the ban on commercial activity on the Internet (what was at that time NFSNet) in 1991; and the release of the first point and click browser, Mosaic, in 1993. In fact it was out of a need to collaborate and share scholarly information among the community of particle physicists at CERN (Conseil Européen pour la Recherche Nucléaire) in Switzerland that the team, led by Tim Berners-Lee, developed the web (Henninger, 2008).

In the 1980s there were many publicly available collections, archives and repositories of scholarly documents such as NetLib, as well as the large proprietary indexing and abstracting databases. While the main system available to search across much of the content of individual databases was ISI's Science Citation Index (at that time accessed via Lockheed's Dialog service),[1] in the public sphere, other than early systems such as Archie or Gopher, there were no tools for searching and retrieving scholarly articles.[2] One of the earliest of the public scholarly search engines was CiteSeer, which was developed at the NEC Research Institute to provide access to cited scientific scholarly literature and was available on the web in 1997. It was really the first decade of this century, powered by robust search engine technology for crawling the Internet and access by agreement or joint venture to some of the large indexes of proprietary databases[3] which saw the development of public, web-based scholarly search engines (see Figure 4.1).

Locating scholarly papers of interest online

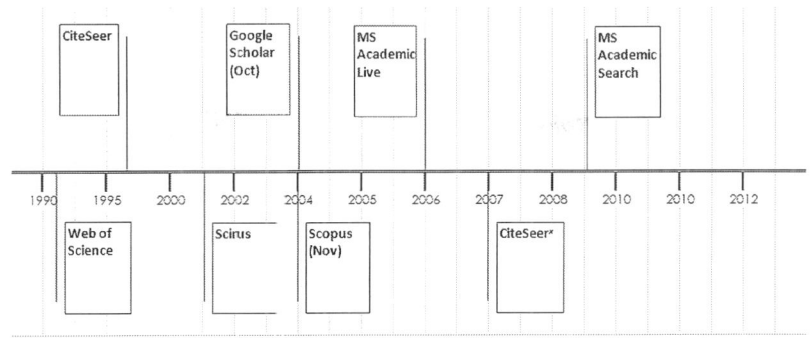

Figure 4.1 Timeline of the release of online academic search engines

Scholarly communication and social media

Before examining the search and retrieval systems, it is important to discuss the meaning of 'scholarly literature'. At a basic level, it is writing done by scholars in the process of expanding knowledge through some review process. This writing may be research results or ponderings; by format it may be books, peer-reviewed journal articles, presentations at conferences, papers or documents deposited in electronic archives or repositories, to name some of the possibilities. As noted above, it's a vehicle for publishing or otherwise disseminating their work. It is this somewhat flexible definition which at times can cause searchers confusion and which differentiates the various services. For example, Web of Science, now part of a broader service, the Web of Knowledge, with its access to many other Thomson databases, originally placed its emphasis on peer-reviewed journal articles and, in particular, those journals which had high-impact value. At the other end of the spectrum is Google Scholar which does not define other than in very general terms what it considers to be scholarly. The details, distinctions, advantages and disadvantages of each of these services are discussed below in the individual service sections.

Scholarly communication, in concept and practice by definition *is* social media. As Christine Borgman (2008) notes, online chat, researchers' blogging and line items in grant proposals for Skype accounts are ubiquitous features in e-scholarship. Nevertheless, in some scholarly communities the uptake of the more informal social media has been reluctant. Christie Wilcox, a blogger at Scientific American, contends that the dissemination of scientific knowledge by social media is the scientist's job, and yet 'when it comes to social adaptation and technology, we're [scientists] more than behind the curve. Although 72% of Internet-using Americans are on Facebook, less than 2/3 of college faculty are' (Wilcox, 2011, para. 2).

However, within the context of this book, the tools of social media have not been readily available with the scholarly search and retrieval services. These services, while providing some insight into scholarly networks through applied citation indexing – 'cited by' and 'related articles' – do not allow tagging, annotating nor the ability to build shared personal or community collections; such functions are the foundations of Web 2.0 technologies. It was not until the mid-2000s that tools such as CiteULike, Mendeley and SearchGate began to fill this space and this development is fully covered in Chapter 5.

Use and purpose of scholarly search services

There are two ostensible uses for scholarly search engines: search and retrieval of literature; and the analysis of the citations in this scholarly literature (bibliometrics). In general, the scholarly search services were exactly that, search engines whose purpose was to search for scholarly literature and to retrieve the full citation. Gradually, they began to provide facilities to discover other similar literature (citation pearl-growing); currently, citation pearl-growing and the delivery of the full text of the document are the major services in both the proprietary and the web-based services.

However, systems which could provide access to very large citation databases enabled the ability to mine these rich resources for other purposes, in particular bibliometric analysis – scholars using these services to track their own citations and to find the most influential journals on a particular subject for promotion and publishing decision-making purposes – and visual mapping of scholarly collaborations and disciplinary networks. The visual maps enable further, and often unexpected, discovery of scholarly communication through citation and co-citation analysis, the work done by bibliometricians using the various versions of the Science Citation databases.[4]

The gradual iterations and versions of the Science Citation databases now provide detailed citation analytical reports (see Figure 4.2) and interactive hyperbolic visualizations of the forward and backward

Locating scholarly papers of interest online

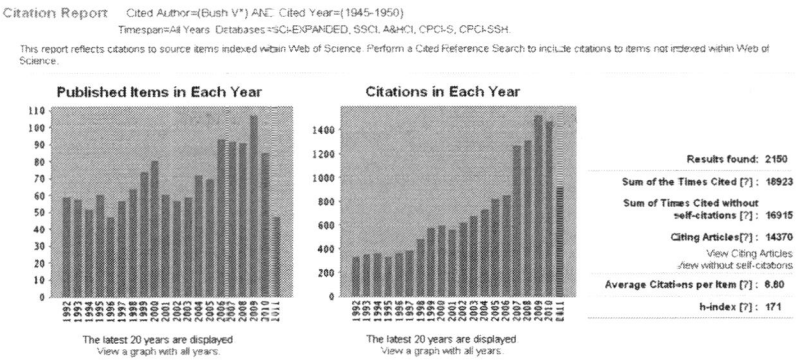

Figure 4.2 Web of Science citation report for the paper, As we may think, by Vannevar Bush

citations, that is, the cited references and citing references of a scholarly paper (see Figure 4.3, p. 64). To date, among the public scholarly search engines, the only serious attempt at this functionality is the more recent versions of Microsoft's Academic Search and, to a much lesser extent, Google Scholar.

It must be said that the use of the scholarly search services, both proprietary and public, for bibliometric analysis engenders much discussion and controversy. The variations in the included and excluded literature in each of the services have been the subject of many studies[5] as well as comparative studies of the ranking algorithms for calculating impact factors, influential journals and citation tracking.

Impact of the Open Access movement

There is a third way, a movement, which provides a vehicle for access to scholarship. The Open Access (OA) movement has had an important impact on access to scholarly literature. This movement, which aims to make the corpus of scholarly literature freely accessible, accelerated with the expansion of the availability of the Internet. While there are initiatives such as PubMed (open access to medical literature) by the journal publishers to make their offerings available after a certain period of time, it is the self-archiving of scholarly papers, the OA green road, and the OA gold road of publishing in OA journals which have increased access to the full text of scholarly literature.[6]

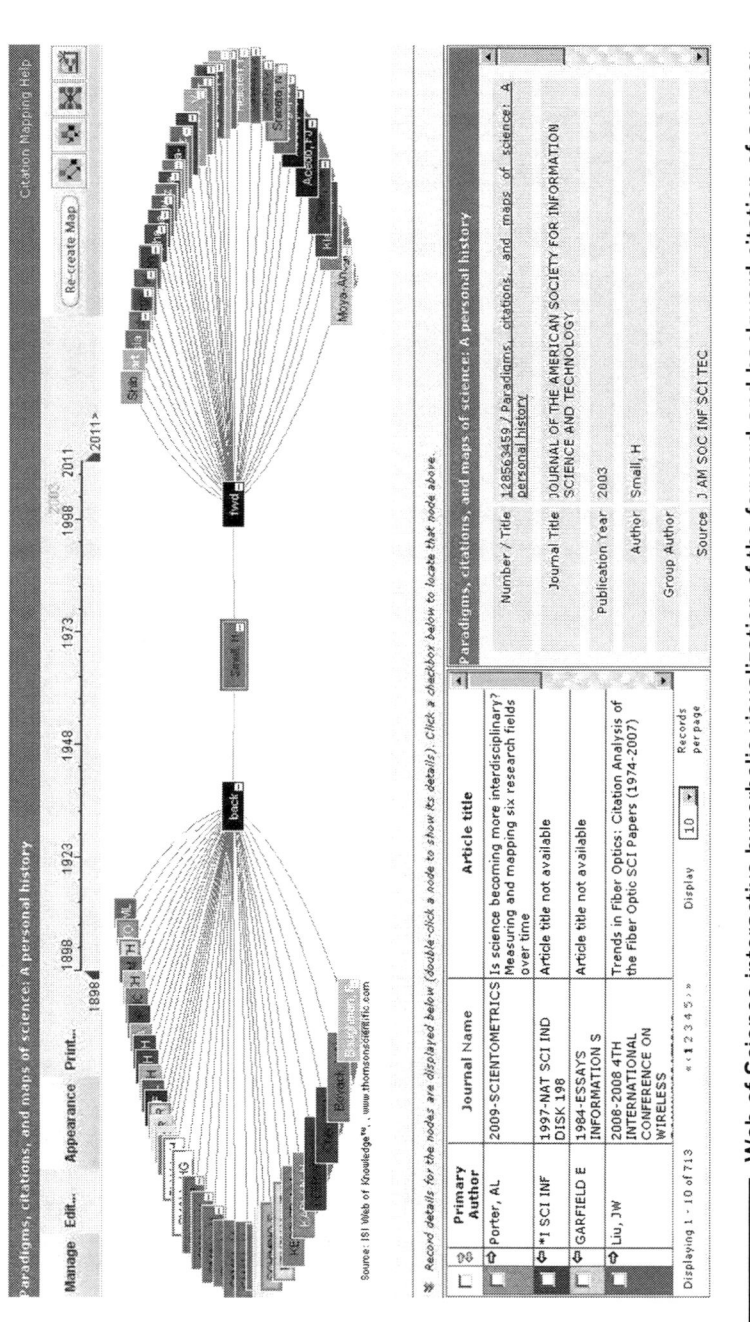

Figure 4.3 Web of Science interactive hyperbolic visualization of the forward and backward citation of a paper by Henry G. Small

Web-based public scholarly search engines can add this content since the online ejournals are open to search engine spiders. In the case of the e-repositories, in reality, it is the bibliographic metadata (title, author, subject, etc.) about the papers which is gathered using the Open Access Initiative-Protocol for Metadata Harvesting (OAI-PMH), the first stable version of which was released in 2003. Proprietary services are also able to use this method to add content to their databases; in the case of Scopus, however, this is not necessary since it owns the public scientific search engine, Scirus.

According to some critics the effectiveness of the web-based services may be compromised since they reparse the OAI metadata rather than simply using it.[7] The OAI-PMH mandates the use of a standard metadata format, Dublin Core, which is more compatible with the metadata, such as subject, document type (article, thesis and review, etc.) and document format, which drives the proprietary services.[8]

Search engine functionality

We now need to discuss briefly how search engines are used. As a rule, the most effective way to use a search engine, although not necessarily the most efficient as demonstrated by the ubiquity of the single search bar, is to utilize the advanced search facility. This allows you to leverage the metadata for more specific queries and provides good filtering and limiting of the results. In the case of general Internet search engines, the searchable metadata is restricted to title, URL, language, file type and sometimes date; these search fields are available in an advanced search interface but you can search in most of these fields in the single search bar, thus combining effectiveness and efficiency. For example,

> intitle: 'scholarly communication' 'information retrieval' inurl: edu.au filetype: pdf

and in most of the public scholarly search engines you can add 'author:' and 'date:'.

On the other hand, proprietary database search systems such as Scopus and Web of Science have highly granular descriptive metadata which is 'on show' in the advanced search interface (see Figure 4.4). As we shall see, the public scholarly search engines have been criticized for not using such rich metadata.

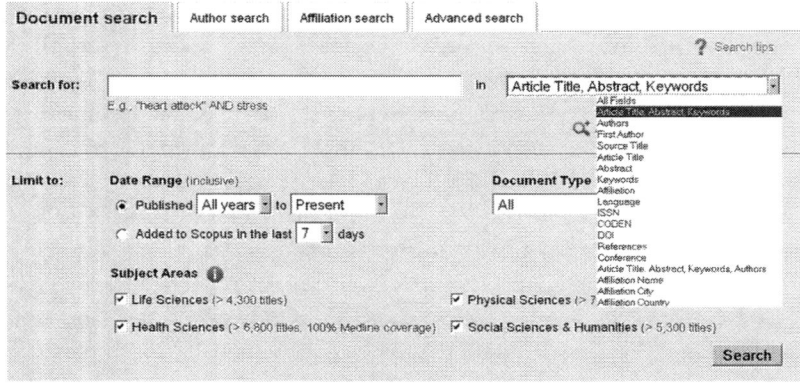

Figure 4.4 Scopus search interface showing searchable metadata fields

Public scholarly search services

In this section we will examine the details of three public web-based scholarly search services: two multi-disciplinary services, Google Scholar and Microsoft Academic Search; and a specific disciplinary (scientific) service, Scirus. In each case, a brief history of the service is given, and a discussion of its content, ranking algorithms, usability, strengths and weaknesses, contribution to the dissemination of scholarly literature, and its use and opportunities within the space of social media are provided. For the specific functionality and features of the individual public search services see the Appendix: Features of web-based public scholarly search services.

Tips for using web-based public services

- If your library has a partnership agreement with the service then it is faster than searching in library databases to get the full-text document.

- Use them when you know the exact title of a paper. It is a great way to build a citation database – it saves typing!

- In Google Scholar, to retrieve only master records once you have done your search filter the results to include 'at least summaries'.

Google Scholar

The beta version of this service was launched in October 2004. At that time, according to Anurag Acharya of Google, the content included 'peer-reviewed papers, theses, books, preprints, abstracts and technical reports' (Acharya, 2004, para. 1); it has since expanded the content – patents in November 2006 and United States legal information in November 2009. There is no doubt that 'search' is the strength of Google Scholar; in Peter Jacsó's words, 'for topical keyword searches, GS is most valuable. But it cannot be used to analyze the publishing performance and impact of researchers' (Jacsó, 2009, para. 4). Part of the difficulty is, firstly, the lack of specificity of what is considered 'scholarly', and, secondly, the inclusion of multiple versions of individual documents, a factor which, conversely, is of great value to the searcher who wishes to be able to retrieve a copy of the full-text article when the original is locked behind a proprietary service.

Content. Currently, 'scholarly' in Google Scholar is defined as follows: 'journal and conference papers, theses and dissertations, academic books, pre-prints, abstracts, technical reports and other scholarly literature from all broad areas of research. You'll find works from a wide variety of academic publishers (though not, unsurprisingly, from Elsevier), professional societies and university repositories, as well as scholarly articles available anywhere across the web' (Google Scholar, 2011a, para. 1). We have already noted Google Scholar content of court opinions and patents. It also includes citations from social media sources Mendeley and CiteULike. It has been pointed out by Beel et al. that much of this content is from 'trusted sources' such as 'publishers that cooperate directly with Google Scholar, as well as publishers and Webmasters who have requested that Google Scholar crawl their databases and Web sites' (Beel et al., 2010, p. 183). However, as Google does not specify the sources of the citations, it cannot be assumed that all are from 'trusted sources'.

The legal content is case law of the United States supreme, federal, state, and appellate courts, which is generally considered the scholarly output of judges. It is certainly easier to use than the traditional Westlaw or LexisNexis systems for case law searching; the ranking algorithm lists results by the highest court opinions first, then by number of citations. It not only returns the list of the citing documents, but it provides the added-value of contextual citations within the full text. However, according to Carol Ebbinghouse (2009), you do not get much of the other material such as the links to statutes and regulations that are available on the database systems.

Patent documents are available via Google's vertical patent search which was added in November 2006 after an agreement with the United States Patent and Trademark Office (USPTO) for a complete download of US patents and trademarks. In Google Scholar you are able to 'include patents' in your search, although it appears that journal articles are ranked more highly than patents, that is, patents often appear after the scholarly articles. If you want to use Google Scholar for finding only patents simply add the word patent to your search.

Ranking and displaying. The ranking algorithm is a combination of several factors; Google states that it 'rank[s] documents the way researchers do, weighing the full text of each document, where it was published, who it was written by, as well as how often and how recently it has been cited in other scholarly literature' (Google Scholar, 2011a, para. 3). In other words, the more cited and relevant articles rise to the top of the results. It is this algorithm, and the fact that it does not make use of the publishers' metadata to parse the documents, which made Peter Jacsó so critical in 2009. While Google appears to have corrected many of these inaccuracies, there is a disclaimer, for example, on authorship: 'author names are often abbreviated and different people sometimes share similar names' (Google Scholar, 2011b, para. 8). Nevertheless, using the available publishers' metadata might ameliorate any residual problems.

Bibliometric analysis. While the use of Google Scholar for bibliometric analysis may be troublesome, for reasons mentioned above, it does provide a gadget, available for online use or for download at *http://code. Google.com/p/citations-gadget/*, which enables a search on an author(s) and provides a total citation count, total number of cited publications and the h-index.[9] You are able to use a variety of query statements in the gadget, for example the search below retrieves the results shown in Figure 4.5:

---

author: "HG Small" "citation analysis" OR "co-citation"

Locating scholarly papers of interest online

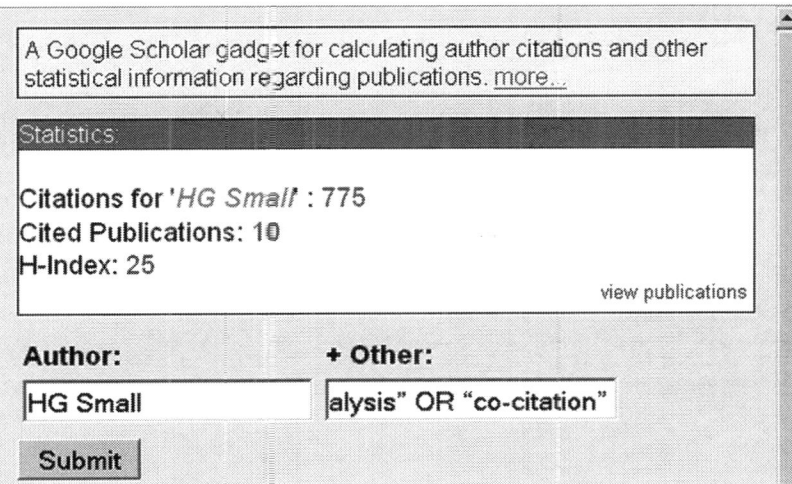

Figure 4.5 Example of a citation analysis in the Google Scholar gadget

Social networking opportunities. There is nothing in the way of built-in social media tools in Google Scholar. However, a citation tracking function, Google Scholar Citations, was announced on 20 July 2011, and on 16 November 2011 the service was made available to everyone. The function builds a profile, which can be either public or private, of the researcher and includes three metrics, the h-index, the i10-index and the total number of citations to the authors' articles. The citations may be sorted by the number of citations or by the date of the reference. It also enables the author to manually update his/her profile by adding a new article or missing articles, correcting bibliographic errors and merging duplicate entries. Figure 4.6 shows the example of a public profile that is available on Google Scholar.

Academic Search (Microsoft)

In April 2006 Microsoft released its original academic finder tool, Windows Live Academic, but suspended it in May 2008. It clearly went back to R&D mode and in late October 2009 launched a much better product, Academic Search, which concentrated on the discipline of computer science. Since its first release Microsoft has been constantly adding content and features, so that the latest release in March 2011 is a sophisticated product and the only one of the public scholarly search services that is moving into the information visualization and social media spaces.

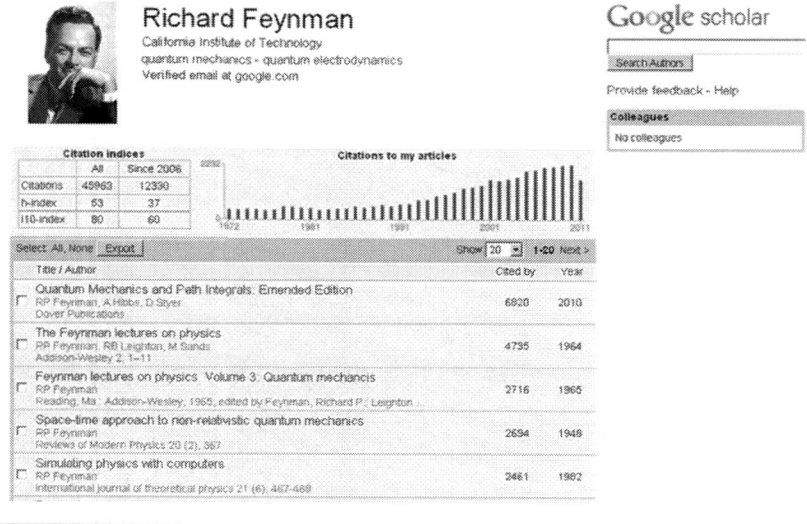

Figure 4.6 Example of a Google Scholar public profile

Content. Academic Search, which is still described as a prototype, initially focused on natural sciences such as mathematics, engineering, physics and life sciences, economics and business and claimed to have 36,684,204 publications and 18,831,925 authors as of 11 November, 2011 (Microsoft, n.d.). One can assume that this is because of the availability of large OA eprint repositories in these disciplines. It recently began to include scholarly papers in the domains of arts and humanities and social science. Nevertheless, from the features and functionalities that are available in this beta service, it is easy to see that it 'also serves as a test-bed for many research ideas in data mining, named entity extraction and disambiguation, data visualization, etc.' (Microsoft, 2011, para. 1) which is being done at Microsoft Research. The fact that the service has had several updates in the past two years, including the addition of content from other domains, leads to the assumption that it should be considered a serious search service.

Academic Search, like Google Scholar, does not specify its sources, therefore it is difficult to know exactly what it considers to be scholarly, other than what is mentioned in the broad statement 'academic publications, authors, conferences, [and] journals' (Microsoft, 2011, para. 2). As to the actual coverage of individual journals, this can be checked by searching on the journal and filter by year, for example:

Locating scholarly papers of interest online

```
jour: (dlib magazine) year>=2011
```

Ranking and displaying. According to the help page, the documents are ranked in the search results according to two factors: their relevance to the query; and their global importance (similar to Google Scholar, i.e., the most cited and relevant rise to the top of the results). The search algorithm is based on objects, not documents, usually recognizable concepts, such as authors, papers, conferences, or journals (this was the basis of the original work that Microsoft Research was doing in the development of Libra, an academic search engine that was the early prototype of Academic Search) (Nie et al., 2005). In practice, this allows good use of the object metadata to display the results in a variety of ways. For example, results are clustered by domains, by a keyword tag cloud, by journal or conference, and by co-authors. The results may be filtered as well as sorted by year. An individual author's results, however, can be sorted in other ways – year, citation and rank – as shown in Figure 4.7.

Bibliographic analysis. As can be seen in Figure 4.7, Academic Search provides a good profile of individual authors, giving information such as number of publications, number of citations, collaborative authors over a period of time, interest domains, and his/her g-index and h-index. Academic Search has some very good visualization features – domain trends, co-author graph, co-author path, and citation graph (see Figure 4.8) – and also has a suite of APIs (application programming interfaces),

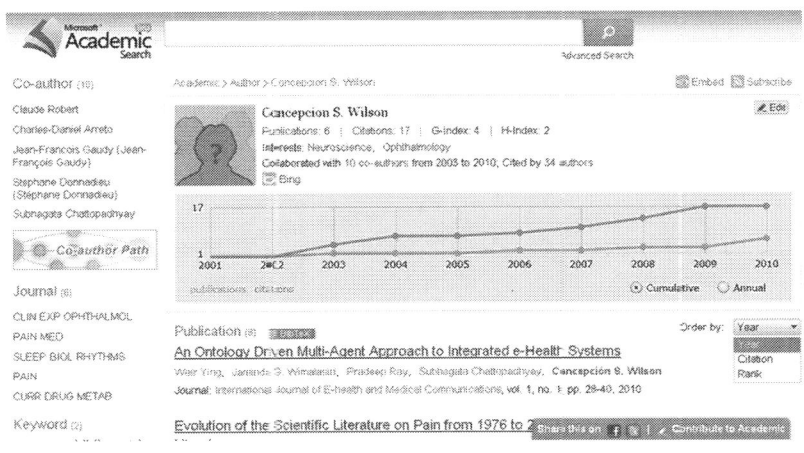

Figure 4.7 Display of results of an author search in Academic Search

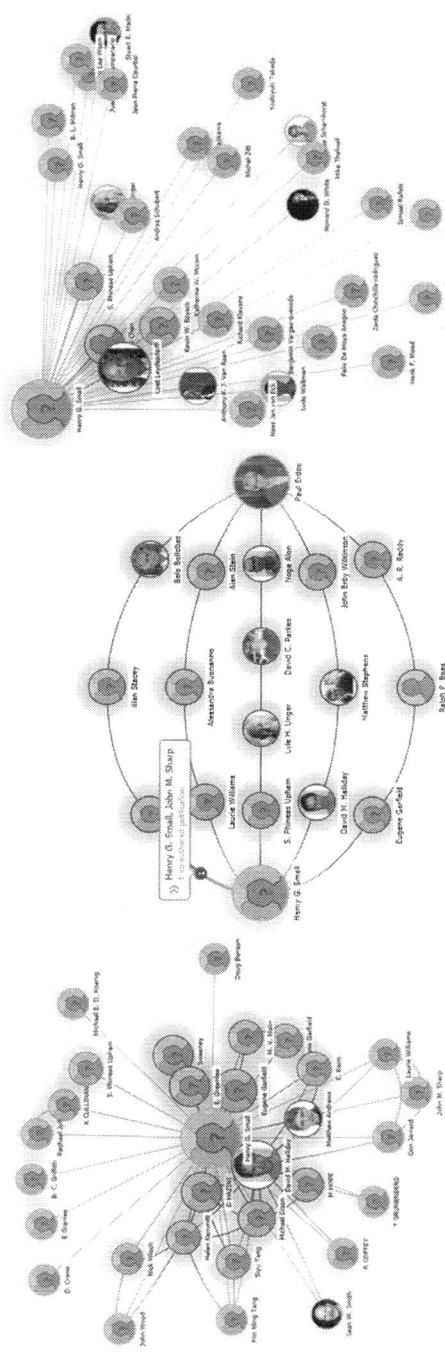

Figure 4.8 Academic Search's co-citation, co-author path and citation graph for Henry G. Small

for example, to build your own ranking of institutions or to build a visual explorer for browsing academic papers in a particular subject.

Social networking opportunities. Currently, of the services discussed in this chapter, Academic Scholar is the only one which has built in a social networking tool – the results of a search can be posted to Facebook (to your own wall, to a friend's wall, or to a Group) and to Twitter.

Scirus

This service, developed by Elsevier in conjunction with the Fast search engine, was first released in March 2001. In a sneak preview of the service it stated it would index scientific websites as well as incorporate proprietary content sources (Scirus, 2001). Today, it is still owned by Elsevier and claims to index over 410 million scientific documents.

Content. Scirus indexes several types of content: scientific websites, institutional and OA repositories' articles, and journal articles from the Elsevier journals, as well as a range of different information types, including all the patents from five patent databases, theses and dissertations, books, conferences and articles in press. Unlike Google Scholar and Academic Search, Scirus not only lists the sources of its content, but provides a complete list of the journals (About Scirus, 2001). Of the academic web-based search services, Scirus has the most content and arguably provides the most complete access to scientific scholarly literature.

Ranking and displaying. By default, the results are sorted by relevance. For websites, Scirus uses an algorithm similar to other general web search engines, that is, term frequency and link analysis. However, it also appears to use the publishers' metadata for the proprietary journal articles and for the e-repository content. The searchable metadata options for Scirus can be seen in Figure 4.9 below.

Bibliographic analysis. Scirus has no bibliographic analytical tools, nor does it provide any social networking opportunities. However, there is a link to SciTopics, also an Elsevier product, which is a 'free, wiki-like knowledge-sharing service for the scientific community. It offers distilled, authoritative and up-to-date research summaries on a wide range of scientific topics ... and designed to be a starting point for researchers to gain an introductory overview of a particular topic' (SciTopics, n.d., paras 1–2).

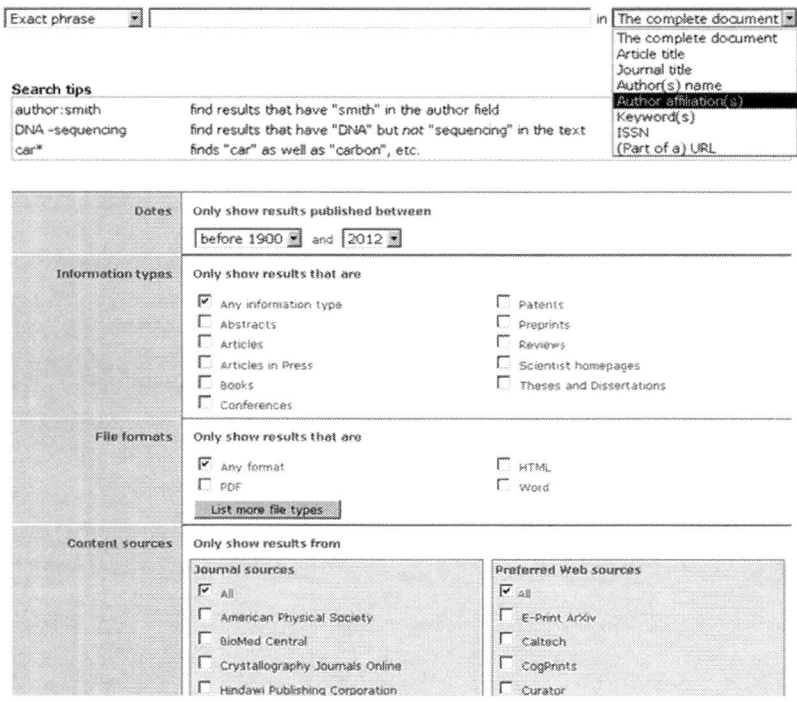

Figure 4.9 Rich searchable metadata options in Scirus

Proprietary scholarly search services

Scopus

Scopus, now officially SciVerse Scopus, is a product from Elsevier and was launched in November 2004 (coincidently within a month of the release of Google Scholar) to be a major competitor to Web of Science. At the time, the service was 'covering 14,000 scientific titles plus 167 million scientific web pages, and delivering the largest collection of abstracts ever collected online in one place, going back forty years" (Elsevier, 2004, para. 3).

Content. Currently, Scopus is an enormous database and according to Elsevier has access to 'over 18,500 titles from more than 5,000 international publishers ... 14.4 million records' (Elsevier, 2011, p. 4). It has its basis in the scientific fields using the citations from its own publications which include peer-reviewed journals, book series and conference proceedings. There is also the advantage of being able to include access to articles-in-press from Elsevier's list of 2,159 journal titles.[10] Recently, Scopus began adding citations in the arts and humanities, thus moving towards a more multi-disciplinary coverage. Scopus, from the search interface, provides a list of all journals and other sources, categorized by journals, conference proceedings, trade publications, and book series.

We have already noted that the web-based scholarly search engines have added listings to their content by agreement and/or joint ventures with proprietary database vendors. In the case of Scopus, the content is extended by the additional harvested listing available on Scirus (see above) which it owns.

Ranking and displaying. By default, Scopus displays the results of a subject search by year in descending order; however, the user has the option of reversing this order, as well as sorting by number of citations, relevance, first author, and source title. There is a very nice feature for selecting items from the results' list and printing a bibliography without having to first export the references into a bibliographic software package.

Bibliographic analysis. Scopus ranks journals according to the h-index, not the impact factor (the formula devised by Eugene Garfield) as done by the Web of Science; however, the data is available to calculate the impact factor. According to Elsevier, Scopus uses a 'next generation context-based' metrics, SNIP (source-normalized impact per paper) and SJR (SCImago Journal Rank).[11] Scopus has some excellent tools for analysis and visualization. For example, there is the usual citation tracker to find, check and track citations, an author identifier to automatically match an author's published research including the h-index and a journal analyser which shows journal performance, which is helpful for publishing decisions (Figure 4.10 gives some examples).

Social networking opportunities. Scopus provides no intrinsic social networking tools. However, Elsevier does have an add-on service, SciVal Experts, which is a directory of research expertise within an organization. It scans and analyses the Scopus publications to produce individual profiles which potentially can be used for collaboration within the organization or to identify external collaborators.

Web of Science

This is the oldest of the proprietary scholarly literature search services which are built around the concept of citation indexing. Its recent

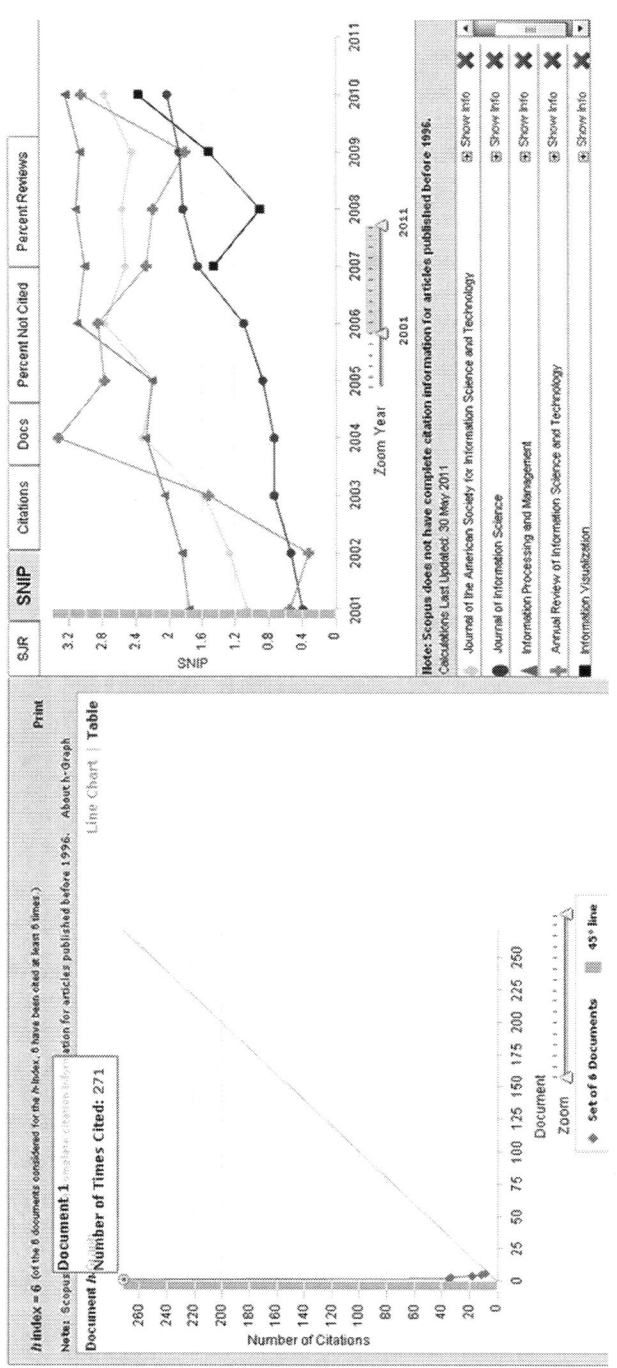

Figure 4.10 Scopus bibliometric visualizations: 1) h-index graph of 7 documents with self-citations removed, and 2) the SNIP (contextual citation impact) analysis of four journals[1,2]

incarnation under Thomson Reuters, the Web of Science, was released in 1992, and while it was long regarded as a premier source for literature discovery, it has been the benchmark service for citation tracking and bibliometric analysis.

Content. The Web of Science consists of five databases covering scholarly literature from 1898 to the present: the three citation indexes of journal articles in science, social sciences and arts and humanities (this last one begins in 1975); and conference proceedings in both science and the social sciences beginning in 1990, covering international conferences, symposia, seminars, colloquia, workshops, and conventions. Web of Science, like Scopus, provides a list of journals included in the different databases; however, you are able to get journal title abbreviations within the search interface, the master list of journals is available at Thomson Reuters.[13] There is also an option within Web of Science to pass your search over to a beta service, Scientific WebPlus, to find web-based documents. This service is a collaborative one with Microsoft and various Thomson editors;[14] and the results come from repositories, news and blogs.

Ranking and displaying. By default, the results are listed by date (newest to oldest); however, the user can select several other sorts, for example times cited, first author, source title. You can also sort by relevance, which is a statistical ranking that considers how many of the search terms are found in each record. In addition, there are options to filter a subject search by almost any piece of metadata (see Figure 4.11).

Bibliographic analysis. While both Web of Science and Scopus have excellent analytical tools, Web of Science provides the very powerful cited reference searching – the ability to track a specific author's work to analyse the extent of the scholarly network in a particular field. This is particularly useful as a starting point in understanding the impact of a seminal piece of scholarship, invaluable for literature reviews for doctoral theses, for example (see Figure 4.3 on p. 64 to view the impact of the work of Henry Small in the discipline of bibliometrics). The service provides many other analytical reports such as citation reports (as shown in Figure 4.2 on p. 63).

Social networking opportunities. Web of Science does not have any built-in Web 2.0 social media tools. However, the beta service, Scientific WebPlus, provides a full range of tools – tagging, bookmarking, commenting, and voting (see Figure 4.12).

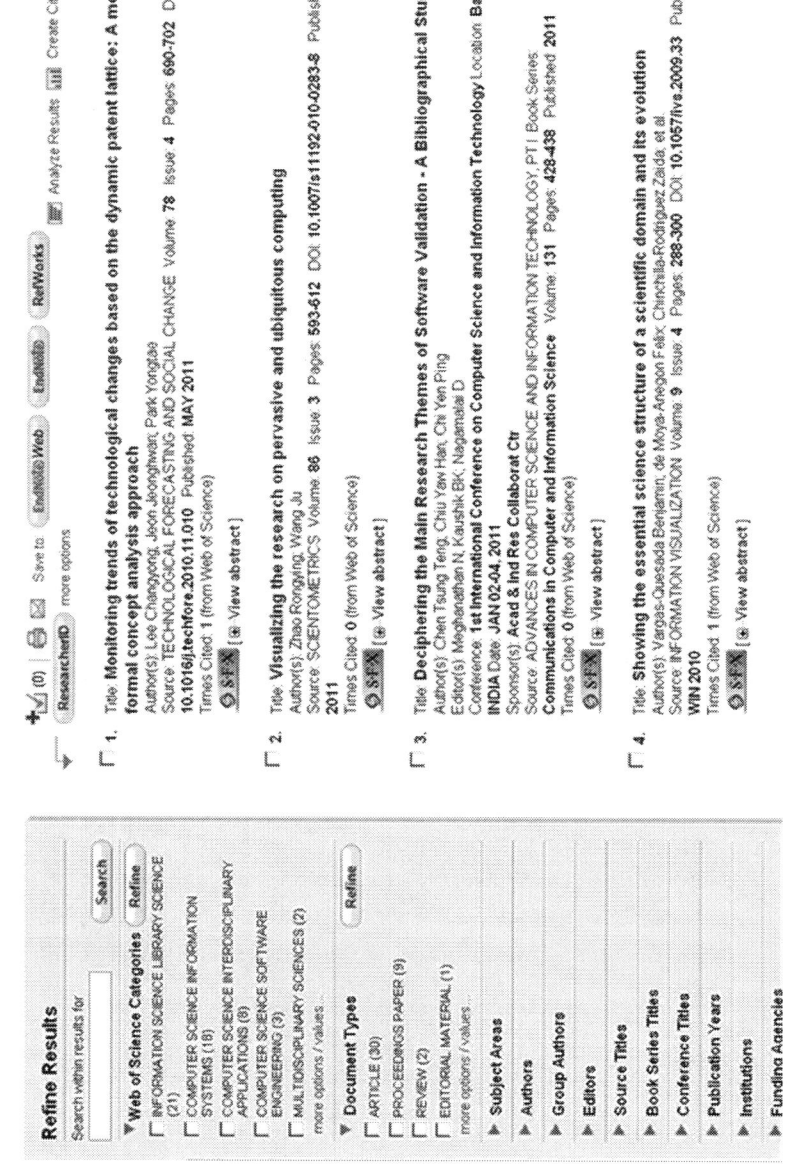

Figure 4.11 Web of Science options for filtering search results

Locating scholarly papers of interest online

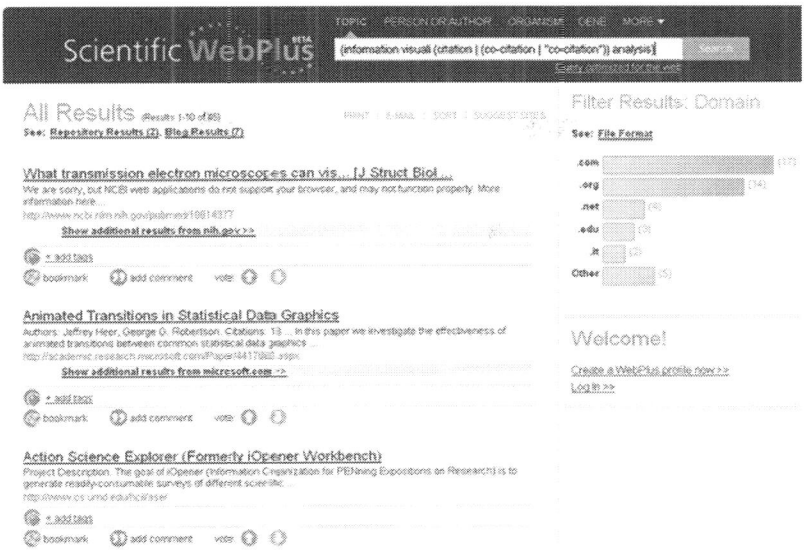

Figure 4.12 Results of Web of Science query passed through to Scientific WebPlus

Social media and public scholarly search

The concept of the social graph, used by social scientists in graph theory, was co-opted by Mark Zuckerberg at the f8 Conference in 2007 to explain the connections made by people within the social networking space of Facebook. While in this context the social graph is metaphorical, in reality social graphs may be visualized using the techniques of visualization from the bibliometrics and scholarly communication communities. Such graphs have been available tools in the Web of Science and now Scopus; however, in the public scholarly search services, only Microsoft Academic Search has the ability to create actual graphical visualizations. Metaphorical social graphs, as will be seen in the next chapter, are the foundations of specific social media reference tracking and sharing tools.

Conclusions

The scholarly literature search services are essential tools for scholarly communication; researchers, academics and students use them for a variety of purposes. These include: the completeness of a literature search; to find out how often his or her own publications are cited since such metrics are considered in hiring, promotion and grant decisions; to find a seminal work as background information; for a few good articles; for mapping scholarly networks. Currently, none of the scholarly services examined uses to any large extent the Web 2.0 social media tools; it is the new web-based services which have moved into this space. Microsoft Academic Search, with its Twitter facility, is the only service which has caught up with Web 2.0 by incorporating social media tools, rather than using an add-on such as Web of Science's pass-through to Scientific WebPlus. Perhaps this functionality comes with 'newness' and, in the case of Academic Search, because of its original function of a 'test bed'. It remains to be seen if the other services, particularly the proprietary ones, Web of Science and Scopus, will see the need to fully incorporate social media communication tools or if they will continue to focus on their strengths of huge databases of scholarly literature and sophisticated tools for citation analysis and the visualization of scholarly networks.

Notes

1. For a history of online information services see Bourne, C.P. and Hahn, T.B. (2003) *A History of Online Information Services, 1963–1976*. Cambridge, MA: MIT Press.
2. By coincidence, Science Citation Index may have included some of the full-text scientific eprints available in early digital archives and repositories. In 1992, Science Citation Index was sold to Thomson Health Systems and became available by subscription as Web of Science.
3. Scirus was developed by Elsevier and therefore had access to their scientific indexes.
4. For example, see Small, H. (1990) *Bibliometrics of Basic Research*. Philadeplphia, PA: Institute for Scientific Information, Inc.; Chen, C. and Boyack, K.W. (2003) Visualizing knowledge domains. *Annual Review of Information Science and Technology*, 37(1): 179–255; and Robert, C., Wilson, C.S., Gaudy, J.-F. and Arreto, C.-D. (2006) A year in review: bibliometric glance at sleep research literature in medicine and biology. *Sleep and Biological Rhythms*, 4(2): 160–70.
5. For differing points of view see, for example, Jacsó, P. (2009) Google Scholar's ghost authors. *Library Journal*, 134(18): 26; Smith, A.G. (2008) Benchmarking Google Scholar with the New Zealand PBRF research assessment exercise. *Scientometrics*, 74(2): 309–16; Meho, L.I. and Yang, K. (2007) Impact of data sources on citation counts and rankings of LIS faculty: Web of Science versus Scopus and Google Scholar. *Journal of the American Society for Information Science and Technology*, 58(13): 2105–25;

and Harzing, A.W. (2007, last updated 20 December 2008) Google Scholar – a new data source for citation analysis. Retrieved 13 September 2011, from *http://www.harzing.com/pop_gs.htm*.
6. For further details see the Budapest Open Access Initiative of 2002, *http://www.soros.org/openaccess/*; and Suber, P. (2008) Open Access in 2007. *Journal of Electronic Publishing*, 11(1).
7. However, other studies show Google Scholar to be effective. According to Walters, 'Google Scholar found 93% of [a specified reference set of articles in OA repositories] covering 27% more than Social Sciences Citation Index.' See Walters, W.H. (2007) Google Scholar coverage of a multidisciplinary field. *Information Processing & Management*, 43(4): 1121–32.
8. Currently, among the public search services only Scirus when harvesting OA content appears to harvest the OAI metadata; see Elsevier (2004, September) *How Scirus Works: White Paper*. Retrieved from *http://www.Scirus.com/press/pdf/WhitePaper_Scirus.pdf*.
9. A relatively simple metric which says that a scholar with an index of h has published h papers, each of which has been cited in other papers at least h times.
10. The current list can be found at *http://www.info.sciverse.com/sciencedirect/content/journals/titles*.
11. See Elsevier (2011) JournalM3Metrics research analytics refined. Retrieved from *http://www.info.sciverse.com/documents/files/scopus-training/resourcelibrary/pdf/journalmetrics_factsheet_web.pdf*, and the white paper, Glänzel, W. (2010) *The Evolution of Journal Assessment: How Research Performance Assessment has Changed Over the Past 50 Years*. Retrieved from *http://www.info.sciverse.com/documents/files/scopus-training/resourcelibrary/pdf/whitepaper9_com.pdf*.
12. For a discussion of Elsevier's SNIP metric see Moed, H.F. (2010) Measuring contextual citation impact of scientific journals. *Journal of Informetrics*, 4(3): 265–77.
13. See master journal list at *http://science.thomsonreuters.com/mjl/*. A nice feature of this list is that within each index the journals are categorized by discipline, e.g., archaeology, with the social sciences.
14. The documentation refers to the Microsoft Live search; presumably this is now using Microsoft Academic Search.

References

Acharya, A. (2004) Scholarly pursuits [blog post]. Retrieved from *http://googleblog.blogspot.com/2004/10/scholarly-pursuits.html*.
Beel, J., Gipp, B. and Wilde, E. (2010) Academic search engine optimization (ASEO). *Journal of Scholarly Publishing*, 41(2): 176–90.
Borgman, C.L. (2008) Supporting the 'scholarship' in e-scholarship. *EDUCAUSE Review*, 43(6): 2.
Borgman, C.L. and Furner, J. (2002) 'Scholarly communication and bibliometrics', in B. Cronin and R. Shaw (eds). *Annual Review of Information Science and Technology* (36, pp. 2–72). Medford, NJ: Information Today.

Ebbinghouse, C. (2009) Judicial opinions now available in Google Scholar [blog post]. Retrieved from *http://newsbreaks.infoday.com/NewsBreaks/*.

Elsevier (2004) Scopus comes of age [press release]. Retrieved from *http://www.elsevier.com/wps/find/authored_newsitem.cws_home/companynews05_00203*.

Elsevier (2011) Content coverage guide: SciVerse Scopus. Retrieved from *http://www.info.sciverse.com/UserFiles/sciverse_scopus_content_coverage_0.pdf*.

Google Scholar (2011a) About Google Scholar. Retrieved from *http://scholar.google.com/intl/en/scholar/about.html*.

Google Scholar (2011b) Citations. Retrieved from *http://scholar.google.com.au/intl/en/scholar/citations.html*.

Henninger, M. (2008) *The Hidden Web: Finding Quality Information on the Net*. Sydney, NSW: UNSW Press.

Jacsó, P. (2009) Google Scholar's ghost authors. *Library Journal*, 134(18): 26.

Microsoft (2011) What is Microsoft Academic Search? Retrieved from *http://academic.research.microsoft.com/About/Help.htm*.

Microsoft (n.d.) Microsoft Academic Search. Retrieved from *http://academic.research.microsoft.com/*.

Nie, Z., Zhang, Y., Wen, J.-R. and Ma, W.-Y. (2005) Object-level ranking: bringing order to web objects. *World Wide Web Conference Series*: 567–74.

Scirus (2001) About Scirus. Retrieved from *http://web.archive.org/web/20010204235l/http://www.scirus.com/about.php*.

SciTopics (n.d.) About SciTopics. Retrieved from *http://www.scitopics.com/about.jsp*.

Wilcox, C. (2011, 27 September) Social media for scientists Part 1: it's our job [blog post]. Retrieved from *http://blogs.scientificamerican.com/science-sushi/2011/09/27/social-media-for-scientists-part-1-its-our-job/*.

Appendix: features of web-based public scholarly search services

Function or feature	Google Scholar	MS Academic Search	Scirus
Syntax			
Boolean			X
Truncation (wildcards)			X
Field search (metadata)			
Author	X	X	X
Document type			X
Document format	X	X	X
Conference		X	X
Content sources			X
Date	X	X	X

DOI			X
Journal	X	X	X
Organization/affiliation			X
Subject categories	X	X	X
Title	X	X	X
URL			X
Display			
Synopsis	Snippet	Abstract	Relevant text
References		X	
Source branding			X
Library partner links	X	X	X
Import			
BibTeX	X	X	Any RIS format
EndNote	X	X	
RefMan	X		
RefWorks	X		
WenXianWang	X		
Save results (future use)			X
Sort			
Rank		X	
Year		X	X
Citation		X	
Citations			
Pearl-growing (similar references)	X	X	X
Context		X	
Ranking	Relevance	Relevance	Relevance
References		X	
Visualizations		X	
Updates or alerts	Email	RSS	
Contribution/submission (individual)		X	X

5

Tracking references with social media tools: organizing what you've read or want to read

Jackie Krause

Abstract: This chapter will address how academic researchers can take advantage of the social media tools for managing bibliographic references online and collaborating with other researchers. Tools such as Zotero, Mendeley, CiteULike, and Connotea take advantage of the best of the new social media by allowing users to seamlessly collaborate with one another and share what they know via online communities. Researchers can post their personal reference libraries, tag references in order to define personal meaning, aggregate tags to form collective meaning among communities of researchers, and collaborate with other researchers in private or public groups. Using online tools means that your reference library is always available. A selection of the leading tools will be examined, providing some pros and cons to help you make your decision.

Key words: reference management, social media, bibliographic, Zotero, Mendeley, CiteULike.

Introduction

Research. As academics, when we think of this word we often conjure up the familiar mantra of publish or perish! That's the refrain which institutions of higher learning around the world espouse and the reality that we all face. Regardless of your role within your institution, you no doubt understand the reality of this common phrase. Whether your research efforts involve simple solo projects or complex collaborations, they follow the typical stages of research design, literature review, execution, analysis, and conclusions. More complex research projects involving multiple researchers require a greater level of effort, coordination and cooperation. Managing these processes and all of the related activities can involve numerous daunting tasks.

One such task involved in the process that has long impacted researchers is that of managing research citations. Often the most difficult and time-consuming process of the research project is that of collecting, cataloguing, validating, and managing bibliographic reference material. Generating a bibliography can be one of the most time-consuming aspects of a research project yet it is considered essential to scholarly work (Norman, 2010). This activity can take away valuable resources for more scholarly pursuits. However, source citation is a critical and fundamental responsibility of all researchers, regardless of their level of expertise (Kern and Hensley, 2011).

There are a number of issues associated with aggregating useful and relevant information about bibliographic data in ways that are efficient and effective. In our new mobile society, the ability to gain access to important citation information when and where needed becomes vital. Increasingly, researchers work virtually rather than co-located with fellow researchers, making for more difficult collaborations. We live in a time when there are vast resources available on the web, challenging researchers to decide what information is relevant and worthy of study. With Internet-related information overload, today's researcher can find it difficult to sift through the endless amount of data available in search of the gems. With better search engines which return vast quantities of valuable data, and more and more data available on the web, we need better ways to save, organize and retrieve citation data (Foley, 2010).

When it comes to managing bibliographic material used within research, some suggest that researchers often stick with the same tools and procedures they learned in graduate school. Many learned to track reference data on 3 x 5" index cards. Some students moved on to use computer-based options, specifically stand-alone bibliographic software. However, most researchers will continue to use the methods of managing references that they used when they were in school, suggesting that 'most social scientists still archive their references on paper' (Muldrow and Yoder, 2009, p. 170). Regardless of the method, academic researchers tend to stay with what is familiar and comfortable (Rosenzweig, 2007).

As academics, we see the emphasis on social networking in so many areas of our practice. We consider social networking for making professional connections with like-minded colleagues to exchange ideas and information. We read blogs, contribute to wikis and watch YouTube to stay current with trends in our fields. We may contribute to any number of social sites that encourage open source sharing of material. We even venture into podcasting, vodcasting or screencasting as a means of providing our own unique voice to our work. Yet, when we consider the tools and methods we use to research, we still cling to outdated notions of effective collection, coordination and management when we gather bibliographic information. Furthermore, when we collaborate with our peers on research and writing projects, we may think of email as the method of choice for sharing our research material (Bramscher et al., 2006). So the question becomes: how can we better share resources, collaborate with one another more effectively and find more of the hidden gems of knowledge and wisdom that others before have found?

In this chapter, we will examine the many benefits of using online social reference manager tools for storing bibliographic reference information. Specifically, we will look at how tools like Zotero, Mendeley, CiteULike, and Connotea can improve the quality of references you find by using the power of other researchers. Finally, we will examine how these tools can assist your research projects by providing you with better collaboration with your peers.

Regardless of whether your bibliographic needs are simple or complex, this chapter has a little something for everyone. Even if you never collaborate with other researchers, you will find that using these online social reference manager tools can provide a positive impact on your personal research process by speeding up your collection and management of bibliographic references and helping you find better-quality references. If you frequently collaborate with peers on large, complex research assignments, you will find the collaborative benefits of using these tools to be invaluable.

Why use online social bibliographic tools?

A brief history of bibliographic tools

As academic researchers, we have heard of tools such as EndNote and RefWorks for managing bibliographic references. These tools have been around for many years and have undergone critical scrutiny and continuous improvement. By no means are EndNote and RefWorks the only tools available for reference management. Other notable tools exist in both the fee-based and open source (free tools) realm. However, EndNote and RefWorks are notably the most popular fee-based reference manager tools available, both having a proven track record. As such, both will be the focus of this very brief overview. For those who may not be familiar with reference manager software, what follows will describe some of the key requirements.

Store your references. One notable benefit of reference manager software is that the user can capture the data once and use it over and over again in other academic endeavours (Rosenzweig, 2007). Every discipline has relevant theorists and reference works. Reference management software provides the researcher with the ability to cite works with ease in many different research projects simply by selecting the appropriate reference from the user's library. Think of this benefit as create once, use many.

Create perfectly formatted citations and bibliographies. Not only do EndNote and RefWorks allow you to store bibliographic material, these tools can create perfectly formatted in-text citations and reference pages based on a large number of accepted formats. EndNote and RefWorks provide simple interfaces with Microsoft Word and Open Office that make the creation of citations and reference pages a breeze. When you identify where you want a citation to appear in your text, you simply select the reference, click the button and the citation is inserted, properly formatted both in-text and on the reference page.

Capture metadata quickly and easily. References can be added to your EndNote or RefWorks library collection either manually, field by field or automatically through a variety of import/export functions. Capturing the metadata associated with a reference can be a time-consuming task when done manually. Most online libraries provide a link to import the citation information, preventing the user from manually inputting this data. Once a reference has been identified, the user can look for a link to import that citation data into EndNote or RefWorks.

Connect directly to online databases. Newer versions of these tools are capable of connecting directly to online library databases directly within the tools themselves, allowing the user to both search and retrieve reference data. Although the process has become somewhat easier in recent versions, connecting to these online databases through reference management software has traditionally been a difficult task. Finally, both EndNote and RefWorks provide the ability to import and export references from a variety of other tools. Using the standard formats, these tools can import bibliographic information from a variety of sources, saving the researcher the time and effort of inputting references manually, all while ensuring that the data input is accurate.

Manage PDF files. Both EndNote and RefWorks allow you to attach PDF files to individual citation records. This ensures that you can always find the full-text document that relates to the reference.

Include notes and annotations. Both EndNote and RefWorks provide fields where users can add notes regarding the citation record. Notes can be searched, making it easier to find the exact citation for which you are looking.

Integrate with Microsoft Word or other word processors. Both EndNote and RefWorks integrate with Microsoft Word, allowing the user to insert citations into their document while composing.

EndNote started as a stand-alone system installed on an individual computer. Newer versions of EndNote allow users to keep their libraries online, so that their references can be accessed from any computer. It is necessary to synchronize the online libraries with the base installed software in order to ensure that the library data is always correct. The synchronization occurs in the background and does not require user initiation. RefWorks has always been an online reference tool. The user's library is stored completely online. At the time of this writing, the only way a user can access their reference library offline (when not connected to the Internet) is to download their entire library to their computer. There is no automated synchronization facility. This means that every time reference material is added to your online library, you will need to download or update your library on your computer. Working with an outdated library can become a problem and the solution is certainly not ideal. Both EndNote and RefWorks are considered the gold standard by which reference management applications should be measured.

It's easy to see how using either EndNote or RefWorks to manage your research references can save time and effort, while improving the finished product. If you are not currently using automated reference management software, I hope this introduction has presented a case for you to consider. Even the novice user can generate great enhancements to their research productivity with just a little effort. However, a 2006 survey of faculty at the University of Minnesota indicated that a full 60 per cent of respondents still use paper and pencil as their method of capturing and recording reference metadata (Bramscher et al., 2006). This is somewhat concerning considering the productivity gains that can be assumed even by the most novice user. While EndNote and RefWorks have considerable associated costs, as well as a significant learning curve, there are a number of free tools available for use that can help even the novice. When we consider the advantages of using online bibliographic tools we begin to take our research to another level.

The benefits of using online reference management tools

Bibliographic tools such as EndNote, RefWorks and other similar products have so much more to offer once we begin to look at using these tools online. Even with significant improvements in the online capabilities of each, EndNote and RefWorks are considered to be tools primarily involved in the preparation of bibliographies (Norman, 2010). The ability to access your bibliographic library of references from any Internet-connected computer is an advantage that should not be taken lightly. Often, academic researchers work in many different locations. Although we are likely to travel with laptop or tablet computers, the effort of synchronizing library databases among multiple computers can be time-consuming and challenging. The ability to access your references online solves this problem. Having your reference libraries available all the time regardless of where your personal computer is located provides a significant benefit (Taraborelli, 2006).

In addition to access, each online reference manager captures 'metadata' associated with a resource quickly and easily. Metadata consists of bits of information such as the source of the material, the author(s), the date, the title, the page numbers, and, if a journal, the issue and volume. The ability to capture the abstract as part of the metadata is especially useful (Muldrow and Yoder, 2009). These tools make it easy to capture references from within traditional online databases as well as other sources as you research, usually with a single click.

Why use social bibliographic online tools?

The concept of social online reference management software suggests that Web 2.0 has indeed invaded how we view citation and reference management. It is appropriate to consider the same reasons we use other Web 2.0 tools as drivers for using social online reference managers. A 2008 survey of 2collab users indicated that 50 per cent of respondents believed that online social applications will have a significant impact on how research is performed in the future (2collab survey, 2008). However, it is important to note that researchers 'have little time for another social work unless its functionality benefits them and improves their research' (Zaugg et al., 2011, p. 32). These tools must deliver on the promises of Web 2.0 principles, as would be expected by scholars, and not be just another Facebook.

More than just a tool to capture citation data. It has been suggested that researchers are looking for more than just automated reference management (Muldrow and Yoder, 2009). Researchers seek new ways to connect, share, collaborate, and discover new information (2collab survey, 2008; Emamy and Cameron, 2007). Social bibliographic tools provide researchers with a variety of ways to connect with one another. Research groups or browsing groups provide a means of knowing what other researchers in your field are reading. Discussion forums allow for the ability to 'chat' about research data. The social aspect of these online tools allows researchers to find others interested in the same topics for possible future collaborations. Finally, social online bibliographic tools allow users to define a professional presence within a community of scholars. See Chapters 2 and 3 for more on virtual collaboration and networking.

Know what other like-minded researchers are reading. Social online services may provide users with dashboards or other displays that indicate what topics are trending within the group, new articles that have been posted in your areas of interest and readership statistics that identify the value of an article in terms of identifying who is reading the article.

Collaborate with researchers within your own domain, or form new research collaborations. Online social reference manager tools provide users with the ability to share their libraries with their peers and fellow researchers. This feature provides a significant advantage over traditional methods of collaborative research by allowing research team members to have access to all that each member has reviewed. Furthermore, each team member has access to the library and can add additional relevant material and add notes and comments to existing material. When multiple researchers are writing separate components of a whole project, team members can easily and quickly capture any reference in the project library and incorporate it into their own piece of the research writing. Prior to online bibliographic options, this level of collaboration among researchers would require considerable effort through email or phone calls, or even the necessity to be co-located with researchers on the team.

Use tagging, 'folksonomy', and soft 'peer review' to validate research for relevancy. Tagging citations truly allows the social side of citation management to come through (Ekart, 2009). Tagging allows a folksonomy to develop among users. As opposed to the traditional notion of a taxonomy, which seeks to classify objects based on pre-defined categories, a folksonomy derives from the ground up as users place their own meaning to objects. 'Tag clouds' form around user defined meanings, allowing users to click on a tag and easily find similar references tagged by other users. By tagging references, the user assigns their own unique relevance to the material, thus self-annotating or categorizing. When these tags are shared among the greater user population, a collective intelligence begins to form (see Figure 5.1).

Researchers have often used 'citation metrics' to measure the quality of references. Citation metrics measure the number of times a research article is cited (Citation Metrics, 2008). In addition to citation metrics, researchers have always counted on the blind peer review process of academic journals to guarantee the quality and validity of the research reported. Social reference management software may provide a new standard for measuring quality (Taraborelli, 2008). Taraborelli suggests that the social nature of online reference managers and the associated capabilities provide a 'soft' peer review which may in fact provide additional ways to assess reference quality. In addition, the traditional formal methods of peer review can be a lengthy and cumbersome process. The notion of distributed evaluation suggests that there may be ways in

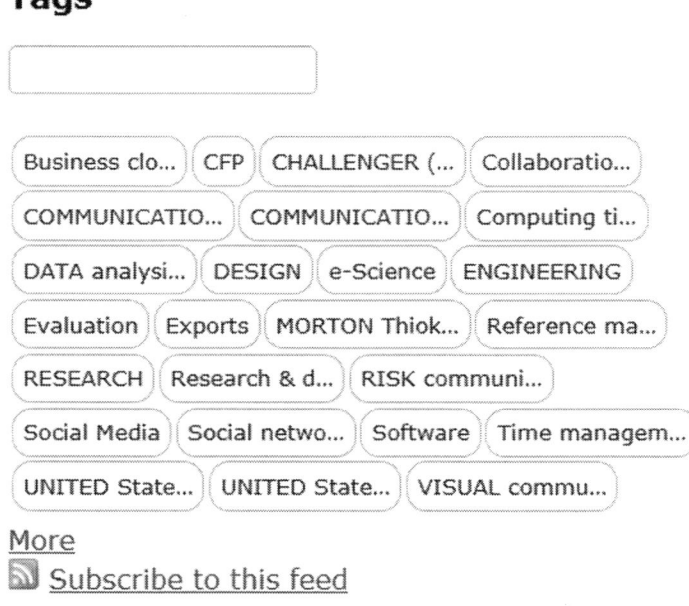

Figure 5.1   Zotero tag cloud

which we can create aggregated metrics as a result of usage, downloads, tags, and other indicators only available from social media metrics, possibly generating equally useful data in a more timely fashion. Usage metrics can indicate the number of users that have bookmarked the reference, downloaded the reference or discussed the reference. While social media aggregated metrics are not intended to replace the traditional peer-review process, these methods may help to provide a scalable solution for managing the ever increasing amount of online reference material.

A look at top social bibliographic tools: Zotero, Mendeley, CiteULike and Connotea

This section is not intended to make anyone an expert in using any of the tools described herein. The intention is to provide a background so that you may determine which of these tools is likely to fit your needs or may be worthy of further investigation. Each tool described has its own merits, advantages and disadvantages. In some cases, one tool may not adequately meet all needs. Regardless, the social bibliographic tools described here should help researchers find better quality material, collaborate more easily with their peers and simplify the process of research writing.

Zotero

Originally developed by George Mason University in 2006, Zotero is an extension, or add-on, for the Firefox browser. As a browser-based solution, Zotero maintains your entire reference library on your local computer as part of your Firefox profile. In addition, Zotero provides a function that allows users to 'sync' their libraries with Zotero servers for access on any computer. At the time of this writing, Zotero only works with the Firefox browser. However, the intention to provide plug-ins for Safari, Chrome and Internet Explorer is expected in future releases. Because Zotero stores data within the Firefox browser, this makes it slightly more difficult to maintain the portability of your reference libraries. One solution is to use a portable implementation of Firefox on a USB drive. You can find all of the required information from Zotero support.

Figure 5.2 Zotero's main page

One way in which Zotero shines among similar offerings is that Zotero can easily identify the metadata from a variety of sources. When searching websites such as Google Scholar or Amazon, the addition of a 'bookmarklet', also called the Zotero book icon, to the browser allows the user to quickly identify a source. Whenever Zotero recognizes metadata on a web page, the book icon is available. Zotero can then capture the metadata on the page and create an entry in your library. In addition, Zotero can identify metadata on most web pages. Clicking the book icon will create a record in the library as well as capture an archive of the page at a moment in time. In addition, Zotero does a good job of identifying metadata within PDF files and extracting this information automatically, creating an entry in your library. When a PDF is found on a website, you can easily store a copy of the file in Zotero with the 'store copy of file' function. This allows you to keep all of your PDF files in a single location. Once references are captured, it is easy to add personal notes to a record. Zotero also allows users to add reference metadata automatically by entering an ISBN number, digital object identifier (DOI) or PubMed ID. Due to the ease with which Zotero can identify and capture metadata, it is an appropriate solution for data found in a large variety of sources.

Possibly the strongest advantage of using Zotero is the ability to share resources with other researchers. You have the ability to connect to existing research groups, thus gaining access to the vast knowledge held within the group, or to create your own research group for centreing on a specific collaboration. These research groups can be private or public, open or closed, and are completely controlled by the group owner. With research groups, you can create a space for collaboration with other members of your project. You can share your own citation sources with the group. Group members can add to the collective project, allowing everyone participating in the project to know what everyone else knows.

Moving beyond the ability to collaborate with your own colleagues, research groups allow you as an individual to become involved in a larger collective of like-minded researchers. You can search through Zotero groups and find other researchers with whom you can connect. In addition, you can view the suggested references as well as a library of additional material. Following the familiar discussion thread found in most Web 2.0 tools, group members can engage in conversations about articles of interest.

Zotero lets you organize your data in collections which resemble iTunes' playlists. An individual reference can exist in multiple collections. Additionally, Zotero supports tagging of individual reference content to add personal relevance and to contribute to the greater wisdom of the collection. Tag clouds then form, allowing you to quickly locate all references around a specific tag.

Finally, Zotero provides many of the features reference manger users have come to expect. Zotero provides integration with both Microsoft Word and Open Office, allowing users to easily add formatted references and bibliographies to their research papers. A wide variety of reference types and bibliographic formats is supported. If you have references in another reference manager, Zotero can import RDF, BibTex, RIS, and MODS data formats. In addition, Zotero can export your library for back-up purposes or for inclusion into another tool.

Mendeley

Mendeley is considerably more than just a reference manager. Mendeley was patterned after the popular music site Last.fm, which recommends music to listeners based on understanding their normal listening patterns. While Zotero and Mendeley share many of the same features in terms of managing references, integrating with word processing software and creating seamless bibliographies, there are some distinct differences that give Mendeley an edge in the online social reference manager tool domain.

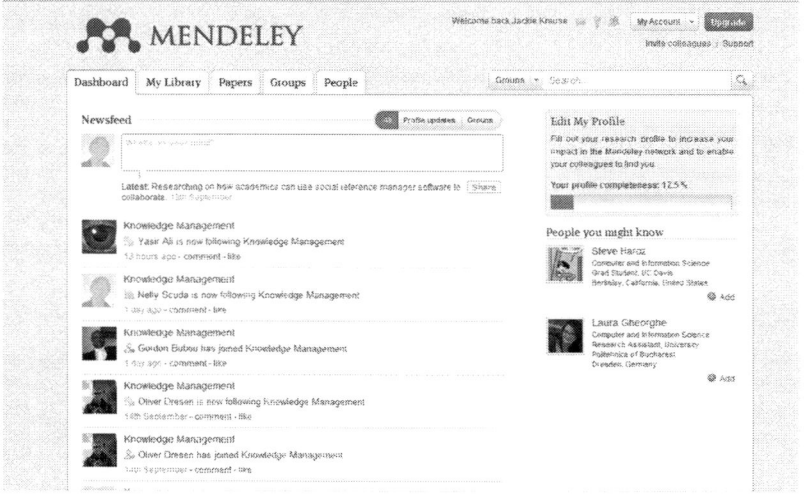

Figure 5.3 Mendeley's dashboard

Mendeley works with two distinct components: a desktop installation and a web interface. The desktop software will synchronize your library with the web so that you will have access to your library from any computer. Both the desktop software and the web interface have distinct advantages. The desktop software provides the ability to add citations and bibliographies to your word processing documents. The web interface provides the social network-like interface for finding and collaborating with other researchers.

Adding references to your library is easy. In the desktop software, you can simply drag and drop a PDF into the Mendeley workspace and Mendeley will extract the available metadata and create the reference automatically. In addition, you can ask Mendeley to 'watch' any number of folders on your computer. When a PDF is added to the folder, Mendeley will automatically extract the metadata and create the reference. However, the web interface of Mendeley does a much better job archiving web-related content. Many online databases provide a link to directly extract and create references from their sources. Should you want to create a reference from a web page, you can install and use the Mendeley Web Importer link in most web browsers, allowing you to capture all available metadata.

Using Mendeley on the web is where the true value of an online social reference manager shines. The Mendeley dashboard provides users with a list of current topics of interest within your research groups. Similar to Facebook's 'status' post, Mendeley offers a 'What's on your mind' feature, allowing users to post comments to the community, and community users can add their own comments or 'Like' what you wrote. Users are encouraged to create a complete profile, which acts as an online curriculum vitae, allowing users to connect with other users who have similar research interests. In addition, you can identify articles you have authored for inclusion in the Mendeley catalogue. Readership statistics identify who is reading the article by discipline, educational status and country, and they are helpful in measuring the popularity of the article.

As one of the largest sources of user-driven content libraries for academic research, Mendeley users can search for papers within the Mendeley community on a variety of topics. When a paper is found, Mendeley will present readership statistics as well as offer possible suggestions for where you can obtain the full-text article. Finally, Mendeley provides a button that allows you to include the reference within your own library.

Much like Zotero, Mendeley provides users with the ability to create public, private or by-invitation-only groups. Again following a familiar Facebook interface, users are presented with an overview tab that displays recent group activity, a document tab which lists all documents within the group, and a members tab which displays all group members. Users can comment and express their 'Like' for group content. However, one especially useful feature is the ability of group members to review and annotate PDF attachments within the group. PDF annotations and notes are then available for all members in a private group. This is a great way to collaborate with colleagues on an active project.

CiteULike and Connotea

Both CiteULike and Connotea are social bookmarking services, designed specifically to capture academic references and their associated sources. While online social bookmarking services such as Delicious, Digg and Reddit were becoming popular among mainstream web users, it became obvious to Richard Cameron, founder of CiteULike, that there was a need to provide academic users with a service that could capture and manage research references as bookmarks on the web (Reher and Haustein, 2010). Both CiteULike and Connotea are true web-based solutions for storing and managing scholarly reference material, and require no desktop appliance. However, unlike Zotero and Mendeley, these tools do not interface directly with word processors to support the creation of bibliographic references.

Because both CiteULike and Connotea are web-based bookmarking solutions, users can easily grab metadata from web pages creating accurate reference entries. Users can click on a bookmarklet that can be installed in any browser to capture metadata from almost any page on the web. In addition, both services provide a capability whereby users can copy and paste a URL for evaluation and identification of appropriate metadata and create a bookmark reference. Many online libraries include a direct link to CiteULike or Connotea, allowing users to create a reference from within the database. In addition, CiteULike allows users to upload PDF files and attach them to references within their library, thus organizing PDFs and providing an additional storage location for these files. Finally, as with other online reference tools, users can add tags and notes to each reference. Tags act like categories to further define the reference with personally meaningful information. Tags further allow for the filtering of library content based on individual tags.

Both CiteULike and Connotea offer a robust search capability, allowing users to search across all bookmarks within their library. However, Connotea's search is a more intuitive Google-like search, searching across all metadata. While CiteULike provides similar search options, its search is considerably more complicated, relying on Boolean search operators to execute. This makes it slightly more complex to master. Both tools were created for researchers, by researchers, and were primarily intended to support the medical and scientific community of scholars.

It is the addition of comments, discussions and tagging that takes reference management and academic bookmarking to the social level by providing the means to share, confer and collaborate with fellow academics. Where both CiteULike and Connotea shine is in the overall social experience. CiteULike users can rate a reference by declaring how many stars the article is worth and review the reference by completing a text-based commentary. These ratings and reviews are available to other users interested in the article. In addition, CiteULike will provide a posting history identifying other CiteULike users that have posted the article to their library, and will allow you to find other related articles posted by these users. CiteULike presents a list that will search for other related articles by tag. Connotea provides users with the ability to discuss

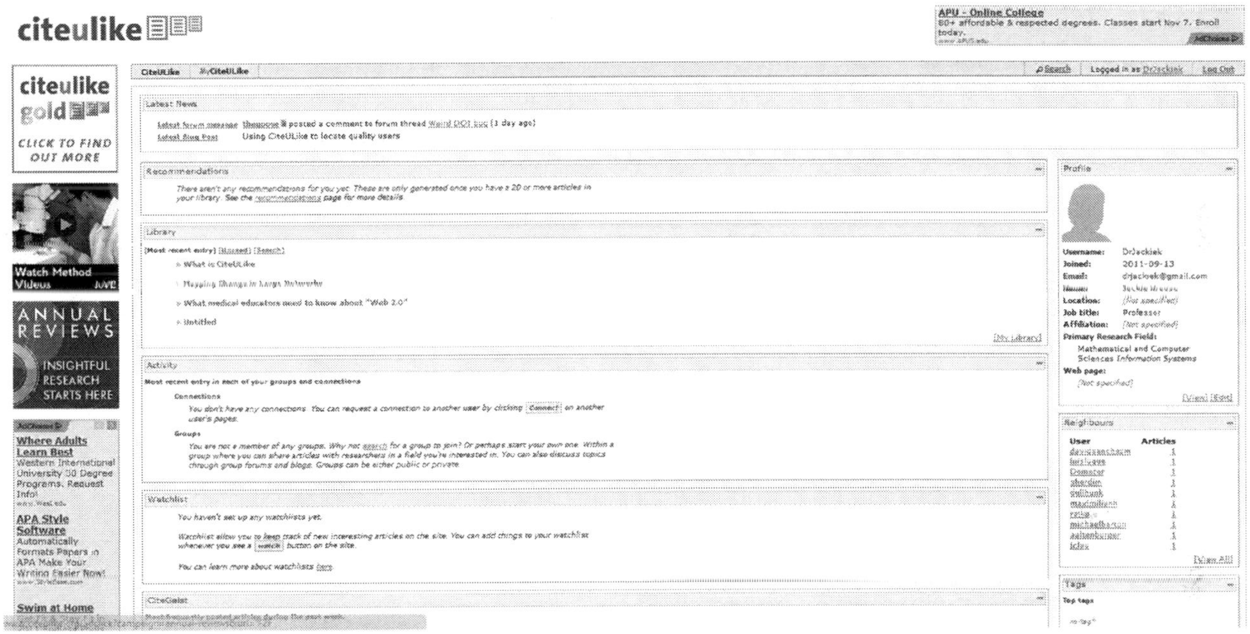

Figure 5.4 CiteULike's portal page

articles through comments. User comments are then aggregated for viewing by all interested users.

CiteULike users enjoy a portal-like home page which resembles a blog or wiki and provides a quick look at your recent additions to your personal library, any activity from your personal connections or any new activity in your watch lists (see Figure 5.4). CiteGeist provides a look at newly added content or content that is trending. The addition of a blog within CiteULike provides an added social dimension. Users can create connections with other users and send private messages to their connections. Finally, CiteULike identifies users that have posted similar content as 'neighbours', allowing you to follow these individuals.

Much like Zotero and Mendeley, users can create both public and private groups in both CiteULike and Connotea. Within groups, users can discuss topics around common research interests. Group users are able to share articles, tag, blog, and discuss articles all within their own forum.

While these tools do not provide direct interface with word processors for the creation of in-text citations and bibliographic references, it is possible to interface with word processors in a less than automated fashion. CiteULike provides a link to display the properly formatted reference in any number of different formats which can then be copied and pasted into your word processor. Connotea allows users to export a list of references (defined by search criteria or tags) for importing into your preferred desktop reference manager software.

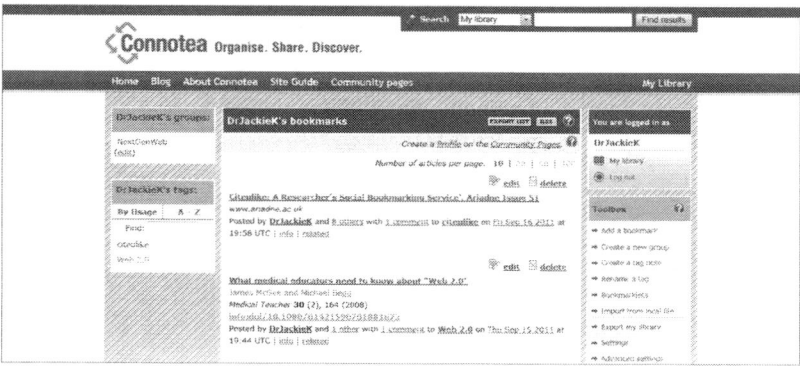

Figure 5.5 Connotea's library view

How these tools can improve your research, writing and collaboration

If as an academic researcher, your main goal is to simply manage the massive amount of reference material that you deal with on a daily basis, then be encouraged by the ease and functionality of any of these tools. However, if you are looking to take research to the next level by making new research connections, finding collaborators, using soft peer review to find additional sources of research or to simply define your own professional presence in the academic research realm, then these tools will help you take that step. While each tool discussed here will help you capture and manage reference data more efficiently and effectively, that is just the beginning of how they can benefit your activities.

Finding connection and improving collaborations over distance may in fact be the strongest reason for choosing an online social reference management tool. The ability to share research libraries with colleagues by defining a collective project space improves the overall productivity of the team. Simply knowing what your collaborators know can provide an enormous benefit in terms of time and resources.

How to choose the right tool for your needs

Each tool we examined has distinct advantages and disadvantages. The tool you use will depend on your own needs, the needs of your collaborators and the needs of your institution. However, the following points should be considered:

Do you need an inexpensive solution? As each solution discussed is free, whatever option you choose will work. Well, almost ...

How big is your library of references? Depending on the size of your reference library, both Zotero and Mendeley *may* cost you. Zotero, while a browser-based solution, stores a synchronized copy of your library online on its servers. At the time of this writing, server space allocated for the free service is 100MB. Users can purchase additional storage for the annual price of US$20 for 1GB to US$240 for 25GB, with many increments in between. It's easy to see how much space you have used by simply logging in to your account and visiting the settings/storage page. Mendeley starts users with 1GB of free space divided into

500MB of personal space and 500MB of shared space. Through shared space, a user is allowed 10 users per private group. If you need more space, you can upgrade to one of two different pay plans ranging from US$4.99 per month for 3.5GB personal/3.5GB shared with 15 users per private group or US$9.99 per month for 7.5GB personal/7.5GB shared with 20 users per private group. Although both Zotero and Mendeley are cost-effective solutions, it is important to note that *free* may in fact cost you something later on down the road.

CiteULike is a free service with no limits on the amount of reference material you can store and is paid for by advertising. However, a Gold service is offered that provides an advertising-free environment, personalized home page, PDF annotation capability, and more. CiteULike Gold is currently US$45 per year. At the time of this writing, Connotea is a free service with no storage limitation and no for-fee upgrades.

Do you need a tool that supports mobile architecture? At the time of this writing, Zotero does not provide a mobile or tablet application for the iOS or Android market. Furthermore, Zotero requires the Firefox browser. While Firefox is available for both the iOS and Android operating systems, a native application is not available. Mendeley, however, provides a mobile application for both iOS and Android devices. The iPhone application allows you to view your library as well as open and read PDF attachments within the application. CiteULike and Connotea are both completely browser based and there is no mobile application available. Safari, the browser found on all iPads, should render pages correctly and allow viewing of PDF attachments with no problem. However, viewing library contents on an iPhone may be tricky without a native application.

Does the tool need to work on multiple browser platforms? Mendeley, CiteULike and Connotea work on all web browsers equally well. Zotero works only on Firefox.

Will I need to maintain access to my bibliographic library after I complete my academic endeavours? Many students have access to EndNote and RefWorks through their school affiliation. Once students graduate, it may be that they no longer have access to these tools. These tools come with a steep price tag. Free tools allow students to maintain their bibliographic library after they graduate and beyond.

Do you need portability? Because free tools are slightly more portable, it is easy to transfer your libraries from one tool to another. Each tool mentioned can easily import or export content following a variety of standard formats. However, Mendeley has the ability to connect to and continue to synchronize with both Zotero and CiteULike databases. Therefore, when you enter a reference in Zotero or CiteULike, it will automatically appear in your Mendeley library. This can solve the problem of the lack of a 'one tool fits all' solution.

Conclusions

Researchers are looking for new ways to manage the information overload that exists as a result of our access to larger amounts of data through the Internet (Rosvall and Bergstrom, 2010), and to find improved relevance and meaning in the search results. In addition, they are looking at the Web 2.0 experience from an academic researcher's perspective. Online social reference managers and bookmarking services provide just the solution. While each has its distinct advantages and disadvantages, the promise of a social experience is fulfilled. Using these tools will allow the academic researcher to connect with colleagues, find new researchers with whom to make connections, collaborate on team-oriented research projects, and learn what others in your domain are reading.

Brynko (2008) suggests that social tools such as those featured in this chapter will play a significant role in the way that researchers professionally collaborate and network. Social online reference management tools take the traditional research process of 'gather, collect and share' and add the critical components of 'network and discover' (Emamy and Cameron, 2007, para. 1). However, there may be a reluctance to embrace these tools within traditional academic environments. One reason academic users may be reluctant to adopt online social reference tools may be similar to the reasons they were slow to adopt electronic journals. Early researchers found that academics were reluctant to adopt electronic journals because of a lack of critical mass (Bonthron et al., 2003). The research revealed that users believed there just were not enough quality journals available online to support legitimate research. Similarly, there may be a perception that there are not enough users of online social reference management tools and therefore there is not enough incentive to entice those reluctant to expend the time and energy to learn something new. However, the more that academics embrace these tools and use them for ongoing research efforts, the more value will be realized through the growing community of scholars.

References

2collab (2008) 2collab survey reveals that scientists and researchers are 'all business' with social applications [press release]. Retrieved from *http://www.elsevier.com/wps/find/authored_newsitem.cws_home/companynews05_00947.*

Bonthron, K., Urquhart, C., Thomas, R., Ellis, D., Everitt, J. et al. (2003) Trends in use of electronic journals in higher education in the UK – views of academic staff and students. *D-Lib Magazine*, 9: DOI:10.1045/june2003-urquhart.

Bramscher, P., Butler, J., Celeste, E., Lougee, W., Marcus, S. et al. (2006) A multi-dimensional framework for academic support [report]. Retrieved from *http://www2.lib.umn.edu/about/mellon/UMN_Multi-dimensional_Framework_Final_Report_Appendices.pdf.*

Brynko, B. (2008) Research 2.0: the age of collaboration. *Information Today*, 25(8): 34.

Citation Metrics (2008) Citation metrics: understanding and finding citation metrics. *AMNH Research Library*. Retrieved from *http://library.amnh.org/research-tools/tips-tutorials/citation-metrics.*

Ekart, D.F. (2009) Tech tips for every librarian: cool tools for back to school. *Computers in Libraries*, 29(8): 46.

Emamy, K. and Cameron, R. (2007) Citeulike: a researcher's social bookmarking service. *Ariadne*, 51. Retrieved from *http://www.ariadne.ac.uk/issue51/emamy-cameron/.*

Foley, S. (2010) Managing the brave new world of online content. *Information Today*, 27(1): 19.

Kern, M.K. and Hensley, M.K. (2011) Citation management software. *Reference & User Services Quarterly*, 50(3): 204–8.

Muldrow, J. and Yoder, S. (2009) Out of cite! How reference managers are taking research to the next level. *PS: Political Science & Politics*, 42(1): 167. DOI:10.1017/S1049096509090337.

Norman, F. (2010) Bibliographic management archives: from Sci-Mate to Mendeley – a brief history of reference managers. Retrieved from *http://blogs.nature.com/franknorman/bibliographic-management/.*

Reher, S. and Haustein, S. (2010) Social bookmarking in STM: putting services to the acid test. *Online*, 34(6): 34–42. DOI:2187696691.

Rosenzweig, R. (2007) Historical note-taking in the Digital Age. *OAH Newsletter*, 35(3): 1, 8.

Rosvall, M. and Bergstrom, C.T. (2010) Mapping change in large networks. *PloS one*, 5(1): e8694. DOI:10.1371/journal.pone.0008694.

Taraborelli, D. (2006, 1 December) Online reference management (part 2): going social [web log message]. Retrieved from *http://www.academicproductivity.com/2006/online-reference-management-part-2-going social/.*

Taraborelli, D. (2008) 'Soft peer review: social software and distributed scientific evaluation', in *Proceedings of the 8th International Conference on the Design of Cooperative Systems (COOP 2008)*. Carry-Le-Rouet, France.

Zaugg, B.H., West, R.E., Tateishi, I. and Randall, D.L. (2011) Mendeley: creating communities of scholarly inquiry through research collaboration. *TechTrends*, 55(1): 32–6.

6

Pragmatics of Twitter use for academics: tweeting in and out of the classroom

Lynne Y. Williams and Jackie Krause

Abstract: Twitter evolved from blogs and is a hybrid between blogging and instant messaging. While blogging is typically a desktop computer activity, Twitter is deliberately designed for easy use with a hand-held device, such as a smartphone. Twitter caters to the mobile blogger by requiring them to keep their posts down to a maximum of 140 characters, which is referred to as microblogging or tweeting. The resulting tweets have an air of immediacy, of what the tweeter is doing in the moment. Tweeters can follow other tweeters with similar interests, and the immediate nature of tweets gives a sense of knowing the tweeter being followed.

Key words: social networking, Twitter, online identity, personal branding.

What is Twitter? An introduction

Of all the chapters in this book, this is the only chapter that concentrates on a single social networking application. Twitter has antecedents and similarities to blogging (as discussed in Chapter 1) and Facebook-style social networking. However, in practice, it's a different beast. It can be easy to mistake Twitter as a vehicle for stimulating two-way conversation within Twitter itself, and while a certain amount of that type of traffic does occur, for the most part, Twitter gets used as a one-way vehicle for disseminating news and information. What follows are some Twitter 'how-tos', and suggestions for the academic leverage of Twitter's unique blend of immediacy and interconnectivity.

While blogging (see Chapter 1) is understood to belong to the old text-based concepts supporting Web 1.0, social networking sites (SNSs) sit firmly in the Web 2.0 category and make the creation of media-rich user generated content much easier than most of the old blogging platforms. More than that, SNSs also provide the essential interconnectivity that allows content creators to easily share their content with others. Kaplan and Haenlein (2010) note these two qualities, stating that SNSs 'allow the creation and exchange of User Generated Content' (p. 11). Although including the ability to generate content as well as self-publish and share content provides almost unlimited opportunities for those users with something to say, there's an unspoken downside to the process. Every day, dozens of blogs and SNS pages are created ... and promptly abandoned. Technorati, a dedicated blog search engine, estimates that there are more than 200 million blogs, not to mention SNS pages, a statistic that continues to climb. By the way, that statistic is only for English-language blogs; with Chinese-language content also included, the figure is much higher. At the same time, Technorati goes on to speculate that almost 95 per cent of these blogs and pages are abandoned almost immediately, but why? Brown (2011) presents five of the most common reasons behind blog abandonment. First, the majority of first-time bloggers seriously underestimate the time commitment necessary to maintaining a compelling blog that others will want to read. The best blogs are constantly being updated with fresh content, so if an author can't devote several hours a week to the upkeep of their blog, they'll probably eventually abandon it due to a lack of time.

Another reason that people walk away from their blogs is that they haven't got a clear purpose or direction for their blog. The concept of presenting their ideas sounded quite attractive until they sat down with that 'blank piece of paper' staring at them from the monitor. Some people are better at writing than designing a good user experience with a blog. Many potential bloggers fail to succeed because they have design or development issues with their blogging platform and don't know where to find help. Closely related to the lack of a focused direction for a blog is the lack of inspiration that can set in after a blogger has effectively exhausted what they had to say about a given area of interest. Sometimes, the purpose of a blog can be too narrowly defined, thus limiting the amount of content that can be presented. Lack of inspiration can also be aggravated by a lack of visitor interaction. If a blog has gone stale, or is just starting out, getting and keeping visitors can be tough, and without that type of interactivity many bloggers lose interest and leave the blog to its fate.

It's probable that most ordinary users simply aren't cut out to be dedicated bloggers. In recognition of this, a more accessible type of blogging, called microblogging, has sprung up. In 2005, Kottke described the uses of microblogging, using the term 'tumblelogs' for the activity. Kottke (2005, para. 2) defines tumblelogs as 'a quick and dirty stream of consciousness', with posts consisting of only a brief sentence or two. While the term tumblelogs isn't used much any more, the microblogging concept itself has caught on and grown exponentially. People who may not have enough interesting material to compose a full multi-paragraphed post can easily come up with a sentence that conveys some thought or action they feel is worth publishing and sharing. And that's where Twitter comes in.

Nations (2011, para. 5) defines Twitter as 'a cross between blogging and instant messaging', while admitting that the definition doesn't cover all of Twitter's potential. Using Twitter, an individual can quickly make short observations whenever they have seen something or thought of something. More than that, these micro-posts can then be instantly shared with a tweeter's followers. A tweeter can have followers who read their tweets, and, in turn, they may also be following other tweeters in whom they're interested. These 'following' activities engender an enormous amount of interconnectivity and can give any given tweeter a steady stream of updated material and information. Examples of ways in which to leverage all this interconnectivity would include music festivals or conferences using Twitter to update participants on upcoming acts or presentations. Politicians use Twitter to keep their constituent followers updated on pending legislation and speaking dates. News media use Twitter to send breaking news stories to subscriber followers, and so on. In all of these examples, the common theme is the ability of Twitter to quickly push information to large groups of people. Come to think of it, that's not a bad definition of what we, as academics, do when we lecture in a classroom!

How can Twitter be used by academics?

Like any other social networking tool, Twitter should be used carefully and appropriately if you plan on including it as a part of your academic work. Mollett et al. (2011) have several recommendations to take into consideration. They advise academics to always keep in mind that social networking will place you in the public eye and that there will be people following you that you may not necessarily be aware of, such as supervisors, students and grant awarding committees. Post nothing on Twitter that you might be ashamed of later; think of the old rule concerning 'angry' emails: count to ten before you hit 'send'. For instance, it's probably not a good idea to tweet after a long, aggravating day when you feel like venting. Those late night thoughts might reach the eyes of various university stakeholders who will be decidedly not amused. Try to avoid taking stances on touchy subjects on Twitter; leave religion and politics to your paper diary or your personal (rather than academic) Twitter account.

While it's possible to maintain separate personas between a Twitter account used for academic purposes and a personal Twitter account, be aware that no matter what you do with your privacy settings, there will inevitably be a certain amount of blurring between the two. The interconnectivity of all social networking sites makes it almost impossible to maintain completely separate personalities online. You needn't allow that knowledge to stifle your enjoyment of your personal account as long as you realize that you'll probably have students or colleagues who come across your personal account and will want to follow you. You'll need to decide whether it's preferable to allow a bit of blur with selected individuals or whether you should keep followers distinctly separated between accounts. If you do happen to tweet inappropriately and have 'tweeter's regret', hover your mouse over the offending tweet to view the pop-up menu and delete it.

How to get started

Hashtags are used to give your followers an easy way of categorizing your tweets. Tech for Luddites (2009, para. 5) describes a hashtag as 'simply a way for people to search for tweets that have a common topic'. Using hashtags provides your followers with a way to sort your tweets according to subject or category. Anyone can create their own hashtags by including one in a tweet using this format: #hashtag (replace hashtag with your own subject word). It's good 'tweetiquette' to do a Twitter search before inventing your own hashtags, in case someone else has already begun categorizing tweets with the same hashtags. Once you've either invented your own hashtags or selected pre-existing hashtags you include your chosen hashtag at the beginning of your tweet to neatly categorize the content of that tweet. Hashtags will take up a bit of your

140 character tweet limit, so you'll want to keep them as short as possible.

When your followers wish to see all of the Twitter content associated with a given hashtag, they'll enter the hashtag in the Twitter search which will then collect all tweets in that category. One of the benefits of using hashtags to categorize research tweets is that often a hashtag will collect tweets from other, related research. You can also combine hashtags to narrow your search. To see how hashtags work, try this quick example exercise:

- Sign into Twitter.
- In the search box at the top of the interface, type in #research #brain.
- You should see a listing of tweets relating to brain research and researchers.

Take care to 'keep it short' in your tweets; remember that you've only got 140 characters (not words) to get your point across. Most seasoned tweeters use an URL shortening service, such as Bit.ly (*https://bitly.com/*) or TinyURL (*http://tinyurl.com/*) for sharing URLs without taking up too much character count.

The @username syntax is used when you wish to mention a particular tweeter. For example, you might want to tweet this:

> Just found @Mias_Kitchen recipe for beef rolls: http://fb.me/XMbQUc6n

Since you've 'mentioned' @Mias_Kitchen in your tweet, the owner of that username will receive a copy of your tweet in his or her mentions and will know that you've passed their recipe along to others. If you'd like to reply directly to a certain tweeter, you place their Twitter username at the very start of your tweet, like so:

> @Mias_Kitchen Tried your recipe, absolutely delicious!

Keep in mind that Twitter will always assume that you're replying when you place a username at the beginning of a tweet. If you simply wish to mention that person in a tweet, be sure to place their username somewhere besides the beginning of the tweet. You can also use the @username syntax to reply directly to more than one person:

> @tweedledee @tweedledum Beware the jubjub bird: http://bit.ly/vX2Fn2

It's considered poor tweetiquette to reply to all of your followers if you actually intended to only reply to a single individual, so don't be lazy, always put the @username of the individual to whom you're replying at the start of the tweet.

Let's say that you've run across someone else's tweet that you'd like to pass along to your followers. To do this, you'll need to 'retweet' (RT) the first tweet, like so:

> RT @audreywatters: Top Ed-Tech Trends of 2011: The Digital Library http://bit.ly/utSMBC

In this example, @audreywatters has found a good tweet from an Ed-Tech source that concerns The Digital Library and wants to pass it along to her followers. Note that @audreywatters did not originate the tweet, her Ed-Tech source did, hence why she's retweeting. One thing that's considered to be extremely poor tweetiquette is to use an RT to reply to someone's tweet; it's a bit like re-gifting that awful Christmas sweater that your Auntie Mable knitted for you last year!

There you have most of the basics for getting started with Twitter, for more information, suggestions and tips, the Twitter Guide Book is a great resource: *http://mashable.com/guidebook/twitter/*.

Research

Academic researchers face an almost constant scrutiny to prove the worth of their research to the public (Dunning, 2011). With greater competition for funding, researchers need to find ways to promote their research in a positive light. Academic researchers have turned to blogs and Twitter to share their research and self-promote their work. Through blogs and Twitter, researchers can make their work available to the public.

Sharing your research, taking advantage of crowdsourcing, finding research collaborators, or finding relevant research in your particular field is made easier through Twitter. Twitter can be used advantageously during a research project for keeping the various members of the research team informed and updated on the project's status. Mollett et al. (2011)

recommend keeping a research blog (as noted in Chapter 1 of this book) that documents the full body of your research, then sending tweets that link to that blog. You can then request feedback and comments from your followers, thus gaining useful insights. To get the best use out of Twitter, you should maintain complete summaries of all of your research work where followers can get to them. Consider including full summaries in your research blog or perhaps in the research repository maintained by your university or college. Whenever something occurs that might impact your research, such as governmental policy or related journal articles, be sure to tweet about it as soon as you see it.

Saunna Davis, an English professor, demonstrates the idea of finding relevant work through Twitter:

> This is where Twitter is such a useful resource for the academic: if you follow those who share your academic interests, they will point you to interesting stuff. When I first joined up I was impressed to find that within the first few days, I'd been directed to two new papers in my field that were very relevant to my work and that I hadn't known about.
>
> (Davis, n.d., para 3)

Consider creating a research 'web' with Twitter that presents your own research tweets alongside related research from other sources. Mollett et al. (2011, p. 7) comment that while this may appear to be a 'case of helping the competition', it's also a good way to draw attention to the entire research area, thus attracting attention and funding to that area. A research network can also stimulate debate which, in turn, improves the research standards for all of the entities engaged in the Twitter web. As academics, we seek to find like-minded individuals with whom we can communicate, exchange ideas, collaborate, and make new connections. Twitter can facilitate these connections on a causal level regardless of geography.

Ingram (2011) discusses a Twitter use that could greatly benefit a research project, in the form of 'crowdsourcing'. Ingram's (2011) example of research-related crowdsourcing involves researchers at Johns Hopkins University who were interested in uncovering public health trends by collecting Twitter search data. The two researchers at Johns Hopkins used 'a software algorithm to filter out approximately 1.5 million messages that referred to health-related issues, by focusing on a variety of terms related to medical issues and illnesses' (ibid., para. 2). One of the researchers makes this comment about their findings:

> Our goal was to find out whether Twitter posts could be a useful source of public health information. We determined that indeed they could. In some cases, we probably learned some things that even the tweeters' doctors were not aware of, like which over-the-counter medicines the posters were using to treat their symptoms at home.
>
> (Ibid., para. 3)

While crowdsourcing does have certain privacy issues associated with the practice, if the usual protocols are observed it has the potential to give a researcher access to enormous data sets that occur practically in real time, making it possible to observe human behaviour in a manner unthinkable just a few short years ago.

In addition to crowdsourcing, researchers use Twitter to post links to their papers or research blogs and to encourage conversation. Researchers are also posting links to podcasts, conference presentations and publications. Savvy academic writers are including #hashtags to create interest around their research and to report new developments (Mollett et al., 2011). Mark Bately (2010) (@markbately) has additional suggestions for generating research interest through Twitter. He suggests that researchers create provocative, short posts that include web links intended to grab attention and encourage interest. When seeking survey participants, Bately recommends using Twitter to send interesting and catchy notices with a link to the survey. Be sure to follow other tweeting researchers to see what they are doing and stay active to build your base of followers.

Crowdsourcing isn't the only way to gather large data sets using Twitter. There are hundreds of 'helper' applications that can help a researcher pull in data in various ways. For example, Twitscoop provides the user with a running visual display of trends, called a 'tag-cloud snapshot'. Tags that are currently being tweeted appear in the display in a size relative to the amount of current usage. The larger the tag, the more activity (or 'buzz') that tag is generating. Clicking on a tag in the display pops up the actual tweets that are using the tags. If your research is informed by watching various trends, Twitscoop provides a quick look at what trends people are talking about in real time.

Guus van den Brekel, an information specialist for the medical library at Groningen University in the Netherlands, recommends the use of another 'helper' application, TweetDeck, to effectively categorize and explore Twitter data (Bauer, 2010). Brekel notes that the default Twitter interface isn't particularly useful for pulling data sets out of groups of tweets, but with a management tool such as TweetDeck, tweets can easily be placed into sets for examining trends, or analysing groups of tweeters.

Twitter also provides a relatively painless method for documenting the monthly activities within a research project. Noting the growth in your followers for the project can be a good way to provide support to funding proposals, and the effect can be further strengthened if you link your tweets with a research blog that also invites comments.

Bately (2010) warns that not all research is appropriate for Twitter. In some cases, the Twitter population may not be the perfect population for certain research studies. However, using Twitter can open up new opportunities to gain respondents that might otherwise have been overlooked.

Teaching

Mollett et al. (2011) suggest using a separate Twitter account for each course in which you plan to use Twitter. This limits the audience to just the students in the class and makes it easier to keep track of the conversations over the course of the term. For each course's Twitter account, design the username such that it reflects the course name; for example, @IT530ComputersandNetworks. Urge all students in the course to become followers; if you have students who are unable or unwilling to set up their own Twitter account, you can provide a substitute in the form of an RSS (Really Simple Syndication) feed that presents the tweets in a list that appears either on your teaching blog or within a learning management system (LMS) such as Moodle or Blackboard. If you aren't an experienced HTML developer or haven't tinkered with RSS feeds before, try using a 'Twitter to RSS' application such as *http://twitter2rss.com/* to handle the coding for you. SoftwareGarden.com provides a good tutorial on RSS feeds for the less technically inclined (What is RSS?, 2004).

Once you have the course's Twitter account set up and running, it can be used to supply students with up-to-the-minute information concerning all course activities. Frequent tweeting during the week can be used as a powerful form of student support; use tweets to congratulate students who have done particularly well on a given assignment, or use Twitter to answer questions that may have been brought up in class. A carefully selected stream of tweets will emphasize your engagement with them and with the course. This type of tweeting support can be especially useful for those academics who supervise graduate students. Graduate school can give students a feeling of isolation or of being disconnected from their committee members; even weekly tweeting can provide a better sense of involvement for them.

Dunlap and Lowenthal (2009) recommend the use of Twitter for online teaching in particular because it can greatly enhance the instructor's presence as perceived by the students. The researchers argue that social interaction between the instructor and students, as well as between students, will elevate the level of engagement in the online course. In most LMSs, such as Moodle or Blackboard, there are already a number of tools available to provide a certain level of interaction, such as asynchronous discussion threads and chat rooms. Twitter differs from these tools in that it allows participants to comment and interact almost in real time, which is quite similar to a live conversation. Dunlap and Lowenthal give a number of compelling examples, such as this one:

> A student is reading something in the textbook and has a question about the chapter on multimodal learning. She immediately tweets (i.e., posts) her question to the Twitter community, and gets three responses within ten minutes – two responses from classmates, and one from Joni (her professor). This leads to several subsequent posts, including comments from two practicing professionals.
>
> (Ibid., p. 131)

From this example, it's easy to understand the exciting immediacy of Twitter in providing content-rich exchanges so quickly. Twitter also provides real-time response to addressing student issues that inevitably crop up. Obviously Twitter is useful for answering student questions that concern assignments that have a deadline, but the immediacy element of Twitter can also allow an instructor to quickly step in and address problems such as conflict between students, especially if the course includes team projects.

In order to derive genuine benefit from Twitter as used in a classroom, whether online or physical, the students must perceive the use of Twitter as relevant to the course and to learning in general. The instructor must provide a clear and focused purpose to his or her tweets, so that the benefits of tweeting are immediately apparent to the students. Under most circumstances, the instructor can't realistically require all students in the course to participate in Twitter. However, if the instructor strongly encourages his or her students to at least give Twitter a try, and then backs up that encouragement with interesting, relevant tweets, the students are more likely to genuinely engage with the medium and garner the benefits.

Professional branding

Labrecque et al. (2011) discuss the implications of having an online identity, noting that a great deal of information about a given person is effectively out of their hands since the information may be provided by a variety of other sources, some of which the individual may not know about. The researchers suggest that individuals should take at least partial control of the type of image that they present online by deliberately crafting their own personal brand.

Just being aware that you have a personal brand online is an important first step towards managing your brand. Labrecque et al. (ibid.) suggest conducting your own audit of your online persona by doing some Google searches using a variety of search terms for your name; if you're a married female, you may also want to search using your maiden name to cover all your bases. If you already have a social media account, you may want to sift through comments that are related to your own posts or shared material. You'll also want to consider how your profile is constructed; Labrecque et al. (ibid.) discovered that viewers of your profile material tend to be negatively impressed if your material appears to be unauthentic. For instance, 'there was a disdain for people who put up many obviously posed pictures' (ibid., p. 45), particularly if the photos had been 'photoshopped' to present a more flattering appearance. Other elements that can affect the perception of your profile are the number of friends or followers that you have. A non-celebrity who has thousands of followers will typically be perceived as someone who is deliberately out to impress the viewer, a trait that will be judged as unauthentic. If you have fewer than approximately 15 followers, viewers will assume that you're aloof or socially disadvantaged. The amount of personal information that you disclose about yourself may also be misperceived; for a professional brand, you may want to consider removing things such as your marital status, religious preference and even your gender.

After taking a careful audit of your online profile, you're then ready to begin crafting your own professional brand. Nanton and Dicks (2011) recommend treating your professional brand as a storytelling exercise, using Twitter as your primary storytelling tool which allows you to keep your followers up to date: 'Twitter is a great place to engage with your audience and keep them up to date on all of your latest adventures' (ibid., para. 2).

The crucial activity from this point is keeping your followers constantly updated on what you're doing in the professional sense. Nanton and Dicks (ibid.) note that your tweets don't have to be exciting each time you tweet, but you should tweet enough to make your followers feel that they're 'in the loop'.

Although you want to be cautious about revealing too much personal information in connection with your professional brand, Nanton and Dicks (ibid.) suggest leavening your work and research-related tweets with the occasional personal tweet. This gives a note of authenticity to your persona and gives your followers the sense that they know you. While you don't have to share a dinner date you've gone on, you might consider tweeting about something relatively harmless, such as a lunch shared with colleagues, mentioning a little about the food and conversation.

Last, but not least, Nanton and Dicks (ibid.) urge you to truly interact with your followers. Many brand-conscious tweeters 'treat Twitter like a bulletin board – they log on a couple of times each week, post something, and then leave' (ibid., para. 5). This type of behaviour makes it difficult for your followers to really engage with you and they'll eventually lose interest. Since Twitter is essentially a mobile platform, if you have an Internet-enabled handset, such as a BlackBerry, try tweeting on the go to give a sense of immediacy to your tweets.

The most important element of professional branding is to accept the fact that, whether you like it or not, if you spend any time at all online, and particularly if you've already been using social media in your personal life, you have a professional brand. It's up to you to take control of your own brand and shape it into the image that you wish to present to your colleagues and your students.

'In the field': academics using Twitter

As we consider ways of communicating with students and peers, we can be encouraged that social media is 'catching on' somewhat with academics. There's plenty of evidence of Twitter usage by a number of faculty and researchers at a variety of schools and universities, all the way from community colleges, traditional on-ground university settings and for-profit online schools. When looking for ways to communicate to a wider audience, the use of both blogging and microblogging provide a means of making an instant connection with those followers.

When considering what to tweet, avid blogger and tweeter, Deevy Bishop, suggests that you simply 'tweet to others things you think will interest them' (Bishop, 2011, para. 22). Additionally, Bishop warns new tweeters not to tweet every mundane aspect of your life. What makes for a good tweet is something useful, insightful, informative, or provocative. Twitter is often used to start a conversation around a topic. By posting interesting information and including URL links, you can share with a greater community and encourage conversation. Those academic tweeters that tweet for students suggest that Twitter makes it easier to connect with a large class of students in a more personal way. Some professors will use Twitter during lectures to encourage student participation. One University of Texas history professor posts questions during lectures and asks students to tweet responses. The results indicated that students who might not otherwise participate in class conversations used Twitter to share their thoughts (Miners, 2010). Other academic tweeters suggest that Twitter allows them to maintain a connection and encourage a conversation outside of the classroom. Some professors will tweet class assignment tips, suggestions or resources and encourage the class to share their own resources through Twitter.

Doug Belshaw (@dajbelshaw), a research analyst and educator, suggests that Twitter can be used in the classroom to 'encourage students to become their own learning network' (Belshaw, 2007, para. 9). Belshaw draws upon the theory of connectivism which suggests that a network of connections can serve to form bridges to a greater knowledge potential (Siemens, 2004). In a learning network formed through digital connections, students can take advantage of the flow of information thereby creating and contributing to new knowledge. Belshaw further suggests that in addition to networked learning, Twitter can support personal learning networks by providing a space where students can communicate with those they know online. Some additional considerations for using Twitter in the classroom include tweeting ideas after the class ends, seeking feedback from students while the class is under way, in effect creating a backchannel, creating asynchronous class conversations, and promoting a sense of community (Gordon, 2009). Gordon also advises faculty to consider using Twitter to brainstorm on topics, take polls, share interesting websites, make announcements, or encourage games such as a Twitter search. Twitter can encourage student engagement at a different level than direct class participation and can, in effect, become a new form of class participation rooted in the digital domain. Bruce Johnson (@DrBruceJ) (2011) encourages students to follow his Twitter feed as a means of developing a connection and a learning network. Johnson comments that, by following student tweets, you can 'develop a sense of who they are based upon what they've written' (ibid., para. 7).

Using Twitter to encourage professional engagement, connection and collaboration

As academics, we seek to find like-minded individuals with whom we can communicate, exchange ideas, collaborate, and make new connections. Twitter can facilitate these connections on a causal level regardless of geography. Debby Kurti (@DebbyK) is a community college professor, educational technology activist and publisher of the Educational Experimentalist Daily. She uses Twitter to connect with a large group of peers for discussion and collaboration. For professional networking, Debby has the following recommendations: 'I have collaborated with others on projects and presentations, shared new ideas and technology, and communicated about teaching challenges and successes. The key is to build up a useful network and then participate. It's not a spectator sport' (D. Kurti, personal communication, 5 December 2011).

Nancy White (@nancywhite) provides a number of examples of collaboration through the use of Twitter in a wiki post (White, n.d.). One such example is the use of Twitter to facilitate professional development. A 'flashmeeting' was tweeted by one of the individuals she was following. She was able to quickly attend the meeting and received word of a new learning tool that she might not have known about otherwise. White provides other examples including using Twitter while attending professional development activities to participate in the backchannel conversations and using Twitter as a virtual water cooler. Here Twitter can be used to connect individuals in disperse locations and to facilitate instant collaborations among individuals.

As universities seek to develop more collaborations with other universities, Twitter can bring individuals together in a way that can help identify and facilitate those partnerships (Anyangwe, 2011). For university researchers seeking feedback from fellow academics, using Twitter in conjunction with an academic blog has been shown to garner quick feedback. Peter Matthews (@urbaneprofessor) writes of his experience in an experiment of open research and collaboration (Matthews, 2011). Matthews decided to incorporate academic blogging in an application for research funding. In his application proposal, he detailed how he would use academic blogging to actively promote his research and engage with policy makers. Admittedly, Matthews was unaware of his audience of blog readers. In an experiment to see just who was reading, he posted his draft proposal in his blog and followed it with a tweet advising interested parties to review his proposal and comment. He was surprised to see how quickly word spread. In addition, there were numerous comments made to the post that were beneficial. He was able to incorporate many recommendations into a revised draft of his proposal as well as rethink some of the approach based on critical feedback from those who participated. This collaboration illustrates how both blogging and Twitter can support crowdsourcing activities in an academic endeavour.

Debby Kurti notes that she has used Twitter to crowdsource updates for a course outline. She had a remarkable number of faculty from all over the country provide suggestions. This same method could be used to find research collaborators through tweeting brief glimpses of the research question and asking the community of Twitter to provide a conversation.

Is tweeting for you?

Zhao (2009) notes that Twitter is typically used in quite a different way to other social networking tools, referring to it as a 'people-based RSS feed[s]' (ibid., p. 245). The brevity and related informality of the microblogging platform make it ideal for making quick, frequent comments on an individual's everyday activities, a bit like swapping stories around the water cooler. The 'real-time' nature of Twitter gives people an impression of understanding what's on the tweeter's mind at the moment. While tweets are necessarily too short to initiate any kind of deep interchange on their own, they can easily act as a springboard to more complex communications. One of Zhao's subjects describes the dynamic in this way: 'By reading someone's updates, you get more present understanding of what's on that person's mind, what he or she has been interested [sic], so that it's more [sic] easily to get a conversation started and flow' (ibid., p. 246).

Tweeters note that the voluntary nature of Twitter means that they are less concerned about the general nature of their tweets, unlike phone calls, IM (instant messaging) or email. The recipients of their tweets are people who have deliberately chosen to follow their tweets, so there isn't a question of invading another person's time and space. Twitter interchanges don't imply that there's any sort of reply required, which frees the reader to quickly read through a section of tweets and filter them out according to interest, rather than priority.

One of the major challenges of Twitter is the almost completely disorganized nature of incoming tweets, at least within the original Twitter interface. Following a prolific tweeter or following a large group of tweeters can easily result in cognitive overload and can be counter-productive to the original intention of learning more about whomever or whatever you may be following. If you find yourself getting overwhelmed by avalanches of tweets there are plenty of tools available to help sort the gold from the dross. For example, TweetDeck allows you to sort people into groups which simplifies sorting out work-related tweets from personal tweets. Filttr (*https://oauth.filttr.com/*) is another application that can help make sense of all that incoming information, allowing you to sort tweets by groups, keywords and priority, as well as allowing you to create white- or blacklists for content or people.

In the final analysis, there probably isn't one single social networking platform that serves every need. Twitter really isn't sufficient for providing highly detailed communications. However, for those academics seeking to start conversations with colleagues and students, or seeking to provide timely updates on research projects, Twitter, with its brief, unobtrusive flow of information, may be just the right tool, especially when paired with Facebook or a blog. The key is matching the right social networking tool with the right purpose. So consider putting down the phone, take your thumbs off that thumboard and get to tweeting!

References

Ammann, R. (2009) Jorn Barger, the newspage network, and the emergence of the weblog community. Paper presented at the 20th ACM Conference on Hypertext and Hypermedia. Turino, Italy.

Anyangwe, E. (2011) Poll: will the partnership between the universities of Birmingham and Nottingham transform academic collaboration? Retrieved from *http://www.guardian.co.uk/higher-education-network/poll/2011/mar/14/birmingham-and-nottingham-universities-partnership*.

Bately, M. (2010, 16 March) The tweetment of research: could Twitter revolutionize academic research? Retrieved from *http://www.psychologytoday.com/blog/working-creativity/201003/the-tweetment-research*.

Bauer, B. (2010) Innovative information and communication systems for scientific libraries: 10 questions about practice and experience covering Web 2.0 to emerging technologies. An interview with Guus van den Brekel. Retrieved from *http://eprints.rclis.org/bitstream/10760/3945/1/2010_E-LIS_ENG_2010_GMS_MBI_1InterviewGuus_van_den_Brekel.pdf?pPage=MOBILE*.

Belshaw, D. (2007) 3 scenarios for using Twitter with your students [blog post]. Retrieved from *http://teaching.mrbelshaw.co.uk/index.php/2007/09/27/3-scenarios-for-using-twitter-with-your-students/*.

Bishop, D. (2011) BishopBlog: a gentle introduction to Twitter for the apprehensive academic. Retrieved from *http://deevybee.blogspot.com/2011/06/gentle-introduction-to-twitter-for.html*.

Boyd, D.M. and Ellison, N.B. (2008) Social network sites: definition, history, and scholarship. *Journal of Computer-Mediated Communication*, 13(1): 210–30.

Boyer, A. (2011) The history of blogging: 12 years of blogs [blog post]. Retrieved from *http://www.blogworld.com/2011/08/24/the-history-of-blogging-12-years-of-blogs/*.

Brown, J. (2011) 5 reasons you will abandon your blog [blog post]. Retrieved from *http://www.heartinternet.co.uk/blog/2011/10/5-reasons-you-will-abandon-your-blog/*.

Davis, S.H. (n.d.) How to use Twitter as an academic – teaching college English [blog post]. Retrieved from *http://www.teachingcollegeenglish.com/2011/10/10/how-to-use-twitter-as-an-academic/*.

Dunlap, J.D. and Lowenthal, P.R. (2009) Tweeting the night away: using Twitter to enhance social presence. *Journal of Information Systems Education*, 20(2): 129–35.

Dunning, A. (2011, 25 August) Innovative use of crowdsourcing technology presents novel prospects for research to interact with much larger audiences, and much more effectively than ever before [blog post]. Retrieved from *http://blogs.lse.ac.uk/impactofsocialsciences/2011/08/25/innovative-use-of-crowdsourcing/*.

Gordon, J. (2009) 100 serious Twitter tips for academics [blog post]. Retrieved from *http://www.bestcollegesonline.com/blog/2009/07/21/100-serious-twitter-tips-for-academics/*.

Ingram, M. (2011, 7 July) Can you crowdsource health information via Twitter? [blog post]. Retrieved from *http://gigaom.com/2011/07/07/can-you-crowdsource-health-information-via-twitter/*.

Johnson, B. (2011) How social networking relates to online learning [blog post]. Retrieved from *http://www.onlinecollegecourses.com/2011/12/05/how-social-networking-relates-to-online-learning-2/*.

Jorn Barger (2011) Wikipedia. Retrieved from *http://en.wikipedia.org/wiki/Jorn_Barger*.

Kaplan, A.M. and Haenlein, M. (2010) Users of the world, unite! The challenges and opportunities of social media. *Business Horizons*, 53: 11.

Kottke, J. (2005) Tumblelogs. Retrieved from *http://www.kottke.org/05/10/tumblelogs*.

Labrecque, L.I., Markos, E. and Milne, G.R. (2010) Online personal branding: processes, challenges, and implications. *Journal of Interactive Marketing*, 25(1): 37–50. DOI:10.1016/j.intmar.2010.09.002.

Matthews, P. (2011, 3 November) Academic blogging and collaboration make demonstrating pathways to impact an easier matter | impact of social sciences [blog post]. Retrieved from *http://blogs.lse.ac.uk/impactofsocialsciences/2011/11/03/blogging-pathways-to-impact/*.

Miners, Z. (2010) Twitter goes to college – students and profs use 'tweets' to communicate in and outside of class. Retrieved from *http://www.usnews.com/education/articles/2010/08/16/twitter-goes-to-college*.

Mollett, A., Moran, D. and Dunleavy, P. (2011) Using Twitter in university research, teaching and impact activities. *LSE Research Online*, 12. Retrieved from *http://eprints.lse.ac.uk/38489/1/Using_Twitter_in_university_research%2C_teaching_and_impact_activities_(LSE_RO).pdf*.

Nanton, N. and Dicks, J.W. (2011) How to effectively tell your brand's story on Twitter [blog post]. Retrieved from *http://www.fastcompany.com/1779578/personal-branding-tell-your-story-on-twitter*.

Nations, D. (2011) What is Twitter? Retrieved from *http://webtrends.about.com/od/socialnetworking/a/what-is-twitter.htm*.

Parry, D. (2008) Twitter for academia. Retrieved from *http://academhack.outsidethetext.com/home/2008/twitter-for-academia/*.

Siemens, G. (2004) Connectivism: a learning theory for the digital age. Retrieved from *http://www.elearnspace.org/Articles/connectivism.htm*.

Tech for Luddites (2009) The Twitter hash tag: what is it and how do you use it? Retrieved from *http://www.techforluddites.com/2009/02/the-twitter-hash-tag-what-is-it-and-how-do-you-use-it.html*.

What is RSS? (2004, 4 July). Retrieved from *http://rss.softwaregarden.com/aboutrss.html*.

White, N. (n.d.) Twitter collaboration stories – how have you used Twitter to collaborate? Retrieved from *http://onlinefacilitation.wikispaces.com/Twitter+Collaboration+Stories*.

Young, J.R. (2010) Teaching with Twitter: not for the faint of heart. *Education Digest*, 75: 9.

Zhao, D. (2009) How and why people Twitter: the role that micro-blogging plays in informal communication at work. Paper presented at the ACM 2009 International Conference on Supporting Group Work. New York.

The academy goes mobile: an overview of mobile applications in higher education

Adam Craig

Abstract: When taken together, smartphone technology and social applications like Twitter and Facebook create an environment which is not only conducive to conversation but to conversation that is no longer limited by physical space. Essentially, we can be connected to one another at any time and in any place. Leveraging the idea of instantaneous social interactions and ongoing collaboration can be an effective means of enhancing teaching and learning at the post-secondary level. This chapter looks at two specific examples of platforms that integrate ideas from social media for mobile learning, as well as a potential means of bridging the gap between users and online content (specifically Quick Response or QR codes).

Key words: mobile learning, QR codes, smartphones.

Introduction

It is no stretch to suggest that we are more connected now than we have been at any point in history. Smartphone technology, wireless networks and social media have created a perfect storm of opportunity for educators to expand the scope of their teaching practice. Electronic learning, despite being a relatively new phenomenon, has made great strides in recent years with regards to effectiveness and accessibility. Where we stand now is on the verge of a new type of learning which is not only remote, but also mobile. With new tools at the disposal of educators, learning can essentially be free of the restrictions of time and space. It could be said that now students can learn anywhere and at any time, whether seated comfortably at a computer terminal or in the middle of an afternoon commute. Moreover, while early experiments in electronic learning were largely text based, modern connection speeds provide access to a media-rich and interactive virtual landscape where podcasts, YouTube videos and blog posts can be called upon in the service of teaching and learning.

Having studied social media in Dr Diane Rasmussen Neal's online class as a component of The University of Western Ontario's Master Library and Information Science programme, and with some experience in the field while working at the University of Toronto Mississauga, I have been in a position to see the convergence of social media, mobile technology and academia from two perspectives: using social learning networks like Edmodo as a student in class, and using QR codes to engage patrons while working in an academic library. From an administrative point of view, mobile technology opens up a whole world of options in terms of student outreach, offering new services and keeping patrons engaged. Similarly, as a student, I thought that using platforms like Edmodo enhanced the social experience of coursework by allowing me to connect and interact with classmates and instructors from anywhere and at any time.

Among the multitude of advantages the mobile approach offers in terms of curriculum delivery is the fact that it allows learners to engage at their own pace and according to their own terms. Working inside the constraints of the material, students are in some respects allowed to generate their own experience, to construct their own classroom and to do so on their own time. To qualify as a formal course of study, there will always be deadlines and instructors and there will always be assignments to be completed for testing retention and understanding, but inside of those parameters there is almost limitless freedom when mobile technology is utilized.

Produced annually in a partnership between the New Media Consortium and the Educause Learning Initiative, the Horizon Report is the result of careful research into new media, technological developments and notable impacts on education. The 2011 Horizon Report helps make a convincing case for adopting mobile technology as a vehicle for enhancing pedagogy when it suggests that 'by 2015, 80 per cent of people accessing the Internet will be doing so from mobile devices' and, further, that 'Internet-capable mobile devices will outnumber computers within the next year' (Johnson et al., 2011, p. 16). Leveraging mobile technology for curriculum delivery and academic study means implementing strategies that make use of existing (or soon to exist) infrastructure, and doing so in inviting and innovative ways.

The use of mobile technology in an academic setting can be divided roughly into two categories based on the sort of information being delivered:

- *In direct support of teaching and learning.* For example, this might mean using mobile technology to deliver content which is explicitly related to learning outcomes, using mobile applications to facilitate online collaboration between students, or capitalizing on the immediacy of the medium to ensure open dialogue between students and instructors. This type of usage is often implemented on a course-by-course or department-by-department basis and, as demonstrated in two examples we will look at shortly, can lean heavily on ideas adapted from social platforms like Facebook and Twitter.

- *For 'marketing' peripheral services.* At present, this seems to be the more common approach when academic institutions initiate mobile-centric programmes aimed at students. This might include delivering information about things like hours of operation for services and facilities, course registration dates and information regarding clubs and student organizations. Typically, when mobile technology is used in this respect, projects are larger in scope and implemented by institution-wide departments (a mobile website maintained by the registrar's office, for example).

In the next section of this chapter, I will look at two examples of the former category which illustrate the notion of borrowing from familiar social platforms, and look at how these ideas can be put to use in delivering course content and generating virtual spaces for student interaction. In subsequent sections, the question of service delivery and, more specifically, service *discovery* will be addressed and explored with respect to some relatively recent developments in barcode technology.

Leveraging the backchannel and immediate collaboration

More and more, we see examples in higher education of faculty and staff using software applications for delivering or supplementing coursework and lectures. In many cases, these projects are geared towards mobile users. Whether as a means of distributing extra content and resources which are tangentially related to course material, or for sending and receiving assignments which are mandatory for course completion, there are examples of platforms which work towards creating learning environments that are not restricted to class time and not limited by physical space and seating arrangements. Developed by Purdue's information technology department, Mixable and Hotseat are examples that illustrate how software designers can elegantly and seamlessly incorporate ideas from social and mobile technology in the service of creating engaging new learning environments.

Released in autumn 2010, Mixable aggregates some of the social networking functions of Facebook with the usefulness of Dropbox (a free online 'storage locker' for files), with the desirable outcome being enhanced communication and collaboration among classmates (Information Technology at Purdue, 2011). By signing in with their institutional credentials, students can join networks for any courses on which they have enrolled. After joining, the user is linked to other students and faculty in a specific class network and given access to any content that others have made available. This content could take shape as links to YouTube videos, podcasts, short text updates, tweets or uploaded files. The intuitive interface sorts the types of material being shared and creates a coherent stream for each user and, with options for desktop computer use, smartphone applications for the iOS and Android platforms, and Facebook add-ons, users are given multiple options for participating.

Mixable checks each contribution a student user makes for the type of content that it contains, and in the case of links or media content a thumbnail image is generated. This seemingly simple function accomplishes two things. First, it allows users to forgo having to call on more than one application (going to YouTube to watch video content, for example), seamlessly blending different types of content into one continuous and easily managed stream. Second, by virtue of allowing content to be pulled into course streams, Mixable generates a rich online environment where curriculum is enhanced by secondary resources. By incorporating the functionality of Dropbox, students are given the opportunity to share documents with their colleagues. Important readings, assignments-in-progress and other course-relevant materials can be passed from student to student in a given network which can be used to make student collaboration more efficient and immediate.

Built into this online environment are a number of options for signing in. By designing a browser-based desktop application, a smartphone application and a Facebook application, developers at Purdue have allowed students to interact according to their own comfort level. Accessing the Mixable interface via Facebook means signing in to one's own personal Facebook account and then a second sign-in with their institutional credentials (i.e., university email address or other identification). When users choose this route, the interface creates potential networks from existing Facebook contacts, and makes suggestions for new contacts from other users who have Facebook accounts. The application generates a list of Purdue students who use the Mixable application and who share classes with a user, which creates an opportunity for building social connections with colleagues. While students can opt out of this in order to keep their academic and social lives separate, the underlying assumption is that by creating a social space inside of a learning environment, the learning process becomes more inviting (Kolowich, 2010).

In short, Mixable functions as a social and mobile system for organizing and managing resources that appropriates ideas from already familiar and well-used platforms like Facebook, in the hope of encouraging deeper engagement and continuous learning. By taking the idea of a study group or lab session and placing it in a virtual environment, Mixable liberates students from scheduling issues and distance issues and encourages ongoing collaboration.

Similar in many respects to Mixable, Hotseat calls on existing social platforms for classroom use. However, it could be argued that where Mixable focuses more intently on assignment and resource sharing, Hotseat borrows a more 'immediate' or real-time approach for the sake of creating an in-class conversation. By making use of open Twitter APIs (application programming interfaces), the developers in Purdue's information technology department have created an instantaneous learning and communication environment which effectively operates in the background during class time. This application works at creating new layers of course-related conversation, superimposed over or running concurrently with lectures.

As with much innovation, the impetus behind developing this sort of conversation-driven software comes from identifying the problem of how to keep students engaged in larger classes. The auditorium-style lecture is nothing new, and because of its relatively low cost to institutions and long history in post-secondary education, classes in excess of 300 students are likely to remain a part of the university experience. Despite being accepted as convention, this type of learning environment has its shortcomings. Chief among these is the fact that someone, somewhere near the back of the room, is likely to disengage. Since many institutions offer wireless Internet access on their campuses, and with the near-ubiquity of mobile phones and laptops, instructors may lose more than a handful of students to Facebook, Twitter and text messaging.

The research and design team at Purdue released Hotseat as what is basically a means of keeping students engaged, but one which does so by leveraging an existing phenomenon:

> A classroom can be divided into two channels: the frontchannel, the official channel for the class, consisting of interactions with the instructor at the front of the room, and the backchannel, the unofficial channel for the class, consisting of interactions among the audience, or perhaps with those outside the class. The backchannel could include whispering, side conversations, or passing notes. In our current technological environment, the backchannel has progressed from paper notes to texts and Facebook updates for students, and Twitter.
>
> (Aagard et al., 2010, para. 6)

Leveraging an existent backchannel for communication amongst students, Purdue has made steps towards creating what could be called a peripheral learning environment in virtual space that complements actual course content, directs students towards desired learning outcomes and consequentially keeps things on track in auditorium-style lectures. With Hotseat, the backchannel is co-opted and runs less of a risk of becoming a distraction. Instead, the conversations those students were already having by passing notes, whispering and 'Facebooking' during class time are being harnessed for the sake of education.

The process for enhancing learning with Hotseat is simple: instructors pose a question and students make use of their chosen mobile device or laptop to answer it. User posts in Hotseat are limited to 140 characters, and they are automatically updated to a class feed and then organized by question. As a result, instructors are made aware in real time of the educational needs of their students, creating a dialogue that is at once constructive for meeting academic needs and also for 'fine-tuning' curriculum. By opening the lines of communication between instructor and audience, classes become dynamic and can be tailored to meet the particular needs of a specific group of students.

Just as Mixable borrowed and adapted ideas from Facebook, Hotseat takes the immediacy of Twitter and SMS (short message service) in order to enhance the large-class learning experience. By managing backchannel communication and enabling real-time dialogue between students and instructors, the application effectively closes the gap that can exist in classes with enrolment in excess of 300 students. Moreover, course-related conversations do not need to start and stop within the time constraints of a lecture. Students can continue their backchannel discussions after class has finished, making group study easier, mobile and available on demand. In both examples, mobility is the key. Accessing either the Mixable or Hotseat platforms from stationary terminals would be a failure to fully realize the opportunities that each offer for collaboration, dialogue and immediacy regardless of location.

In addition to uses in a strictly academic sense, mobile technologies can be an effective means of pushing information about peripheral services to the student population, such as library hours of operation, course registration dates and procedures and information about campus tours and orientation. Post-secondary institutions generate rich and active communities simply by virtue of gathering large numbers of people in close proximity to one another and, that being the case, many institutions find themselves looking at ways of offering signposts to navigate what could be a confusing and overwhelming experience. Since students are busy and perpetually 'on the move', it stands to reason that an effective solution for keeping them informed is through channels which allow information to reach them at any time and regardless of where they are in physical space.

There is no shortage of options available when it comes to the problem of disseminating administrative information to students. Whether this takes shape as an official Facebook page, Twitter account or YouTube channel, or along more 'traditional' lines as in handbooks, signage and pamphlets, institutions often have large teams of professionals available solely for the purposes of communicating to students what they need to do. When it comes to electronic means of delivery, issues arise in terms of driving users to the resources that they need. If we want our students to engage and receive administrative information through a registrar-maintained Facebook or Twitter account, for example, how do we let them know that those resources are available?

For platforms like Hotseat and Mixable, or the widely used Blackboard and Moodle course management systems, the answer is as simple as enlisting instructors to prompt their students to log in. Facebook, Twitter and YouTube on the other hand rely heavily on user discovery, and since institutional presence in these environments is a relatively new phenomenon, administrators are ultimately gambling with time and resources. If people are not searching Facebook for their institution's page, or if students don't know that a Twitter account exists to find information about important deadlines, then pursuing these avenues can be a costly misstep. Two-dimensional codes, or QR codes, offer something in the way of a potential solution.

QR codes: creating linkages to online content in physical space

Research, development and implementation for QR codes started in 1994 with Toyota subsidiary, Denso Wave. As a global automotive and robotics manufacturer, Denso Wave developed this technology as a means of tracking parts' shipments. The company identified a need for barcodes that could store more information as well as more *types* of information, and that could be scaled in order to accommodate physical space limitations. To track and display complex information about shipments of seatbelts, mufflers and door panels, Denso Wave decided that traditional barcodes were insufficient. The result of their research and design was the two-dimensional or QR barcode.

Where traditional barcodes store information only from left to right, QR technology allows for reading and writing bits of information on two axes, left to right and bottom to top (see Figure 7.1). According to Denso Wave documentation from 2010, whereas a one-dimensional barcode is capable of storing roughly 20 characters, QR codes are capable of storing and displaying 'several dozen to several hundred times more information' (from Denso Wave, 2010; no longer available online). This new approach to information transmission had benefits beyond the

Figure 7.1 Scanning pattern of one-dimensional vs. two-dimensional barcodes

volume of data that could be stored. Reading along two axes meant that data could be stacked, and thus QR codes could be compressed into a much smaller space compared to barcodes.

Aside from the increased storage space offered by this new technology, the results of Denso Wave's design project offered a number of other advantages over standard barcodes, including flexibility and resilience. By using position-sensing markers at three corners of each design, QR codes can be read regardless of the reader's relationship to the code. Traditional barcodes require hardware readers to be pointed directly at and on the same plane as their target, whereas QR-reading technology is able to sort information around 360 degrees. These markers also allow codes to be read even when placed on uneven surfaces that might distort or bend the pattern.

The flexibility offered against distortion that comes from adding positional markers to codes is further complimented in many QR generators by offering varying degrees of data correction. In some cases, codes can be worn, damaged or have large chunks missing altogether and can still be read. With the free, web-based code writer found at *http://www.delivr.com/*, for example, users can choose to encode their final product with up to 30 per cent correction. This means that almost one-third of the actual code can be missing or damaged and the design remains readable by most software. With higher degrees of error correction a code will be more 'dense' or will be comprised of more individual points, but ultimately will be more resilient.

Despite holding the patent on QR code technology, Denso Wave has thus far chosen not to exercise it. This has given carte blanche to users and developers when it comes to what can be done with creating programs for reading and writing QR codes. The proverbial door has been flung wide open for both the public and the private sector with regards to this new technology, and the list of applications for their use is almost boundless in scope. The versatility of these barcodes, the openness and availability of the technology and the ingenuity on the part of developers and designers has meant a gradual, but consistent, expansion in uptake.

In 2008, the Information Technology Standards Committee in Singapore gathered substantial data on the background technology that drives QR technology. Included in their report was page after page of examples of QR codes at work in the private and public sector. The list (while not comprehensive) gives some indication as to the potential scope of use:

1. Hospital patient identification in Japan, Hong Kong and Singapore.
2. Passenger management on a luxury cruise line in Japan.
3. Livestock tracking in Australia.
4. Recording sales and stocking information of jewelry in France.

(Information Technology Standards Committee, 2008)

By virtue of the storage capacity these codes provide we see examples emerging where the technology has been put to good use for quality control and consumer education. In Taiwan, codes that point towards the Council of Agriculture mobile website can be found on packaged vegetables which consumers can scan to retrieve information about freshness and grower information. This process also allows for easier recalls in the event of contamination and provides customers with a sense of confidence in the products they purchase. Here we see mobile technology being put to use in the interest of public health and safety.

The above examples illustrate some creative uses of QR technology outside of North America, and it should be noted that the US and Canada have seen a considerably slower build-up in terms of users and developers fully recognizing the potential tool at their disposal. Overseas use has been significantly ahead in terms of the innovation at work and the sense of experimentation with regards to QR codes. That said, in recent years, and inspired by the near ubiquity of smartphone use, North American marketing companies, government bodies and other institutions have begun making steps towards including QR technology in their projects. Gradually, two-dimensional barcodes are beginning to appear on passport applications and building permits, fashion advertisements and on billboards in Times Square.

Due in large part to the fact that the underlying technical specifications for generating QR codes are open, there seems to be no shortage of freely available online applications for their creation. Anyone with an Internet connection has access to the necessary technology for creating QR codes and, moreover, anyone with a camera-enabled smartphone has access to applications for reading and displaying their contents. In many respects, anyone wishing to build projects around QR technology will find that much of the infrastructure necessary to get started is not only already in place, but is also cost-effective and easy to use.

For developers who wish to use QR codes in their projects, the options available are numerous and mostly free with more advanced code creating applications that will allow for a wider array of options in terms of what sort of data can be encoded. At *http://www.qrstuff.com*, users can choose to create codes with a direct link to Twitter or Facebook profiles, formatted contact information that will be added directly to smartphone address books, or VCalendar entries. Once a code has been generated through the chosen application, users are either asked to download as an image file, or are able to copy and paste the image directly from their browser. After being saved to the user's hard drive, these codes can be implemented in print or digital form, manipulated in photo-editing programmes or distributed via the web.

As with code writing software, open standards for program development have meant a surge in reading applications. In many cases, readers are developed by the same companies that offer code generating applications. Kaywa offers free application downloads for Nokia, Motorola and Sony phones from the same site from which users can access their code generator. Readers run the gamut from bare-bones applications like the Kaywa reader mentioned above or TapMedia's QRReader which simply translate and display data contained in codes, to more multi-purpose tools. As an example of the latter, a more comprehensive class of reader, RedLaser, has developed a mobile application which not only has full functionality for scanning two-dimensional codes but also for reading standard barcodes as well. The RedLaser application features full integration with smartphone calendars and address books and a history function which saves information gathered from scans (see Figure 7.2).

RedLaser illustrates the potential inherent in this technology. On a very basic level, the software functions as a 'bridge' between users and information existing online. Wrapped in this notion of camera-enabled smartphones acting as mobile portals to digital content through scanning technology is a wealth of possibilities for educators, librarians and other professionals who find themselves generating largely digital content. When the usefulness of information is contingent on how easily it is accessed, it becomes exponentially more important to ensure that the proper mechanisms are in place to make delivery effective, audience-appropriate and reliable.

Looking at the examples included earlier in this chapter it may seem a stretch to include QR codes in the toolbox at the disposal of educators and institutional administration; disseminating information about food freshness is a far cry from disseminating information about course curricula, class registration dates and campus services. On some very basic level, however, QR codes are still a means of dissemination and in that respect are similar to handouts and pamphlets. With that in mind,

Figure 7.2 RedLaser QR code scanner in use

the responsibility for making the most of this technology lies squarely in the hands of whoever is using them. Mirroring the pace of uptake in the business sector, education has been slow to adopt QR codes. That said, the tentative steps that have been taken are promising and illustrate some degree of creativity and willingness to experiment.

Two such examples, similar but different in scope and execution, took place at the libraries of Syracuse University and Boise State. The former included QR codes on bookmarks distributed to students, posters, pamphlets and table-top signs in order to drive students to a virtual tour of their facilities and virtual resources in their collection. Boise State also used QR codes to lead users to content at a mobile-friendly website, but used signage in the physical space of the library to an official Twitter account and blog. In both cases, library web resources include comprehensive guides for the use of QR codes. If it can be said that one of the downsides of implementing a QR campaign is underutilization due to unfamiliarity, including informational content for students is an attempt at a solution. Both libraries provide a brief background on QR code technology, some of the motivating factors that led to their implementation, and recommendations for which readers to use.

Ryerson University in Toronto began its experimentation with QR codes by using them to drive traffic to downloadable audio resources. Based on the success of that project, in 2010 they began to implement a large-scale project in which codes were added to library catalogue entries and contained location, call number, title and author information for items in the collection. After scanning codes that appear on-screen in the library's online public access catalogue (OPAC), users are able to save information to their mobile device for retrieving physical resources at their convenience. After noting a positive response to this project, Ryerson released its own mobile application that included a built-in code reader for accessing information contained in both ISBN and QR codes (McCarthy and Wilson, 2011).

Outside of the library walls, the potential for QR codes is no less impressive and requires little in the way of time and resources. Here are just a few examples:

- Include QR codes on course syllabi with instructor contact information (email addresses, office hours and locations). Students can scan codes and add them directly to their phone contact lists for easy access.
- Embed QR codes with links to supplementary course content such as videos, websites and articles of interest which can then be accessed from anywhere and at any time.
- Create institutional 'placards' or campus signposts to help students navigate and learn about their school. In this example, the codes themselves could be used to express short pieces of information about buildings and services, or to point students towards more detailed online descriptions.

- Create digital calendar entries for students which can be scanned and added directly to smartphone day planners using QR codes. Added to syllabi, posted online or used in class, codes are a quick and easy way to ensure that students are reminded of upcoming assignments or tests.

The list of possibilities for incorporating QR codes into the post-secondary student experience is only limited by willingness to experiment. For administrators and instructors with an interest in adopting new technology in the service of coursework, institutional promotion and information delivery, QR codes are an easy-to-use and inexpensive option.

Comparing the costs against the potential benefits of a QR code campaign is likely to demonstrate little in the way of risk. Because the applications necessary to run a project of this sort are largely free, institutions can approach them with an attitude that says 'nothing ventured, nothing gained'. The Ryerson example mentioned earlier is special if for no other reason than the scale, and since it represents a more in-depth and all-encompassing approach to using QR technology the risks actually became somewhat more immediate. To not only include codes in Ryerson's library catalogue but to build software that makes use of those codes would be a substantial investment of time and resources.

Treading lightly in uncharted territory

Understanding and looking critically at a project before taking the first steps is absolutely crucial, and this is true particularly when investigating the viability of new technological solutions to problems. The following only really scratches the surface of a list of questions that need to be asked before charging headlong into e-endeavours:

- *Does it have a shelf-life?* Is the project being planned going to be a long-term investment, or will the technological infrastructure be out-of-date before the next cohort of students has a chance to make use of it?
- *Is it accessible?* Can projects meet the needs of people with disabilities? If not, can steps be taken to amend this?
- *Is it affordable for students?* Is the hardware required for use available to all of those students who are being asked to use it, regardless of economic background? In the case of QR codes, smartphones and service charges may not be within the financial reach of everyone.

- *Do we have the expertise to support this?* Successfully running a technology-oriented campaign demands that an appropriate troubleshooting and informational system be put in place. If students ask questions, do we have the background to answer them?
- *Is it safe and secure?* Could the privacy of student users be compromised in any way when using the planned services? In situations where login information is required, students are being asked to risk compromising their online 'selves' which may make programme administrators liable.
- *Is it appealing, inviting and innovative?* Student uptake, particularly where technology is concerned, may ultimately hinge on the way a project is framed and so the question needs to be asked: 'Can the initiative being planned be easily "sold" to its intended audience?'

When asking these questions during the planning stages of new projects, organizers may be forced to make difficult decisions about viability. Technological initiatives may not meet all of the criteria outlined above, but ultimately may prove to be no less valuable. With that in mind, the most important question to be asked is how well a project fits with institutional imperatives. In other words, *does it meet the needs of the student?*

In this chapter, we have looked at two considerably different but nonetheless related applications of technology; first, Mixable and Hotseat represent advances in student-centred social software. Borrowing popular ideas from the dominant platforms embedded in student culture, these two programs are potentially powerful tools for enhancing teaching and learning. They effectively address a need for immediacy, dialogue and collaboration in education and they do so in simultaneously novel and enticing ways. By leveraging concepts from Twitter and Facebook, the developers at Purdue have almost guaranteed success in terms of student buy-in.

The second part of this chapter looked at QR codes, a technology whose motivating principle is ultimately nothing revolutionary. When all is said and done, QR codes are simply an effective means of expressing information in a manageable form. A fitting analogy for two-dimensional barcodes would be a blank sheet of paper, in that their value comes embedded in the ways in which they are used. Without being encoded with meaningful content, QR codes are simply constellations of square dots inside a box. That said, in the right set of hands and under conditions where students are likely to put in the effort to acclimatize themselves with the 'ins and outs' of QR codes, this method of information delivery could revolutionize the way services and resources are accessed.

What ties platforms like Mixable or Hotseat to tools like QR codes is mobility, and the way in which wireless connectivity is being used to create connections to online content. Mixable and Hotseat create a virtual forum for discussion that can be accessed anywhere and at any time. QR codes provide access points in real space to virtual content that would otherwise require users to be stationary. In both cases, the end result is increased and enhanced access in the service of enriching the experience of online content. When used creatively, and with the best interests of students in mind, the new tools available could represent a paradigm shift in electronic learning.

References

Aagard, H., Bowen, K. and Olesova, L. (2010) Hotseat: opening the backchannel in large lectures. *EDUCAUSE Quarterly Magazine*, 33(3). Retrieved from *http://www.educause.edu/EDUCAUSE+Quarterly/EDUCAUSE QuarterlyMagazineVolum/Hotseat/OpeningtheBackchannelin/213668*.

Denso Wave (2010) QR code features. Retrieved from *http://www.denso-wave.com/qrcode/qrfeature-e.html*. (No longer available online.)

Information Technology at Purdue (2011) Mixable: a social learning environment centered on the classroom. Retrieved from *http://www.itap.purdue.edu/studio/mixable/*.

Information Technology Standards Committee (2008) Section 3: QR code [report]. Retrieved from *http://www.itsc.org.sg/pdf/synthesis08/Three_QR_Code.pdf*.

Johnson, L., Smith, R., Willis, H., Levine, A. and Haywood, K. (2011) The 2011 Horizon Report [report]. Retrieved from *http://net.educause.edu/ir/library/pdf/HR2011.pdf*.

Kolowich, S. (2010) Mixing work and play on Facebook [blog post]. Retrieved from *http://www.insidehighered.com/news/2010/10/06/facebook*.

McCarthy, G. and Wilson, S. (2011) ISBN and barcode scanning mobile app for libraries. *Code4Lib Journal*, 14(5). Retrieved from *http://journal.code4lib.org/articles/5014*.

Part 2
Putting social media into practice

8

Incorporating web-based engagement and participatory interaction into your courses

Maureen Henninger and Diane Rasmussen Neal

Abstract: This chapter presents ideas for delivering online course content and communication in ways that will increase student participation and engagement. Diane Rasmussen Neal discusses options for using social media such as discussion forums, synchronous chat, social networking, and collaborative workspaces to reach students online in exciting ways. Additionally, she outlines advantages and disadvantages of using these tools in class. Maureen Henninger presents a case study of social media use in the forms of (1) providing a mentoring space for incoming students, and (2) embedding social media tools in courses.

Key words: student engagement, e-learning, social media, case study.

Online engagement and interaction: what does it mean?

As university instructors, we are all at least somewhat skilled in engaging with our students when we are in front of a class. Whether you use humour to keep a class of 500 undergraduates awake in English 101 (with varying degrees of success), or you pose thought-provoking questions to your doctoral students over coffee, we are all passionate enough about our fields to pass them down to our students.

But, the equation changes when we start teaching online. I (Diane) have been teaching online since 2004, and I enjoy it, but it's just different. Personal connections can feel less tangible. You might not ever meet your students in person, and they don't show up during office hours because they are sending you emails at 2 a.m. instead, in expectation of your response by 6 a.m. You feel overwhelmed by all the communication, and despite the amount of typing you do to keep in touch with your online students you never feel like you're teaching a class, but rather serving as a robotic secretary at the other end of the Internet. You want to be able to connect with your students, and you want them to develop those peer relationships that are so important in college/university, but you just do not see how that's possible. Does this sound like you – or like it could be you if you had to teach online?

If so, please do not worry. Based on my conversations with faculty colleagues over the years, these frustrations are quite common. Institutions vary in their levels of support for online courses. Ideally, we would have instructional designers at our disposal, content creation advisers, and teaching assistants to maintain all the conversations and all the grading. But typically, reality sets in – and we're on our own! Students and colleagues have told me stories about their negative experiences with online courses: the instructor only communicated with students via email; the instructor only sent out a syllabus and told students to get to work; the instructor never responded to messages; the list continues. So what can we do? We call up social media and related engagement techniques.

If you recall my discussion in the introductory chapter, Web 2.0 philosophy encourages participatory conversation, and it somewhat levels the playing field for those involved. As the instructor, it is your job to provide a consistent, reliable springboard of tools and environments for students to explore the material, but they can take it from there. This does mean that your comfortable 'Lord of the classroom' approach to teaching changes somewhat, but it is still up to you to lead the engagement. When the materials and the tools are there for students to participate in a conversation as they co-create their own learning experience – individually and collectively – amazing things can happen. Some ways to do this are outlined below.

Lead the conversation, but not too much

In Akin and Neal (2007) we introduced a model of presenting discussion questions in online courses. With each topic, it can be useful to present questions that encourage students to engage with the material and with each other, in a format such as an online discussion forum. However, just like a good research question, a good discussion question has several elements; writing them in appropriate ways encourages discussion in the right direction. We provide tips for designing the following elements: 'the cognitive nature of the question, the reading basis, any experiential possibility, style and type of question, and finally ways to structure a good question' (ibid., para. 1). We also suggest that while it is important for the instructor to be 'present' in the discussion, an overbearing presence can decrease the chances that students will participate. It is up to you to set this tone.

Keep it fresh but manageable

Today's students are used to our 'always-on' world. Texting, Facebooking, and tweeting is second nature. If you don't believe me, just observe them walking across campus; they usually do not even look up from their phones as they cross the street! Examining their reality, in which five minutes between texts is an eternity, not providing content to your students on a frequent basis will make them lose interest. Make a social contract with them at the beginning of the semester: they will be expected to report in to class at least once a day, and you will be expected to provide discussion questions, links to relevant websites and other useful items as frequently as possible.

That said, you can't post links at 3 a.m. To maintain a semblance of a life and to help your students know what to expect from you, I would like to suggest creating a 'communication policy' for your syllabus. For example, my communication policy states that I may or may not be available on weekends, holidays, or after 5 p.m. on weekdays. But, I also promise responses within 24 hours, or as soon as possible. Some online faculty hold 'online office hours' when they will be available via instant messaging software. Even if students do not choose to contact you, that extra availability can comfort them – and, if they don't 'show up', you can get some writing done while you're logged in! Email is also a consideration for your communication policy. Students appreciate the 'instructor immediacy' (Akin and Neal, 2007) associated with email, and it's generally reliable, safe and rapid if we respond as quickly as possible. On the other hand, our email inboxes are already clogged with correspondence related to our research and service duties. This is a personal choice, but I encourage students to post course-related questions to the course discussion forum area (in whatever form that might take). When they do that, not only can the entire class benefit from one consistent answer, but sometimes another student will answer the question before I even see it, which increases peer engagement (and saves me time)!

If they have a confidential question, I ask that they send me a private message through the learning management system. With this approach, their questions will not clog my inbox and my student communications are naturally organized in time and space.

Make it count

Many of us give participation points for in-person classes, and online classes should not be any different. In fact, I believe that participation should count even more online than in face-to-face classes. Set out your expectations at the beginning of the class, and hold them to these standards. For example, you might expect them to post related links, comment on discussion questions, blog once a week, and log in to weekly chat sessions for 20 per cent of their final grade. The problem with this kind of participation, of course, is that it can be difficult to measure qualitatively, and strict quantitative measures can feel draconian. At the same time, we have similar issues when measuring face-to-face participation. As the instructor, it is your responsibility to set whatever online participation activities you feel are necessary for your subject matter and appropriate for your personal style. The students' job is to meet those expectations.

Once, a very conscientious student contacted me to ask me whether she was participating 'enough'. She was one of the most frequent contributors in class, so I told her not to worry. The ones you need to worry about are the ones who never participate; you may have to send them a reality check a few weeks into the class to remind them that an online class is not a 'do a little bit whenever you feel like it' kind of course; in fact, it is the opposite. Online learning requires substantial personal motivation, but you can ease this if you provide the tools, content and infrastructure that will make students feel less isolated. As one of my efforts in this direction, I post weekly 'lessons'. For example, students might be expected to complete the activities and discussions for the previous week's lesson by Monday evening, and I post the new lesson on Tuesday morning. This routine provides structure in an otherwise relatively unstructured learning environment.

Choose the right tools for the job

From a nuts-and-bolts perspective, there are many tools that help you build opportunities for participatory engagement into your online courses. The options you choose may depend to some extent on your subject matter, the number of students on your course and your available technical support. Let's explore a few possibilities. Let's explore a few needs, and a few options.

Giving lectures

At some point, whether online or face-to-face, professors have to lecture; it's what we do! When I first started teaching online, I wrote PowerPoints and posted them online. Some faculty create PowerPoints with voiceovers for each slide. While these can be familiar and effective, they are 'one-way' and don't promote discussion. You could still present slides and talk about them, if that is what you are comfortable with. But, instead, you could record the activities on your computer screen (the slides, demonstrations, etc.) with a screen recording tool such as Camtasia (*http://www.techsmith.com/camtasia.html*), upload the video to YouTube or Vimeo and open it up for comments from your students. These could take the form of a podcast or vodcast. This approach would allow your students to access them via RSS feed (see Chapter 1 for more about RSS), download your files to their laptop, iPhone or other compatible device, and listen to them in the time and place that their preferences dictate.

If you are able to meet with your students synchronously (meaning that everyone is together online at the same time and place), you could give lectures via a tool such as Skype (*http://www.skype.com*), which allows people to hold text chats and group audio calls for free. With Skype, you can add your students as contacts, and then add the students to a 'group'. You can then 'call' or 'chat' with the group as a whole – and give your lecture virtually. A nice feature is that Skype also keeps a record of text chats, so students can refer to them later.

An emerging wave of streaming tools, such as *http://www.twitch.tv*, allows you to broadcast your screen and sound to viewers. You simply download a tool, provide the link to your viewers and lecture away! For a lecture on video games in my social media class, some gamer librarian friends and I provided my students with a live demonstration and narration while playing World of Warcraft. We were able to demonstrate the basics of the game (character creation, completing your first quest), some advanced play (rated battlegrounds) and lead a discussion at the end of the chat. It was a fun, productive session for everyone, and it encouraged students to think critically about video games and how they could play a role in library settings.

Lynne Williams, a co-author of Chapter 6 and the author of Chapter 10, uses Adobe Connect (*http://www.adobe.com/products/adobeconnect.html*) and Elluminate Live (*http://www.elluminate.com/services/training/elluminate_live!/?id=418*) to give lectures and hold synchronous discussion, respectively. I do not have personal experience with these tools, but she reports:

> Adobe Connect ... has a good interface, so you can run your lecture in the center of the screen while keeping an eye on the chat to the left of the screen ... we also have ... the Elluminate Live platform, which is good for drawing one or two students aside and answering questions 'live,' along with slides or demos via watching you walk through actions on your desktop. The good thing about Adobe Connect and Elluminate is that all sessions can be recorded, then stashed as recorded webinars for later viewing by students who may have similar questions.

(Lynne Williams, personal communication, 13 December 2011)

Blogging is another excellent option for providing lectures. In a blog, you can write your thoughts, link to online readings, embed videos or screencasts, and allow students to comment on your posts. I like to use course blogs as my main method for providing lessons, because every type of material I include can be linked from a weekly blog post. Also, if there are issues that come up during the course – if something proves more difficult than you expected, or you want to provide blanket feedback on an assignment – you can write a special blog post.

Infrastructure options for student engagement and participation

Asking students to create blogs that document their experiences and thoughts during the course can be beneficial. In Neal and Xiao (2011) we explored students' experiences of blogging for my social media course; you can read a first-hand student view of this particular course in Chapter 12. I used only social media tools to teach social media, but the class was still organized and maintained a predictable structure. The Neal and Xiao paper noted that the unfolding of their learning trajectories could be viewed in their weekly posts. This student's quote from a different semester of my social media course demonstrates why I find this method of engagement so encouraging:

> As I think back on this semester, I remember myself engaging with content in a way that I hadn't before ... I was introduced to a number of tools that I now feel comfortable using ... I have enjoyed our weekly Skype chats. It was important for me to 'hear' my classmate's [sic] opinions and ideas about social media in libraries so that I can build on my own thoughts.
>
> (tiredstarlingsocial, 2011, paras 1, 3 and 4)

Utilizing popular social networking and microblogging services is another way to increase active student participation. You could, for example, create a Facebook group, a Twitter hashtag or a Google+ hangout. This not only goes where your students already are, but social interaction is naturally built into the tools. With this option, however, you have privacy and identity issues to consider: do you want your students to see your personal profiles and updates, or should you make separate accounts for class purposes? (See Chapter 10 for more on this issue.) Additionally, students may have their own privacy concerns: they may not want their professor to see their social conversations on these networks, and may not want to create separate accounts to keep their identities separate. I will leave this deliberation for you to consider.

Collaborative work tools such as wikis and Google Docs can be a practical option for class projects. Students can use them for group work; this is an important feature in an online classroom setting because students are frequently geographically dispersed. Such tools probably improve the quality of student–student interaction because they give them a shared workspace and they are not subjected to the version control frustrations of sending email attachments. See the section, 'Wikis in the classroom', below, for more on this teaching and learning tactic. Collaborative tools and social media sites are also fun options for class activity collaboration; the possibilities are only limited to your pedagogical creativity. Wikis are not the only way to accomplish this. For example, Hoffman and Polkinghorne (2008), within an academic library instructional context, described their use of collaborative Flickr photograph tagging to demonstrate the differences between user-provided tags and library-provided index terms in describing and searching for photographs.

Putting it all together: learning management systems

Along with the use of all these tools comes a quandary: is it too much? With all the places a class can convene, post and comment, will the instructor and students forget which channels of communication are available? One solution to this problem is the use of a learning management system (LMS), which organizes all elements of an online course in one place. Examples of currently popular LMS options include Blackboard (*http://www.blackboard.com/*), Moodle (*http://moodle.org/*) and Sakai (*http://sakaiproject.org/*). They feature options such as the ability for the instructor to post course content, receive and grade assignments, manage student lists, create discussion forums, and so on. As Dalsgaard (2006) notes, integrating social media tools within the structure that an LMS provides is advantageous because LMSs do not provide a social constructivist approach to learning. Frequently, universities require that professors use a particular LMS for online course delivery.

At the time of writing, my university, The University of Western Ontario, uses WebCT (a product that merged with Blackboard), and is moving to Sakai soon. These are institutionally sanctioned systems, and the campus supports the technologies, but faculty are not required to use them for e-learning out of respect for academic freedom. I am fortunate to use Edmodo (*http://www.edmodo.com*), a 'social' LMS. It provides many LMS features such as assignment submission and a grade book, but it also operates very much like a Facebook wall or group. You can create a 'group' for each class, and students access it via a code that you provide to the class. Best of all, it's free and it's cloud-based, so no campus IT support is required! Figure 8.1 shows an Edmodo group for one of my courses.

I've focused on the use of social media for online course delivery but there are many other uses for social media in student engagement. In the remainder of this chapter, Maureen Henninger presents case studies of social media tools at play in her local setting for the purposes of embedding social media tools in courses as well as new student mentoring. The uses of these tools are wonderful, and I especially hope that Maureen's mentoring case study helps you think creatively about the currently unrealized potential of utilizing these tools in the academy.

Incorporating web-based engagement into your courses

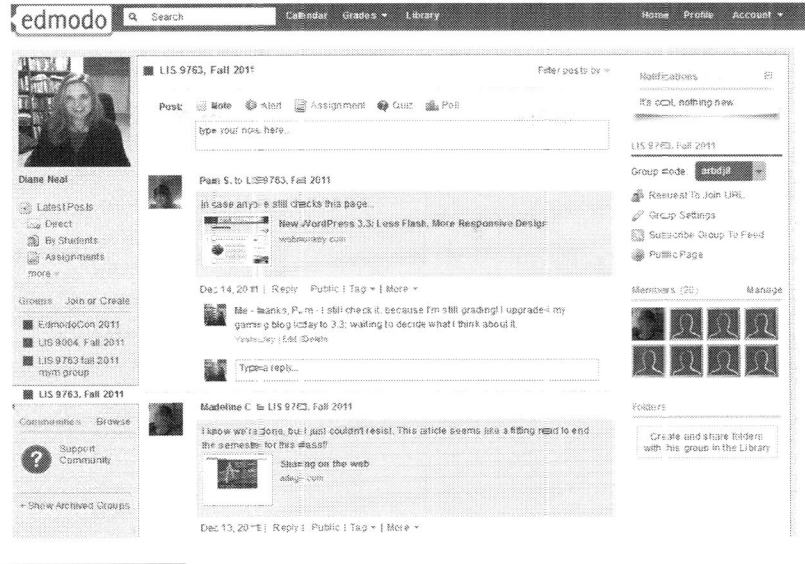

Figure 8.1 Edmodo, a 'social' LMS

Social networking services in the classroom: a case study

Concerns for student apprehension and uncertainty in a new and seemingly chaotic environment and the potential for significant attrition rates led an initiative to set up a mentoring space for the incoming undergraduates in the BA in Communication (Information and Media) programme at the University of Technology, Sydney (UTS). The ubiquity of Facebook (according to Socialbakers, during the week of 24 October 2011, 10,659,580 Australians logged into Facebook)[1] makes it an obvious social networking service choice for high-school leavers (Millennials) entering university. The UTS initiative, however, was about more than simply providing a platform for student informal chat and information sharing. It was about building a community of first-year students and providing a platform for mentoring services.

This was done in two steps. Firstly, a small cohort of final-year students was identified, and the students were asked to be mentors to the incoming students, with the aim of having one mentor for 8–10 students. An email was sent out – Do you want to be a mentor? – with the message: 'it can be as much or as little work as you wish to make it. We will be setting up a Facebook group for the mentors and their "mentorees" so that they can ask questions, share stories, etc., and we would ask you to introduce yourselves to your group of new students.' Every one of those contacted agreed; in fact, they were very enthusiastic, saying that they would have liked to have had such support when they were 'newbies'.

Once we had our mentors, Doodle was used to schedule the first (and only) meeting between the academics and mentors. At the same time, the Facebook group was set up, and within 48 hours over 50 per cent of the incoming students had joined. By the middle of the semester, 95 per cent of new students were part of the community (see Figure 8.2). The mentoring programme was then advertised with a post by an academic and the mentors introduced themselves to the community:

> *Academic*: Hey everyone we are setting up a mentoring program – Connie & Sarah are 2 of 9 mentors – more about this program in the next couple of days.
>
> *Mentor*: Hey guys! I'm Ryan, a 3rd year Info and Media Student with Media as my sub major. I'm also the temp Digital Preservation Officer over at UTS eScholarship for the next few months. It's great to see you all doing Information and Media as your major. If you have any problems, or just want to have a yarn, feel free to drop me a line.
>
> *Mentor*: Hey guys! I'm Joanne and I'm currently in my third year of info & media and am also doing a law degree. Feel free to drop by if you have any questions or any trouble – or even if you want to vent about your frustrations :) looking forward to working with you!!

In the first week of the programme, each mentor set up a face-to-face meeting with their mentees in which they chatted and swapped email

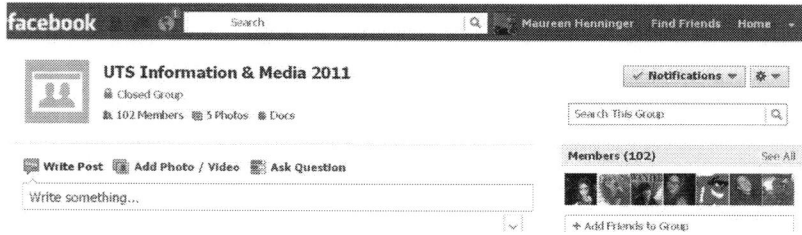

Figure 8.2 Mentoring service for first-year undergraduate students

addresses and phone numbers in case they wanted to ask or discuss a situation of a more sensitive nature. In the first week of the semester, the mentors were very active in monitoring and answering fairly routine coursework and 'how to' questions posted on Facebook.

> *Student*: hi everyone, i couldnt come into uni today because i'm sick and i was wondering if anyone has notes from the Creative Information Design lecture that they could email me?
>
> *Mentor*: Hey Guys. Generally you can find the lecture slides and tutorial notes on UTSOnline in the folder for that week.

Questions of a more personal nature were not posted on Facebook. According to the mentors, these questions were emailed or discussed face-to-face over coffee or a beer.

It was envisaged that there would be little input from the academics but by the middle of the semester it became obvious that Facebook was the preferred method for asking questions of tutors and lecturers. In spite of advertising the fact that the Blackboard discussion boards were the Faculty's preferred vehicle for questions and answers about classes, Blackboard was rarely used for communication purposes. In fact, over the three core subjects in the major (Information and Media), there were only two questions, one of which was from a student who did not join the Facebook group.

Although no formal survey was carried out to evaluate the mentoring programme, the mentors reported informally on a few instances of 'tears' and personal questions, for the most part via email. Anecdotally, the students reported that they found the idea of having a mentor 'very welcoming', and that it 'made some of the settling-in stages much easier'. At the end of the first semester, the attrition rate was 3.9 per cent, a big improvement on the year before, and we would like to think that the Facebook mentoring programme may have played some part in this.

Wikis in the classroom

Most academic institutions now use online learning environments such as the proprietary Blackboard or the open source systems such as Sakai and Moodle. The following three case studies show ways in which social media tools can be embedded in coursework, using the wiki space of Blackboard in order to build collaboration and participatory interaction.

At UTS, this is done within both the postgraduate and undergraduate degrees, and the following case studies are from the Information and Knowledge Management programme: two from postgraduate subjects and the third from an undergraduate subject. The postgraduate degrees at UTS can be completed either part time or full time, and indeed many of the students attend class in the evening as they are employed and often have work commitments which interrupt their studies. As Diane noted, this situation can pose difficulties for students' group work and assignment presentation. Here are two case studies which, using online spaces (wikis), enable students to fully participate in the subject in a flexible manner not bounded by time or space. Both involve group work. The first demonstrates the creation of a body of new knowledge; the second, an online presentation and peer evaluation of a group assignment.

Case study 1

There are two subjects in the Information and Knowledge Management degrees that revolve around the use and management of information objects and knowledge: Knowledge Management in the Organization and Enterprise Content Management. Embedded in both is the notion of sharing information and knowledge; in particular, the concept of communities of practice. In order to emulate and give a reality to online communities of practice, there is a group assignment in which members of the group share ideas and build content in a wiki environment over a period of several weeks. One of the criteria against which the students are assessed is to 'work collaboratively in a group to design content by writing and contributing ideas and research uses'.

Figure 8.3 shows an example of a resource on cloud enterprise content management (ECM). The wiki provided the facilities for uploading diagrammatic documentation (mind and concept maps), group contract agreements and textual content, which was easily edited.

The comments area within the Blackboard wiki was used for editorial and planning processes, and the group noted that for the most part this was successful. Other comments highlighted the well-known challenges of virtual collaboration: 'our face-to-face team meeting was really interesting and valuable but not recorded; it was a challenge to bring the same energy into our wiki based discussions', and 'understanding the balance between the neutral voice needed for the master wiki and the opinion allowed in the discussions [sic]'.[2] Overall, across all the groups in these subjects, the wiki environment enabled the collaborative, at times

Incorporating web-based engagement into your courses

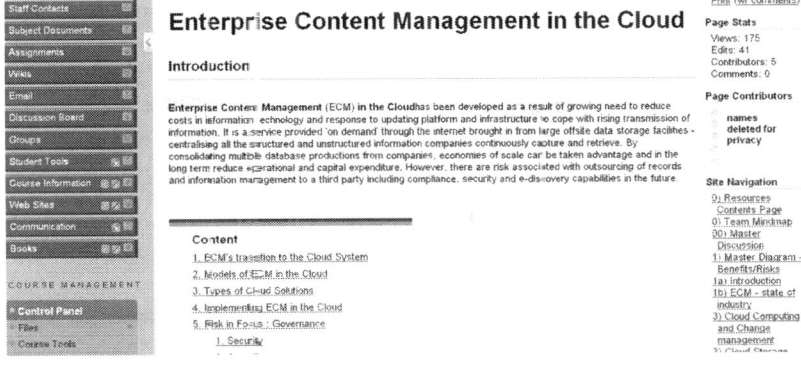

Figure 8.3 A new information resource – Wiki: ECM in the cloud

innovative, creation of new information resources without the constraints of time and location.

Case study 2

In a subject, Investigative Research in the Digital Environment, students, in pairs, have to deconstruct an information product (an environmental scan, a briefing report, for example) in order to tease out the research processes and data sources. Once done, this has to be presented to the class. Again, because of work and time constraints the work is done collaboratively in a wiki. The final work, generally a PowerPoint presentation, is made public to the entire class three days before the assignment is due. At this time, all students must go through the presentations and make evaluative comments in the wiki (see Figure 8.4).

In face-to-face presentations, students are often reticent to offer critical comments, and, particularly at night when they are tired, often don't want to take the time to do so. However, in the online environment, several interesting things happen. As the time frame is three days, students have the time to really examine the presentations in order to make considered comments. Not only do they make good critical comments, they tend to ask questions, such as 'How did you do that?' and 'What was your thinking behind the validation of that dataset?', thus setting up a conversation not only with the original presenters, but with the rest of the class who offer further insights and suggestions. Finally, the students have all commented in the subject feedback that they find this method very satisfying because of the ability to have

Figure 8.4 Online presentation and peer evaluation

a conversation in which not only do they get good feedback, but they also get tips and strategies for the research processes – the sharing of information and knowledge.

Tools for virtual conferences: a case study

First-year undergraduate students in a BA in Communication (Information and Media) programme had a final assignment that required them, in groups of three, to collaborate in creating a digital poster which critically examined a theme or issue associated with information discovery and access. A digital poster was deemed to be any type of digital presentation, and they were encouraged to be creative and to use any tool or technique they considered effective to 'get the message across'. The week before the conference each group had to post three questions concerning their poster topic for a three-day online discussion by the class (the virtual conference). This discussion was then synthesized and incorporated into the group's final poster presentation, which was uploaded to the class wiki for further discussion.

Students were allowed to use any collaboration tool for discussing and designing the poster as well as sharing their research. Blackboard collaborative spaces, wikis, discussion boards and synchronous chat were made available and all three were used; in addition, students used email and set up Facebook groups. Unfortunately, no statistics were kept on this part of the communication process.

The following is an example of one digital poster on the topic of 'Access to online health information by patients and carers: risks and benefits'. The group who created this poster made extensive use of social media tools (see Table 8.1) and, coincidently, much of the online health information for their annotated bibliography came from social networking sites (SNSs) as well as from traditional scholarly and/or authoritative resources.

The group used Facebook to get started on the project, but soon moved over to the Blackboard wiki space for composing and editing content – the traditional use of a wiki – and commenting on and discussing the content and the project. They conceived their poster as a wiki (built inside the Blackboard wiki space) that had a customized interface with the following elements and content:

- navigation by resource types (blogs, tagging and bookmarking services, journal articles, websites, and wiki and SNSs);
- discussion questions posted in the wiki, but class discussion done via MSN Messenger service;

| Table 8.1 | List of elements and tools incorporated into a digital poster presentation at a virtual conference |

Element or tool	Description
Group collaboration	Wiki, Facebook group
Poster description	Customized interface for Blackboard wiki
Poster elements	<ul><li>PowerPoint presentation</li><li>Information categories, e.g., blogs, tagging and bookmarking</li><li>Questions – discussion summaries – solutions (outputs), e.g., radio podcast</li></ul>
Class discussion	MSN service and wiki comments

- a summary of the class discussion of each question, done by an analysis of the MSN logs;
- three creative solutions (outputs) for dissemination of health information to patients and carers; and
- an overview of the poster in the form of a PowerPoint presentation.

Of particular interest is the innovative 'output' for two of the questions:

- *Numerous online sources indicate that the information provided should be taken as advisory and a guide only. It falls to the user to be responsibly informed about their health-related decisions. How do patients/carers differentiate between advice and information?*
- *Is it possible for the Internet to provide health information in an educational manner in an understandable and entertaining fashion?*

The group analysed the logs of the MSN class discussion of these two questions and decided that, in the first case, a radio podcast would be an appropriate resource and, in the second, an online health survey would be appropriate. The group wrote, recorded and embedded a podcast, and, using the Facebook application, QuizCreate, designed and embedded the survey, both of which can be seen in the collage of the poster elements (see Figure 8.5). It should be noted that the output for the first question was a series of well-designed postcards.

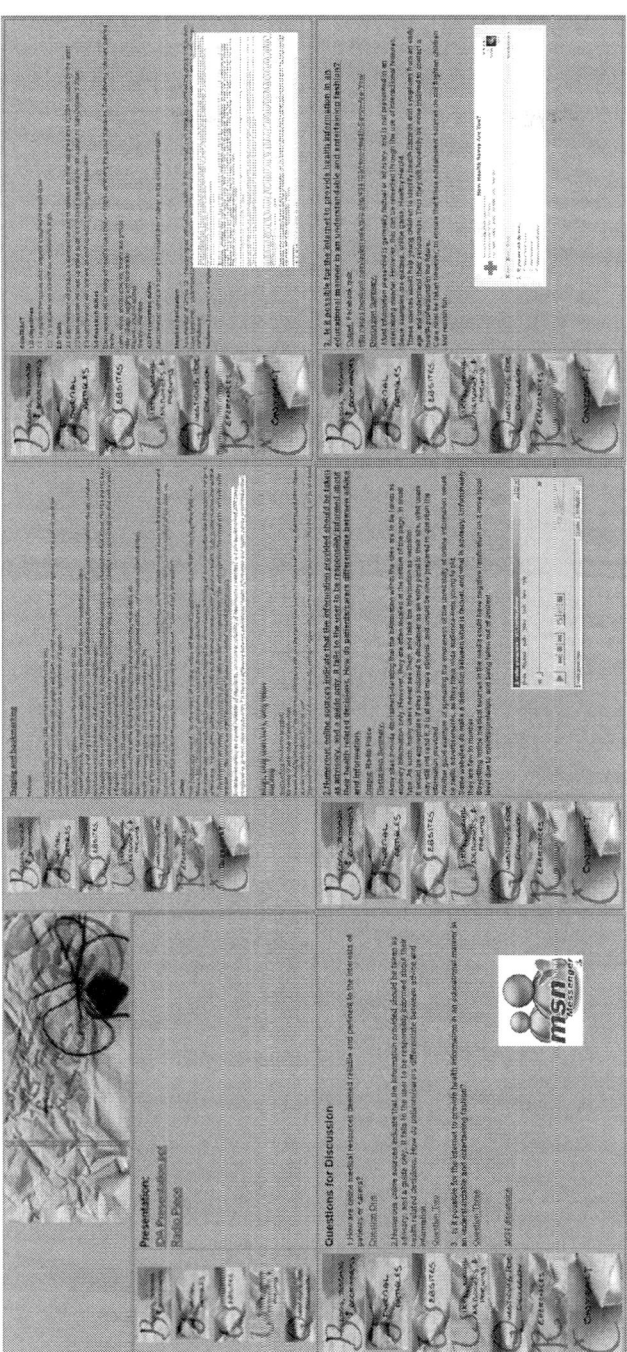

Figure 8.5 Elements of a student digital poster in a virtual conference

Overall, this case study provides a striking demonstration of Millennials' familiarity and ease with social media services, and, even more impressively, their ability to use them in a creative and innovative way to communicate serious ideas and issues.

Conclusions

This chapter has reviewed a suite of choices for providing online engagement and participatory tools to your students. A point to reiterate: while some of the tools discussed (such as certain learning management systems) require your institution's financial and technical support, many of these tools are free and cloud based, which means you can start using them immediately, with minimal start-up time and expense required. It is a satisfying feeling to know that your students are working with emerging technologies in their educational journeys; technologies that matter to their generation and to society. You are also providing them with new forms of digital literacy that they may not possess yet. While they might text and Facebook and tweet all day, this does not necessarily mean that they know which tool to use for the work task at hand, or how to use them appropriately. You can provide a safe environment for them to develop these types of critical thinking skills as you provide the infrastructure and support for them to learn these essential 21st century abilities. This might sound clichéd but for your students, and their eventual employers, the future is *now*.

Notes

1. For social media statistics, including weekly updates of Facebook statistics, see Socialbakers *http://www.socialbakers.com/*.
2. This facebook group is a closed group and can not be accessed by the public (*http://www.facebook.com/#!/groups/202528896423886/members/*).

References

Akin, L. and Neal, D. (2007) CREST+ model: writing effective online discussion questions. *Journal of Online Learning and Teaching*, 3(2). Retrieved from *http://jolt.merlot.org/vol3no2/akin.htm*.

Dalsgaard, C. (2006) Social software: e-learning beyond learning management systems. Retrieved from *http://www.eurodl.org/materials/contrib/2006/Christian_Dalsgaard.htm*.

Hoffman, C. and Polkinghorne, S. (2008) 'Sparking *Flickrs* of insight into controlled vocabularies and subject searching', in P. Godwin and J. Parker (eds). *Information Literacy Meets Library 2.0* (pp. 117–23). London: Facet Publishing.

Neal, D. and Xiao, L. (2011) 'The use of weblogs in LIS online courses: a case study', in I. Huvila, K. Holberg and Maria Kronqvist-Berg (eds). *Proceedings of the International Conference on Information Science and Social Media 2011 (ISSOME 2011)* (pp. 107–16). Åbo/Turku, Finland: Åbo Akademi University. Retrieved from *http://issome2011.library2pointoh.fi/wp-content/uploads/2011/10/ISSOME2011-proceedings.pdf*.

tiredstarlingsocial (2011) tiredstarlingsocial. Retrieved from *http://tiredstarlingsocial.wordpress.com/*.

9

When good research goes viral! Getting your work noticed online

Diane Rasmussen Neal

Abstract: It is possible to use many online outlets to make your research go viral, or popular with many people online. This chapter provides an overview of how to do this. You can use social media tools such as blogs, Facebook, Twitter, Google+, and YouTube for promoting and providing your research to your academic community. Additionally, this chapter explains how you can influence Google search results to your benefit with techniques such as search engine optimization, and why you should care about search result rankings. Other pointers include using your Google Scholar Citations profile as well as your university's existing Internet infrastructure to prominently position your research online.

Key words: viral marketing, social media, search engine optimization, Google.

Introduction

Many of us academics have a research component in our job descriptions. I work at a research-intensive university; on paper, research is a full 40 per cent of my job, and research really counts more for tenure and promotion decisions than does teaching. Clearly, it is important for me to win grants, hire capable research assistants and publish in peer-reviewed journals. Equally, or more, important is the task of getting my research noticed by my academic peers. Today's journals (and, increasingly, books) are mostly only accessed online but this can work to our disadvantage. In today's digital environment, we are constantly inundated by more and more online information. The relatively level playing field of online information access means that we compete for our colleagues' online attention alongside every other researcher in our field (not to mention photos of our friends' children, clips from last night's *The Big Bang Theory*, and so on). Certain tools are at our disposal to help us manage all the information, such as publishers' table of contents email alerts when new journal issues are published online, but there is still no guarantee that our research will get noticed, read or cited because so many elements are working against us. Is there anything we can do? I'd like to suggest in this chapter that we can make our research go viral using both social and traditional tools.

What exactly does it mean when something 'goes viral'? The idea has been present in business for some time now; essentially it means that you can make your customers do your marketing for you (Scott, 2010). The masses have the power to make online items popular by posting links to them on their Twitter or Facebook accounts, writing about them on their blogs, commenting on YouTube videos they like, emailing them to 200 of their closest friends (we all know people who do this!), and so on. We tend to follow people and organizations we know, trust and like online, which makes us likely to be interested in viewing content that friends or respected organizations recommend.

We have seen this play out in popular culture over the last few years in many contexts. YouTube videos are a good example. As early as 2006, the 'Diet Coke and Mentos' YouTube videos started garnering hits on YouTube, providing people with a quick laugh; see *http://www.youtube.com/watch?v=hKoB0MHVBvM* if you've never seen this experiment. Regardless of what you might think about his singing abilities, popular music star, Justin Bieber, was discovered after videos of him singing and playing guitar were posted on YouTube and viewed by large numbers of teenage girls everywhere. The 'Old Spice guy' commercials went viral instantly in 2010, receiving over 50 million views in just a few months (Wiancko, 2010).

This model works well in business and popular culture, but how would we apply it to academic research? Are 50 million people going to care that a biologist made a new discovery about the eating habits of one frog species that lives in northern Manitoba? That's not likely, unless this discovery can cure cancer, but we can use similar techniques to help our peers notice what we are doing. This chapter explores ways to do that.

Social networking: Facebook, Twitter, LinkedIn, YouTube, and so on

Facebook

Using social networking to make our research go viral corresponds with Chapter 2, 'Non-academic and academic social networking sites for online scholarly communities'. Since this brief chapter draws largely on my own practice and experience, I will be completely honest in stating that most of my viral self-marketing takes place on Facebook. Keeping in line with what Chapter 2 discusses, this is true for me simply because it's where I connect with most of my colleagues. While I have friends, family and colleagues on my sole Facebook account, I tend to post mostly professional content on Facebook because it's the least personal common denominator. (My family doesn't always understand what I post, but my seemingly enigmatic posts provide good conversation fodder at holiday gatherings.)

Let us say that I get the fortunate news that a journal has accepted one of my articles. Since I have waited months for this decision in many cases, I'm obviously excited, and I want to share it with people I know. I post two words and a smiling emoticon as my Facebook status:

> article accepted!:-)

What happens when I do this? Unfailingly, a respectable number of my Facebook friends, mostly colleagues, 'Like' the status; it seems to be human nature (or Facebook nature) for us to appreciate positive status updates. Additionally, if I don't give away too much information in the update, I get comments on the status, such as, 'Congratulations! What's the topic? What journal?', which builds 'buzz' around the update.

After the article is published, I can take advantage of the online nature of today's scholarly communication and post a link to the journal article in Facebook. Since I have worked hard to build a friendly and consistent – but not overpowering – presence on Facebook, people do seem to watch my links and updates even more than I necessarily realize. Often, a faculty colleague or doctoral student will see me in the hallway and say, 'I saw your article on Facebook! It looks interesting! I'm looking forward to reading it.' I don't always get direct feedback about the work itself on Facebook but it gets noticed, which is all we can hope for sometimes. These Facebook tactics can work for not only journal articles but conference papers, monographs, exhibitions ... whatever 'research' means in your field. I also post occasional observations, frustrations or successes I have in my research life. On the day I drafted parts of this chapter, I posted:

> ... thinks it's practically self-indulgent to have a research day!

This comment prompted posts from a colleague about avoiding the telephone on a research day. The exchange wasn't anything major but it put the idea that research is on my schedule into colleagues' minds. It also builds rapport: we can all commiserate about how busy academic life is, and how hard it can be to find uninterrupted time for research.

Twitter

Twitter is another social networking site you can use to promote your research. Twitter can be a complicated place for new initiates. Chapter 6 covers Twitter usage in great detail so I won't discuss it too much here. I would like to say here, as Lynne Williams and Jackie Krause say in Chapter 6, that Twitter is more of a one-way communication tool than a two-way discussion tool. For this reason, as well as the fact that it just isn't as well-populated with my colleagues as Facebook, I cannot say that I participate in Twitter very often. However, if you and your peers use (or want to use) Twitter you can use similar tactics on Twitter. Especially if you are fortunate enough to be a research leader in your discipline, it is possible to build a following if you post often. You can also take advantage of the relatively one-way nature of Twitter (again, that is my opinion) by posting not only announcements related to your productivity but thoughts about your research area, such as thoughts about a new article, your recent research questions, and so on. Since people go there to get news updates, there is no reason why academic researchers can't share ideas there as well. Invite your closest colleagues to follow you, and see if your following grows as you continue to post thoughtful comments and announcements about your research productivity. Even if this doesn't get conversation going, hopefully it will at least make people think about your comments.

LinkedIn

As Anatoliy Gruzd notes in Chapter 2, LinkedIn is 'a social networking website for career-related networking'. LinkedIn is a much more active site for private sector professionals than for academics, but it's definitely worth having a presence there. LinkedIn allows account holders to provide their employment history, education and other CV-related details. LinkedIn members can make 'connections' with each other, which is similar in concept to 'friending' someone on Facebook.

LinkedIn excels with potential viral capabilities in its ability to recommend people for connections. There are some privacy concerns with LinkedIn, however; it may search your email address books and so on. It is unclear exactly how LinkedIn finds suggestions for connections. Recently, LinkedIn recommended connecting to a personal trainer I worked with about five years ago, and I'm not even sure we exchanged emails! Also, LinkedIn allows your connections to 'recommend' you by writing on your profile what they like about you as a professional colleague. When people find your profile, these connections might create some buzz about you. One more piece of potentially viral information LinkedIn provides is how many people have searched for you in the last month. This information in itself is not viral but it can give you a sense of how many people are looking for you – especially if you compare that number to how many people have added you as a connection in the past month.

YouTube

As illustrated by my earlier examples, YouTube videos can go viral for many reasons. It might be unreasonable to think that a video of you talking about the mice in your lab will garner 23 million views in a week but it is certainly possible to gain the attention of students and colleagues in your field.

The standard lecture or 'talking head' video format is prevalent. This has been used for many years in contexts such as distance education classes and it can certainly convey important messages. In some circumstances, these can go viral, especially if they get attention from non-academics. For example, the video at *http://www.youtube.com/watch?v=dBnniua6-oM*, which features Dr Robert H. Lustig of the University of California, San Francisco, discussing the negative health impact of eating sugar, has had over 1.8 million views at the time of this writing. You can tell by reading the comments that many of the viewers have not been academics. If you want your research to reach an audience that exists outside of academia, it may be necessary to either: 1) change your research agenda, which would entail too much work; or 2) find an angle that makes your work interesting and relevant to the general public. (Think Carl Sagan.)

It is also possible to present work and ideas in a non-standard lecture format. Many people create instructional videos with software such as Camtasia, which records anything you do on the computer screen and your voice, so you can narrate as you demonstrate. This is an effective tool for online classroom demonstrations but it can be used for conference-style presentations or other demonstrations as well. The possibilities are limitless!

Once you've started creating YouTube content, or at least have a plan for content, consider creating a YouTube 'channel'. YouTube users can 'subscribe' to channels that interest them, so they get updates when their favourite channels receive new content. Individuals and organizations create channels to hold and organize their YouTube content; a directory of these can be found at *http://www.youtube.com/channels*. Universities, too, create channels; for example, the University of California's channel at *http://www.youtube.com/user/UCtelevision* contains a video of Dr Lustig's lecture and many others. If your university or department has a channel, you should definitely consider contributing content. If not, create your own channel. The link to the channel should be listed in your email signature as well as your Facebook page/LinkedIn profile/Twitter account – whatever social media platforms you decide to utilize. As your social media profile becomes noticed, your YouTube channel will get known too.

Blogs

In Chapter 1, Carolyn Hank reviews academic blogging basics so I will avoid exploring details about blogging in this chapter and just discuss some promotional ideas. While blogs can be a wonderful way to get your research noticed, keep in mind that if your blog isn't in your adoring public's minds, it won't get read. Just like your official publications, you can link to your blog on your Twitter, Facebook and LinkedIn profiles, and mention when a new post is available. Likewise, place links to your Twitter, Facebook and LinkedIn profiles on your blog. The blog I co-edit, 'tl-dr.ca: where gamers and information collide', is linked on the faculty profile page hosted by my university's website and I do get blog readers referred from that profile page. Ensure that it is easy for people to follow your blog by using Really Simple Syndication (RSS) feed aggregators such as Google Reader. This involves placing a link to your RSS feed on your blog; WordPress themes will typically assist you with this via an RSS widget. This is very important to do because many people rely on RSS-based services to keep current with all their online news sources, and you want your blog to be one of those sources.

Google, you and 'the filter bubble'

On today's Internet, Google is the indisputable leader in providing our starting point to online content, and social media further directs us to online content. According to Alexa (2011), a company that provides web metrics, Google is the top website in the world, followed by social media sites Facebook and YouTube. 'Googling' a topic – even our own name – has become a household word. On social media, if we ask a question about something, other people sarcastically tell us to 'just Google it'. My research into how young people find and evaluate online mental health information (Neal et al., 2011) has revealed, however, that although people typically start with a Google search, they do not always find the accurate, reliable information they want. Additionally, most people do not look beyond the first page of Google's search results (McTavish et al., 2011). Therefore, as hard as we might work to make our research go viral, if Google doesn't rank our work prominently when someone Googles our name or research area, it will be disadvantageous. As Bailyn (2011, back cover) wrote, 'If you aren't at or near the top of Google searches, you won't be found.' We must understand and plan against the factors affecting this phenomenon as much as possible.

Nobody really understands the mechanics behind how Google's search result list ranking works except Google itself, but we do know a few things about it. Google's ranking order, which is known in the information retrieval system terminology we use in my field of information science as 'relevance ranking', is based on something Google calls PageRank. When Google founders, Sergey Brin and Larry Page, started Google as graduate students at Stanford University, they built their search algorithm on the idea that the importance or relevance of web pages was based on how many other web pages link to it. So, the more web pages link to a site, the higher the Google PageRank (Bailyn, 2011; Langville and Meyer, 2006). Influences on PageRank's evaluation of a website's importance constantly evolve, and the influence of social media sites is an increasing factor: how many times a page is linked on Twitter, Facebook or Google+, for example.

Clearly, then, it is important to get as many sites to link to sites containing your research output as possible (and to link to them yourself on social media sites), but there are tactics around it as well. There is an entire industry called search engine optimization (SEO) that focuses on increasing websites' search engine rankings. Understanding how to implement SEO for your sites is a little technical, but not insurmountable. For an introduction to SEO's workings and implementation options, see one of many resources such as Bailyn (2011) or Tossell (2011).

Another factor influencing people's Google search results is what Eli Pariser (2011) calls 'the filter bubble'. A video of Pariser's talk about this concept is available at *http://www.youtube.com/watch?v=B8ofWFx525s*. Essentially, he points out that every individual's Google results are personalized based on one's computer, browser, geographic location, and so on. You do not have control over what he calls this 'personal unique universe of information'. Based on this principle, the faculty member next door to you could do a search identical to yours and get different results than you because she is using a MacBook as opposed to your PC. I have seen this at play as well when I travel to different countries: I get *google.ca* results at home in Canada, *google.com.au* results in Australia, and so on, all with country-specific rankings. Somebody browsing the web with Google Chrome may get different results than an Internet Explorer user. This makes it difficult to predict exactly how Google's search results for my name will appear on the first page of any one person's 'hit list'. To demonstrate this, Figure 9.1 displays the hits on *my* first page of results for 'Diane Rasmussen Neal' on *google.ca* in December 2011, using Windows 7 and Firefox.

The first result is my profile page on my university faculty's official website. This is a very good result to have listed first; see the following section for more thoughts on this. The second and third results are my Twitter and LinkedIn profiles, respectively. Next is a discipline-specific website with information about my dissertation and associated 'academic genealogy' information. Surprisingly, the next result is a letter I wrote to an editor in a blog post written by my friend that referenced me; this makes me a little uncomfortable because while it is a discussion about chronic illness misinformation, I am not sure how much I want my colleagues to know that I suffer from this disease. Next is an invited book review I wrote for the *Journal of the American Society for Information Science and Technology* (*JASIS&T*). It is 'only' a book review, but I am very proud of it, since the editor really liked the review, and the book won the Society's Information Science Book of the Year

Diane Rasmussen Neal - Faculty of Information & Media Studies ...
www.fims.uwo.ca › People › Faculty
Faculty. **Diane Rasmussen Neal** Assistant Professor. North Campus Building Room 258. Phone: 519-661-2111 x81034. University of Western Ontario London ...

Diane Rasmussen Neal (@bellydancer360) on Twitter
twitter.com/bellydancer360
Sign up for Twitter to follow **Diane Rasmussen Neal** (@bellydancer360). techie information science assistant professor, music lover, and bellydancer.

Diane Rasmussen Neal - Canada | LinkedIn
ca.linkedin.com/pub/dir/Diane/Rasmussen
View **Diane Rasmussen Neal's** (Canada) professional profile on LinkedIn. LinkedIn is the world's largest business network, helping professionals like **Diane** ...

MPACT
ils.unc.edu/mpact/mpact.php?op=show_tree&id=4880
27 Jun 2008 – Dissertation Information for **Diane Rasmussen Neal**. NAME: - Diane **Rasmussen Neal**. DISCIPLINE: - Library and Information Science. SCHOOL: ...

Endometriosis Advocacy and the Media — ChronicHealing.com
chronichealing.com/endometriosis-advocacy-and-the-media/
10 Feb 2010 – **Diane Rasmussen Neal**, PhD London, Ont The publication of this letter to the editor to The Intelligencer is excellent news because there have ...

Atlas of Science: Visualizing What We Know - Rasmussen Neal ...
onlinelibrary.wiley.com › ... › Journal Home › Vol 62 Issue 6
by D Rasmussen Neal
Atlas of Science: Visualizing What We Know. **Diane Rasmussen Neal**. Article first published online: 17 MAR 2011. DOI: 10.1002/asi.21497. © 2011 ASIS&T ...

Diane Rasmussen Neal - Google+ - this is funny!
https://plus.google.com/112814512869960879220/.../KqmyK26yBp...
27 Jul 2011 – **Diane Rasmussen Neal** is using Google+. Join Google+ to connect with the ... **Diane Rasmussen Neal's** profile photo. **Diane Rasmussen Neal** ...

DBLP: Diane Rasmussen Neal
www.informatik.uni-trier.de/~ley/db/.../Neal:Diane_Rasmussen.html

Figure 9.1 Search result list for 'Diane Rasmussen Neal' on google.ca

award in 2011. Next is a Google+ post of little consequence, a citation database that attempts to link information scholars by shared publications, *http://www.peekyou.com* (one of those pesky 'people search' engines that does not represent anybody in a flattering way!), and a link to a site containing the presentations for a panel I sat on at the Annual Meeting of the American Society for Information Science and Technology in

2011. As this demonstrates, all these sites relate to me, and some of them are 'social' sites. None of my published peer-reviewed articles shows up, which is unfortunate. However, these results are better than what I would get if I searched Diane Rasmussen Neal without quotes, or just Diane Neal – in which case I get gossip pages about the *Law & Order* actress, Diane Neal! Feel free to Google my name from your computer and see what results you get.

In Chapter 4, Maureen Henninger discusses Google Scholar (*http://scholar.google.com*) in some detail, including its ability to help you find other scholars' papers of interest. Figure 9.2 shows a screen shot of the Google Scholar results for 'Diane Rasmussen Neal' (again, in quotes).

I find Google Scholar to be quite accurate in its results for scholars' names, and extremely accurate for paper titles. For this reason, it's important to make sure that your Google Scholar Citations profile is up-to-date.

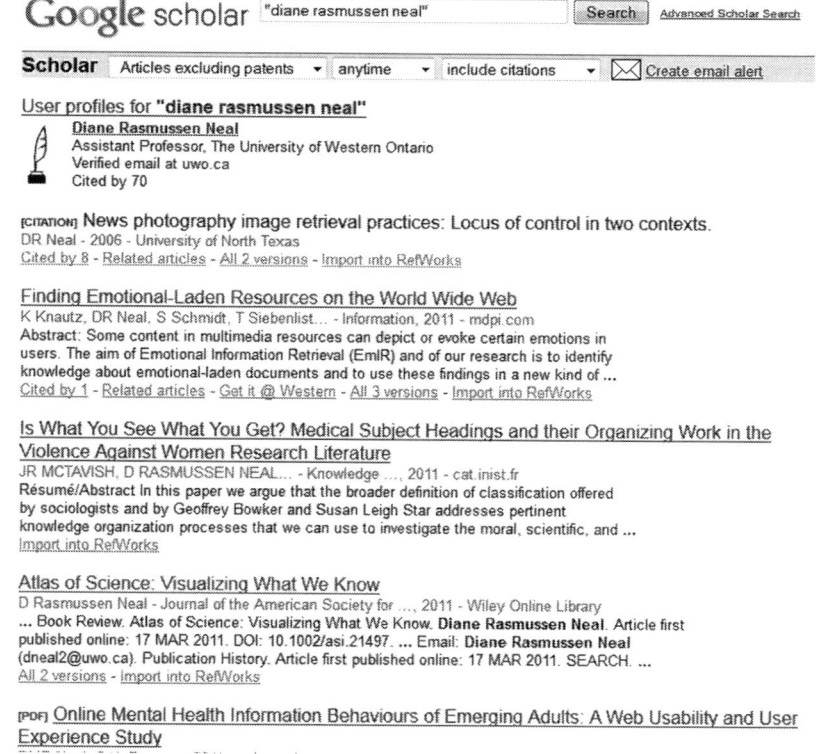

Figure 9.2 Google Scholar results for 'Diane Rasmussen Neal'

To learn more about Google Scholar Citations, see *http://googlescholar.blogspot.com/2011/11/google-scholar-citations-open-to-all.html*. Based on the connections Google Scholar made for my Google Scholar Citations profile, it was excellent at determining which 'Diane Neal' needed to be linked to me. I should know better as a librarian but I have published under different versions of my name (Diane Rasmussen Neal, Diane M. Neal, Diane Neal, etc.), which makes my citation counts look lower than they are. This is one pitfall to avoid, whether you get married and use your husband's last name or just cannot decide if you like your middle initial.

Official university pages: viral is not always better

Despite the shiny newness of social media, there are still some 'old school' web outlets that rank prominently in Google's hits. University websites are one such example. Since we have a content management system (CMS) in my faculty and I am allowed to edit my page, I keep the page very current with lists of upcoming and recent publications as well as brief teaching and service descriptions. As previously mentioned, I also link to the blog I co-moderate, 'tl-dr.ca', on this page. I want to note here that it is very important to keep your faculty profile page as current and up-to-date as possible! Simply because that page is tied to the university website as a whole it will probably receive higher search rankings than almost anything you create yourself, because the domain name has been in existence for years and receives frequent hits from many stakeholders. If you create your own website (such as *DianeRasmussenNeal.ca*, for example) it will be difficult to receive higher search engine rankings because the site is not part of that larger infrastructure. Blame PageRank. Not every academic department is fortunate enough to have a CMS, but if it is possible to at least ask your local web contact to link to some publications on a perfunctory faculty profile page for you, you will notice a difference in how many people read and cite your research.

Another option for promoting your research within your university's existing online infrastructure might be its 'institutional repository' (IR). In this model, the university library provides an option for researchers to place electronic copies of published work on a university server and people can access your work there for free. There are licensing issues to be worked out with certain publishers, especially if it is the type of publication in which you must relinquish copyright, but these details can be worked out. When copies of your work are available in an IR, people can find all your work (not just journal articles but other forms of literature such as presentation slides, conference abstracts, etc.) in one place. You can see my university's IR, called Scholarship@Western, at *http://ir.lib.uwo.ca/*. If you are not sure whether your university has an IR, ask the library. IRs are an emerging mode of providing scholarship; faculty have legitimate reasons to avoid placing their work in them (Brown and Abbas, 2010). However, if we all agree to work through the challenges and start using them we can work through the issues collectively. If it becomes easier for people to access and cite our work because of increased IR activity we can only benefit from this service.

Conclusions

As I conclude this chapter, the question arises: How viral do you want to be? Lynne Williams demonstrates in Chapter 10 how all your online 'yous' can blur, and unless you go off the grid you may not be able to avoid this completely. One suggestion is to employ different usernames. If you are BioDoctor65 on your professional YouTube videos, you might want to be HotMama99 when you post YouTube videos of you and your dogs playing in the park. Your academic circle does not need to know that you dress your chihuahua in purple sweaters, but that's something I do!

Also, it is important to use only the viral outlets that appeal to you. For example, if you find that Twitter's constant update stream is too busy for your tastes, consider spending more time on building your LinkedIn presence or just link your papers on your university faculty profile. Conversely, if you find it helpful to tweet ideas as you think and write you are likely to gain followers. Whatever you choose, make sure that: 1) it fits with your personality; and 2) you do it consistently and thoroughly. Nothing reflects worse on your online, professional, viral self than a lingering Twitter profile that you have not touched for over a year – especially if it is the first hit in a Google search for your name! Perhaps the most important thing we can do is to make sure that only the things you want colleagues to find online, are online ... and nothing else.

References

Alexa (2011) Top sites. Retrieved from *http://www.alexa.com/topsites*.

Bailyn, E. (2011) *Outsmarting Google: SEO Secrets to Winning New Business*. Indianapolis, IN: Que.

Brown, C. and Abbas, J.M. (2010) Institutional digital repositories for science and technology: a view from the laboratory. *Journal of Library Administration*, 50(3): 181–215.

Langville, A.N. and Meyer, C.D. (2006) *Google's PageRank and Beyond: The Science of Search Engine Rankings*. Princeton, NJ: Princeton University Press.

McTavish, J., Harris, R. and Wathen, N. (2011) Searching for health: the topography of the first page. *Ethics and Information Technology*, 13(3): 227–40.

Neal, D.M., Campbell, A.J., Williams, L., Liu, Y. and Nussbaumer, D. (2011) 'I did not realize so many options are available': cognitive authority, emerging adults, and e-mental health. *Library & Information Science Research*, 33(1): 25–33.

Pariser, E. (2011) *The Filter Bubble: What the Internet is Hiding From You*. New York: Penguin Press.

Scott, D.M. (2010) *The New Rules of Marketing and PR: How to Use Social Media, Blogs, News Releases, Online Video, and Viral Marketing to Reach Buyers Directly*. Hoboken, NJ: John Wiley & Sons.

Tossell, I. (2011) Handle SEO with care. Retrieved from *http://www.theglobeandmail.com/report-on-business/small-business/digital/web-strategy/handle-seo-with-care/article2015296/*.

Wianko, R. (2010) And the 'Oldspice Maneuver' is created, blows the doors off of advertising [blog post]. Retrieved from *http://ryanwiancko.com/2010/07/15/and-the-oldspice-maneuver-is-created-blows-the-doors-off-of-advertising/*.

10

Who is the 'virtual' you and do you know who's watching you?

Lynne Y. Williams

Abstract: Navigating the minefield that comprises the privacy settings for the majority of social networking websites is at best a frustrating experience which leaves the user with the vague feeling that although they've left the house, the gas oven is still turned on. At worst, the host vendor of the social networking website deliberately prevents the user from modifying the privacy settings in such a way that the user's privacy is genuinely protected. In all cases, the verbiage spelling out the user's privacy rights as supported by a given site tends to be so convoluted that even the most hardened lawyer would have difficulty teasing the sense out of it. The consequences of engaging in social networking without taking precautions can be severe, ranging from identity theft to being stalked online and abuse of personal information by a third party. Because user privacy is not in the best interests of the social networking vendors, it's up to users to look out for their own privacy and to set up safeguards that protect their social data, their identity and, ultimately, their 'virtual self'.

Key words: privacy, identity theft, tags, Facebook, Twitter, profiling.

> 'Stay, quoth Reputation/Do not forsake me; for it is my nature/If once I part from any man I meet/I am never found again.'
>
> (Webster, 2000, line 156)

Awareness of data privacy, digital footprints, maintaining separate work and personal online identities, and other types of identity concerns

Researchers from the Pew Internet & American Life Project have found that the number of Americans using 'social networking sites (SNSs) in 2011 has nearly doubled from the number of SNS users in 2008' (Hampton et al., 2011, para. 3). The Pew Internet & American Life Project also notes that users of social networking websites are becoming more aware of the identity and privacy issues associated with social networking.

When considering issues of identity, personal data and privacy, it's important to avoid using the terms interchangeably because the effectiveness of the various approaches to safeguarding each category depends on the type of data being safeguarded. Another element that has to be taken into consideration is the relative sensitivity of data when it can be connected with other chunks of data and placed into a particular context. While the numbers '100954' mean very little standing on their own, if you connect the numbers with the context of 'birthday' they then acquire meaning.

What is an online identity?

So what exactly do we mean when we say 'identity' or 'personal data?' Castells (2009) makes a number of interesting points concerning cultural and collective identity, stating that '[i]dentity is people's source of meaning and experience' (p. 6). This statement implies that identity is something that people derive from some external agency, such as their local culture, events that they've experienced, or some other collection of cultural attributes that define who they are.

In the most tightly defined sense, it could be said that an online identity is that collection of individually descriptive data that is contained within a person's online profile. Feizy et al. (2010) use this definition exclusively: 'In online social networking sites, people define an identity through the definition of information within a profile' (p. 1). Particularly when signing up for social networking membership with any of the vendors, the user is strongly encouraged by the website to include a wide variety of identity-related data, such as the user's birth date, address, contact information, preferences, and so on.

The implications are noted by Neal and Williams (2009): 'as in the Aristotelian saying, "The whole is greater than the sum of its parts", the aggregated whole may represent a body of personal data that [implies] ownership, such that the user would have defensible rights over the aggregation, if not the disaggregated pieces' (p. 4). Further, users have little control over how personal data residing with a variety of entities can be linked together to create their online identity. Neal and Williams (2010) observe that, in the US, current privacy legislation essentially allows SNSs to aggregate and link the data residing on their servers in any fashion that they wish. Users of US-based SNSs who physically reside outside the US are at equal risk of having their personal data linked or exposed in unintended ways.

Taking our search for a definition a step further, we already know that the context of data can transform that data from a meaningless set of characters into meaningful information. Context is an element that can't be easily controlled by the individual and provides a useful method for drawing a true picture of that individual's online identity (Madden et al., 2007).

Even when an organization actively employs one or more 'depersonalization' techniques on stored personal data, none of them can guarantee to safeguard the more sensitive data in 100 per cent of all cases. Given the business model on which the majority of SNSs are based, depersonalization is actually a disadvantage to the SNS hosts. It's difficult to market purple people-eating zinnia clippers to your users if you can't clearly identify those customers who have expressed a rampant interest in purple people-eating zinnia clippers!

What is privacy?

As with identity, for the purposes of our discussion here, we need to look at privacy through the lens of an online environment. Gavison (2011) remarks that many current legal definitions of privacy are the subject of much debate. In most definitions, privacy includes a '"right to be left alone", covering a general interest in not being interfered with in any way that violates human dignity' (pp. 400–1).

Williams and Neal (2009) note that, with the advent of more powerful data mining techniques, the aggregation of seemingly innocuous personal data across a range of social media makes it fairly straightforward to put together a disturbingly detailed profile of the data's originator. Although the originator may have been careful when giving information to the individual websites, the ability to aggregate data belonging to that originator across a variety of sites creates an unintended consequence. Because the originator has no way of knowing when this kind of data aggregation will occur, or who the gathering entity may be, it's impossible to safeguard your personal data against being aggregated. The only viable option is simply to not participate in social networking, although that approach will still leave any data residing in organizational online databases available and vulnerable in many cases.

Another element that muddies the privacy waters is the fact that total privacy, that is, an absolute limitation on what can be known about a person, is undesirable and could be potentially harmful. Consider the case of a convicted sex offender; while it can be assumed that the offender would desire to keep his or her criminal history entirely private, the community in which the offender resides would almost certainly disagree.

What is a digital footprint?

Weaver and Gahegan (2007) define a digital footprint as 'a high dimensional and constantly growing space characterized by digital transactions, augmented by surveillance, and influenced by associations and patterns through space and time' (p. 330). What on earth does that mean?

This definition encompasses almost everything that the average American does on an average day. Let's follow Joe Average as he goes about what he thinks is his own business. When Joe awakens in the morning, he rolls out of bed and has a shower. While drying off, he turns on the television to watch some news. His set-top cable box keeps track of every channel to which he surfs and reports his viewing habits back to his cable company. Whether he knows it or not, the set-top box also keeps track of what his digital programme recorder records and reports that information back as well, including the *Debbie Does Fort Worth* adult movie he watched last night. While having his coffee, he checks his email on his mobile phone, which is tracking both his location and his habits. An application that he downloaded to his phone a couple of months ago for receiving tips on nearby restaurants continually updates where his phone is and sends that information back to the application's developers.

When he arrives at work, he searches his favourites and opens a news website to catch up on the national news. The website keeps track of all of the links that Joe clicks as he reads various articles, and logs his interests. The EULA (end user licence agreement) that Joe signed when he signed up for the website allows the site to not only keep track of his news reading habits but also to sell that information to third parties, such as marketers, which is how the news site makes most of its revenue. The news site isn't the only entity tracking Joe's viewing habits. His employer uses monitoring software to keep track of what employees are doing with their company computers. The company maintains a fair use policy that allows employees some leeway for checking their personal email or doing some online shopping in their lunch hour. If an employee spends more than their fair use allowance on personal web surfing they receive a warning which goes into their employee records.

On his way home after work, Joe calls his brother on his mobile phone. His phone company logs the minutes he's using, the number he has dialled and also records the location of the phone. After supper, Joe pays some of his bills online. Each transaction is logged on the various websites for his phone company, his utility company and his bank. Joe watches a little television after he has paid his bills, still being tracked by his set-top box and finally goes to bed, which is practically the only action he has taken all day that hasn't been recorded, logged and stored in a database somewhere.

This just describes a single day in the life of a digital footprint. Every day, companies collect data about all of us, our television viewing habits, our banking and credit profile, even the route we take to drive to work, grow larger at an exponential rate. Gantz and Reinsel (2011) estimated that the amount of personal data stored online would top 1.8 trillion gigabytes by the end of 2011. They went on to note that while 75 per cent of the data stored online is generated by or about individuals, the liability for around 80 per cent of that data falls on commercial entities. 'Less than a third of the information in the digital universe can be said to have at least minimal security or protection; only about half the information that should be protected is protected' (p. 1). The majority of those entities who actively seek to acquire and store personal information have based their business focus on the value of something called 'big data'. Big data isn't a thing so much as a phenomenon. It's the result of increasingly less expensive storage technologies that are also capable of storing ever greater quantities of data. The data in and of itself doesn't have much value to anyone aside from the person to whom the data refers. But when you add context, such as not just the person's location, but what the person was doing at that location, then you begin to obtain value. Big data is all about extracting as much commercial value from this rapidly expanding storehouse of personal data as can be managed without actively running afoul of any pesky privacy laws. Your digital footprint spells profit for these commercial entities and it is not in their best interests to protect your privacy.

Maintaining separate personal and professional online identities

Very few of us are exactly the same person 100 per cent of the time. With our parents, we're their children; at work, we're colleagues; and in our leisure time, we're yet another person with our friends. The divide between our personal and professional identities is probably the deepest out of the range of identities that we wear on a daily basis. Rozuel (2011) refers to this internal separation of identities as 'compartmentalization', where we each place bits and pieces of our work selves in one main box, and other bits and pieces into our personal selves' box.

The online blurring of roles is becoming steadily more common as commercial entities deliberately attempt to convince users to weave every aspect of their lives, both public and private, together into a single amalgamated alloy of roles. A good current example of the increased overlap between online personal and public identities is a new social networking initiative deployed by Google called Google+. Google+ includes much of the same interactivity that Facebook does, with some twists. Since Google's primary business is searching and organizing data, it intends to make all of the social networking data within Google+ publicly searchable. From the Google privacy policy: 'We may combine the information you submit under your account with information from other Google services or third parties in order to provide you with a better experience and to improve the quality of our services' (Google, 2011, para. 3). If you have more than one Gmail account (or multiple Google Calendars, Google Docs, etc.), all of your data – regardless of whatever separate accounts you've used – will be lumped together to make it easier for Google and any third parties of their choosing to target your interests and habits.

Arguments about finding a balance between work and personal lives aside, is it wise to combine the work role with the personal role, so far as information is concerned? The answer to this question almost certainly depends upon a person's own feelings about the work–personal space separation. Perhaps an individual simply doesn't feel that it's any of their work colleagues' business knowing that they design doll house furniture as a hobby or that they enjoy geocaching. On the other hand, particularly if a person is self-employed, it may be perfectly acceptable to combine both business and personal roles without a problem. Generally speaking though, the majority of us do seem to prefer at least a modicum of separation between work and personal life. For example, a teacher may prefer to maintain a certain amount of professional distance between herself and her students.

The monetization of personal information has ramped up the pressure on individuals to blur and combine their personal information, which makes it easier for commercial entities to build up and optimize an individual's 'big data' profile. An example of this type of pressure is Facebook's 'Connections' feature. Essentially, anything in a Facebook profile, such as friends, family, interests, religious views and anything else used to personalize the account, can be searched by any third-party entity, whether or not they're directly affiliated with Facebook. Rather disingenuously, although Facebook states that this information isn't 'visible' to anyone other than those who the user has explicitly allowed to view the information, visibility has nothing to do with the 'searchability' of the information. Facebook's privacy policy also leaves the door open to new avenues of searchability: 'Facebook does not give third party applications or ad networks the right to use your name or picture in ads. *If we allow this in the future*, the setting you choose will determine how your information is used' (Facebook, 2011, para. 1; italic added by author). If and when public third parties are allowed to search all of your Facebook information, regardless of how many separate Facebook accounts you may maintain, those compartmentalized bits of your life will be blended regardless of your own preferences.

Many of the previous concerns are founded on the ability of various types of software to make textual connections. However, searching and making connections between all sorts of information is about to get much more interesting as Google has apparently figured out how to semantically search images: *http://images.google.com*. If this rumour (in early 2012) proves to be true, it will greatly enhance (for better or worse) the ability of Google's image similarity algorithm to match up online images of yourself with personal information. The key here is the concept of a semantic search. A semantic search not only looks for keywords but is also capable of interpreting the meaning behind the words used for the search terms. Thus, if you misspent at least part of your youth and then decided to share the digital snapshots with your friends on the SNS of your choice, there's a strong possibility that any images you uploaded from spring break on the beach in Puerto Vallarta can now be linked to your professional profile photo on LinkedIn. If this same search is semantically enhanced, the chances of linking your images with your personal information become considerably greater. Google isn't the only game in town when it comes to semantic image searching; TinEye© and Picsearch© are also working on their own proprietary image searching methods. With employers increasingly using web searches to get a look at the private life of potential employees, the ability to connect images with not only context but meaning as well could dramatically change the job search process.

Data privacy and the 'virtual' you

With all of these corrosive threats against your personal data, what should concern you in particular as an educator? Are there areas within the overall personal data debate that may be especially sensitive within an education setting?

In many ways, these questions will lead us to new wine in old bottles, that is to say that social networking and the availability of increasing amounts of personal data only exacerbate the same ethical dilemmas that educators have always had to face. For instance, if you keep a personal Facebook page and a student sends you a 'friend request', should you accept? Should you be concerned if students find and read your personal Facebook page? Is there a significant difference between the information on your Facebook page and your LinkedIn page? None of this really differs from traditional concerns, such as forming inappropriate friendships with students or having students discover personal information about you that you might have preferred to keep personal.

Where online ethical dilemmas differ from traditional ethical dilemmas is both in the potential lifetime of the data as well the availability of the data. Once your data goes online it will potentially persist online in some form for an indefinite period of time, certainly for years. Even if you go back to the site where you originally uploaded the data and delete everything, copies of the data will remain tucked away in various places, such as the site's backup files, Archive.org or third-party entities that have used the information for marketing purposes.

Dealing with students disgruntled over a low grade or a disciplinary incident acquires a significantly higher risk of retaliation when the educator engages in social networking. Hacking most user accounts on Facebook is a relatively simple exercise; once inside your account the hacker can easily change your profile information and friends list. Rusli (2010) describes the ease with which your Facebook profile can be hijacked. Debatin et al. (2009) then provide an eye-opening example of what can happen after the hacker has got in:

> The first time [that Brian's Facebook account was hacked], the hacker changed some of Brian's groups and altered his "interested in" selection to insinuate (incorrectly) that Brian was gay. He brushed the incident off as a joke, changed his password, and "went on with everyday life." At that time, he was not aware of privacy options. Then, the hacker again entered his profile, changed his password back, and altered some things. Brian changed them back again and wrote on his status, "ok, you know, enough is enough ... the joke's over, this isn't funny anymore." On the third day, his profile was completely changed, including groups and interests, and his profile picture showed a combination of his head and a porn star's body. The hacker had also put in a relationship request with Brian's freshman-year roommate and changed his status to "I was just kidding. I'm having a hard time coming out of the closet right now." To Brian's dismay, all these changes were made public through the news feed.
>
> (Ibid., pp. 98–9)

There are also a number of privacy and security issues related to collaborative work with colleagues. A variety of sites, such as Office Live, offer collaborative tools that make it simple to maintain a single master copy of a research document, while at the same time allowing a group of researchers to edit and modify the document. Google Docs is a popular example of this type of collaborative tool, but as with other forms of social networking there are risks that accompany the benefits.

Barkah (2009) details three risk scenarios inherent in the use of Google Docs. His first scenario involves the difference between security settings between the master document and any images embedded within that document. When you upload an image that accompanies your text document, Google will assign that image a URL that points to the image's location on the Google server. Inserting the image into your Google Doc requires that the document uses the image's URL in order to locate it. Here's the trick: because the document and the image exist on Google's servers as two separate items, the security settings for each of them can (and usually do) differ. So, although you may have tightened up who can share and manipulate your text document, your image file is freely available to anyone who finds it. Obviously, if your research encompasses ideas that could be patentable this is a major concern as any figures embedded in a Google Doc can easily be copied and used by any stranger surfing by. Even if you delete the text document that contains the embedded images, they still linger on because they reside on the server as a separate entity.

Should you become sufficiently paranoid about the possibility of image snitching and lock down your sharing permissions, you still probably haven't managed to close the barn door. Under certain circumstances, anyone to whom you've ever granted sharing permissions can still access the previously shared document even if you've removed them from your group of approved collaborators.

So, what are some safe options for engaging in social networking? If you've already been active on a variety of SNSs for several years you should probably begin to take some time about once a month or so to do some damage control. Facebook, Twitter and other forms of social networking all allow for a certain amount of privacy tweaking. Let's take a look at the top three SNSs according to their August 2011 market share (see Figure 10.1).

Facebook is currently the 800 pound gorilla, with YouTube and Twitter bringing up the rear. YouTube was not purpose-built as an SNS, having simply evolved through its use of communities and subscriptions into a sort of visual social network. LinkedIn, although not in the top three at the time of writing, is closer to Facebook in format than YouTube.

Keeping in mind that many, if not all, of the following 'best practice' directives may change in the future, you can still get a general idea of what to look for when seeking to better manage your privacy settings as you engage with various SNSs.

Facebook privacy best practices

- Look at the bottom of any Facebook page. You should spot the privacy link; this will give you information concerning Facebook's most current set of privacy policies. If you don't quite understand how a given policy will affect how others view your profile, use the profile preview to double check. Try to remember to check the privacy policies about once a month (Sophos, 2011).

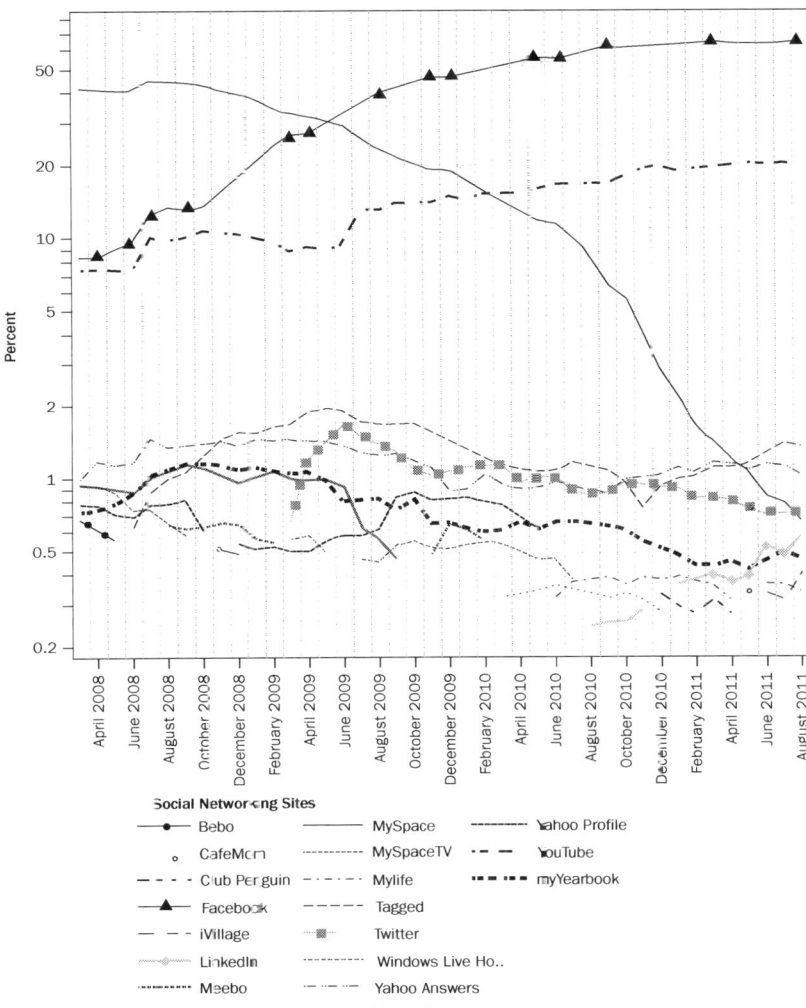

Figure 10.1 Top ten social networking sites by market share, August 2011

Created by Pritt Kallas @ http://www.dreamgrow.com. Data from http://www.marketingcharts.com/categories/social-networks-and-forums/. Note that the Hitwise data featured is based on US market share of visits as defined by the IAB, which is the percentage of online traffic to the domain or category, from the Hitwise sample of 10 million US Internet users. The market share of visits percentage does not include traffic for all sub-domains of certain websites that could be reported on separately.

- Be very choosy about who you accept as a friend. Keep in mind that anyone designated as a friend can access a lot of your information, depending on your settings (ibid.).
- Turn off all options that you don't routinely use (ibid.).
- In your account settings, don't provide a nickname that could easily link your account to other accounts you own. Don't include personally identifying information in your nickname, such as your date of birth (ibid.).
- In your account settings, reduce the permissions given to Facebook advertisements; the more that third parties know about your 'likes', the more you leave yourself open to social engineering attacks as well as marketing spam (ibid.).
- Facebook applications are probably the greatest single risk to your personal data because there's no reliable way of knowing whether the developer is trustworthy or how the developer will use the information to which you give them access. Limit the number of applications that you allow to the bare minimum of what you actually use. Also limit or completely disable information accessible to your friends (ibid.).
- Turn off 'Instant personalization'. Click the down arrow to the right of the home link in the upper right-hand corner of your Facebook page. Click on 'Privacy settings'. Click on 'Edit settings' in the 'Applications and websites' section. Click on 'Edit setting' in the 'Instant personalization' section then deselect the 'Instant personalization' box.

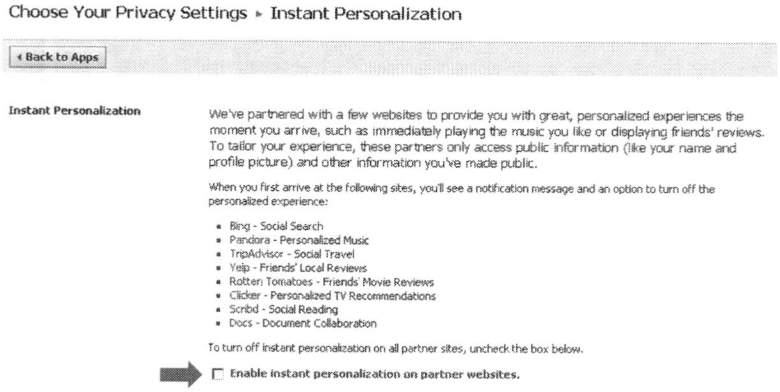

Figure 10.2 Instant personalization

- Also in 'Applications and websites', turn off 'Public search'.
- Stay offline in Facebook Chat; Chat gives away your online status and can be used to scam you using hijacked credentials from a friend's account (ibid.).
- Customize your privacy settings. Keep in mind that even if you have every setting locked down to 'Friends only', there's a growing possibility that some of your friends haven't been as careful as you have and have had their accounts hacked, in which case the hacker can then access your information (ibid.).

LinkedIn privacy best practices

All of the best practices noted in the Facebook section above also apply to LinkedIn. Interestingly, you seldom hear the same privacy horror stories about LinkedIn, which is probably due to the site's emphasis on workplace connections rather than purely social links (Anna, 2011). Even though most LinkedIn users are on their best behaviour you still need to be careful about what you're sharing and who you're sharing it with. By now, just about everyone knows that they aren't supposed to click on unsolicited attachments, with the emphasis on 'unsolicited'. But what about email that appears to come from a friend? Would you automatically open an attachment that you received from a colleague, even though it doesn't appear to relate to any current dialogue?

Many, if not most, people would, despite years of cautionary tales, simply because humans are hard-wired to trust people they know. Making your contact information too widely available on LinkedIn can make you more vulnerable to this type of social engineering attack, so share your contact information sparingly.

Twitter privacy best practices

- Remove as much of your personal information from your Twitter account as you can get away with. You want to avoid providing unknown followers with enough information to link up your Twitter account with any other SNSs that you may be using (O'Donnell, 2011).
- Turn off your 'Tweet location'. It's never a good idea to let too many people know when you're not at home. Remember that it's easier to pick up followers on Twitter than it is to make friends on Facebook. Don't provide complete strangers with your location (ibid.).

- Turn on the 'Protect my tweets' feature. It won't protect you from any followers that you've already picked up but it will allow you to approve (or not) any new followers that appear. Get rid of any unknown followers you already have by clicking on the gear icon next to the follower's alias and selecting 'Remove' (ibid.).
- Review all of the previously stated best practices for Facebook and LinkedIn!

Tracking your digital footprints

There are two distinct sides to the digital footprint discussion: those who actively use their digital footprint as a self-marketing tool and those who are concerned about their privacy. In either case, if you use the Internet regularly, and especially if you spend much time on SNSs, it's a good idea to know not only the general size of your digital footprint but the breadth of it as well. Whether you like it or not, your digital footprint is the 21st century equivalent of your reputation and it will provide others with a picture of you that may be less than flattering.

An easy first step to measuring your digital footprint is to do a Google search on yourself. Be sure to use different combinations of your name to make sure that you dig up as much information as you can. The Innovative Educator (2011) also recommends some additional tools for measuring your digital footprint. Google Alerts (*http://www.google.com/alerts*) will allow you to monitor your own Google results. Should anyone post any information about you online that can be searched, Google Alerts will email you with the results. You can do a visual search using Spezify (*http://spezify.com/*); the results are placed in a type of connected table to give you an idea of which result is connected to other results and can give you an interesting look at how your digital footprint pieces are interlinked.

Keeping your work 'you' and your personal 'you' apart

There are plenty of people who have no desire to separate their private and public lives. If you are an entrepreneur it's possible that you actually use social networks as an important marketing tool and wish to leverage your virtual influence as much as you can. However, many of us want to retain our compartmentalization and, as educators, would like to keep a respectful distance between ourselves and our students. Amber Mac (2011) provides some useful tips in this regard.

First, and easiest, is to use completely different SNSs for each compartment of your life, perhaps using Facebook for your personal networking, while restricting work-related networking to LinkedIn. You'll need to hold firm on the people with whom you're connected on each site; it won't do you much good to try to maintain separate networking personas if you allow people from LinkedIn to become friends of yours on Facebook.

If Facebook is your SNS of choice you can still maintain a certain degree of separation by creating separate accounts for your personal and professional selves. Facebook allows users to create company pages that are set up explicitly for marketing purposes. By clicking on the 'Pages' link you can set up a business page for a business, company, public figure, brand, or community cause. To maintain separation, you'll need to remember not to blend your personal friends with your professional fans.

In addition to creating a business page on Facebook, you might also consider moving your business contacts over to Twitter. While Twitter lacks many of the networking tools included with Facebook and LinkedIn it's still useful for keeping clients and colleagues updated on your current activities.

Depending on Facebook's privacy policy at any given time, you can also place various friends into particular groups, then restrict or allow access to your information based on the group. Use the 'Privacy settings' link to dig into the various pathways through which your data is shared to create different groups of people with varying degrees of permission. You can also place people into lists, based on whatever they have in common, such as real-life friends, family or professional contacts. Select your account drop-down menu, then select 'Edit friends'; on the left sidebar, select 'Lists' and 'Create a new list'. Depending on into which list you've placed a person, they'll be able to view only the content that you allow for that list. Keep in mind that, on Facebook, visibility does not preclude searchability and if an individual on a restricted list is really determined to see some of the information to which they don't have access there are still avenues that allow searching and possible discovery.

Probably the most effective way to maintain truly separate public and personal personas is simply to take yourself offline altogether. If that sounds too extreme, then just remember never to upload anything to an SNS that you wouldn't feel comfortable seeing on a billboard by the side of a busy road.

If you do decide to take your online self offline, every SNS has the option to delete your account. For example, to delete your Facebook account, go to *https://ssl.facebook.com/help/contact.php?show_form= delete_account*, and follow the steps. Once you've reached the final step, it's important that you do nothing else and simply close the page. It takes two weeks for Facebook to actually remove your account, so if you log back on at any time before the two week deadline is up your account is automatically reinstated. If you use Facebook Connect to log into sites other than Facebook itself, using Connect to log in will also automatically reinstate your account.

What should you know in order to adequately protect all of your 'you's?

Over the past decade, a number of businesses have sprung up that claim to safeguard your overall identity for a fee, such as LifeLock and IdentityGuard. In general, companies like LifeLock do little to help protect your social networking activities, being more concerned with guarding your credit score and preventing illegal use of your financial information. While identity protection companies do provide a certain degree of convenience, they really don't do anything that you can't do yourself.

For those of us living in the US, our financial identities are defined by our ratings with the three big credit reporting agencies: Experian, TransUnion and Equifax. Although Experian also operates in the UK, if you live elsewhere in the world you may need to do some searching to discover the credit monitoring scheme for your locality. In general, wherever you live, you should be able to request a copy of your particular credit rating document and should do so annually.

In the US, to protect your financial identity there are a few simple steps. First, check your credit report each year to make sure that your profile information is correct. Despite the television commercials advertising free credit reports from a variety of sources, you'll find that these sources, such as FreeCreditReport.com or CreditExpert.co.uk, won't give you any information until you've subscribed to their services for a fee. The US Federal Trade Commission provides information on getting your US credit report without subscribing to anything; see *http:// www.ftc.gov/bcp/edu/pubs/consumer/credit/cre34.shtm*. Consumers in other countries can follow a similar procedure, depending on how their credit ratings are maintained. By taking the time to request your information from your local credit agencies each year you can keep an eye on whether your information has been tampered with and who has been accessing it.

In the final analysis, you alone must take responsibility for anything that you upload to an SNS, as well as for how you link your various online identities together. All of the tips and tricks in the world can't substitute for good judgement concerning what you decide to share. Take charge of managing your digital footprint by carefully assessing what you want people to see. Become adept at tweaking your privacy settings within any SNS profile that you maintain. Trust no one you 'meet' online and be very picky about who you allow to befriend you. If you value your online privacy and the rights to your online identity, it is well worth making the effort to keep yourself secure, because, as the not-so-old saying goes, the Internet never forgets.

References

Anna (2011) An introduction to LinkedIn privacy and security [blog post]. Retrieved from *http://safeandsavvy.f-secure.com/2011/09/23/linkedin-privacy-and-security/*.

Barkah, A. (2009) Security issues with Google docs [blog post]. Retrieved from *http://peekay.org/2009/03/26/security-issues-with-google-docs/*.

Castells, M. (2009) *The Power of Identity* (vol. 2). Hoboken, NJ: John Wiley and Sons.

Debatin, B., Lovejoy, J.P., Horn, A. and Hughes, B.N. (2009) Facebook and online privacy: attitudes, behaviors, and unintended consequences. *Journal of Computer-Mediated Communication*, 15: 83–108.

Facebook (2011) Data use policy. Retrieved from *https://www.facebook.com/about/privacy/*.

Facebook Ads (2011) Isctope twothirtynine. Retrieved from *http://www.facebook.com*.

Feizy, R., Wakeman, I. and Chalmers, D. (2010) The transformation of online representation through time in relations to honesty and accountability characteristics. Retrieved from *http://www.sussex.ac.uk/Users/dc52/infweb/Papers/asonam-2009.pdf*.

Gantz, J. and Reinsel, D. (2011) *Extracting Value From Chaos*. Framingham, MA: IDC.

Gavison, R.E. (2011, 13 July) 'Privacy: legal aspects', in *Blackwell Encyclopedia of Political Thought*, pp. 400–1, 1987. Retrieved from SSRN: *http://ssrn.com/abstract=1885008*.

Google (2011) Google privacy policy. Retrieved from *http://www.google.com/intl/en/privacy/privacy-policy.html*.

Hampton, K., Goulet, L.S., Rainie, L. and Purcell, K. (2011) Social networking sites and our lives Retrieved from *http://www.pewinternet.org/Reports/2011/Technology-and-social-networks/Summary.aspx*.

The Innovative Educator (2011) Discover what your digital footprint says about you [blog post]. Retrieved from *http://theinnovativeeducator.blogspot.com/2011/08/discover-what-your-digital-footprint.html*.

Kallas, P. (2011) Top 10 social networking sites by market share of visits. Retrieved from *http://www.dreamgrow.com/top-10-social-networking-sites-by-market-share-of-visits-august-2011/*.

Ketabchi, F. (2010) Digital footprint and virtual social influence [blog post]. Retrieved from *http://java.sys-con.com/node/1312494*.

Mac, A. (2011) 5 tips to separate personal and professional life online. Retrieved from *http://www.fastcompany.com/1754431/5-tips-to-separate-personal-professional-life-online*.

Madden, M., Fox, S., Vitak, J. and Smith, A. (2007) Online identity management and search in the age of transparency [report]. Retrieved from *http://pewresearch.org/pubs/663/digital-footprints*.

Neal, D. and Williams, L.Y. (2009) The digital aggregated self: a literature review. Unpublished manuscript, The University of Western Ontario, London, ON; Kaplan University, Ft Lauderdale, FL.

Neal, D. and Williams, L.Y. (2010) The ethical concerns of data mining: the aggregated self. Paper presented at the The Fifth International Conference of Interdisciplinary Social Sciences, Cambridge, UK.

O'Donnell, A. (2011) Who's following your child on Twitter? Retrieved from *http://netsecurity.about.com/od/newsandeditorial1/a/Whos-Following-Your-Child-On-Twitter.htm*.

Opsahl, K. (2010) Six things you need to know about Facebook Connections. Retrieved from *http://www.eff.org/deeplinks/2010/05/things-you-need-know-about-Facebook*.

Plaisant, C., Shneiderman, B., Baker, H., Duarte, N., Haririnia, A. et al. (2005) 'Personal role management: overview and a design study of email for university students', in V. Kaptelinin and M. Czerwinski (eds). *Integrated Digital Work Environments: Beyond the Desktop* (pp. 143–70). Cambridge, MA: MIT Press.

Rozuel, C. (2011) The moral threat of compartmentalization: self, roles, and responsibility. *Journal of Business Ethics*, 102: 685–97.

Rusli, E. (2010) Extension lets you hack into Twitter, Facebook accounts easily [blog post]. Retrieved from *http://techcrunch.com/2010/10/24/firesheep-in-wolves-clothing-app-lets-you-hack-into-twitter-facebook-accounts-easily/*.

Sophos (2011) Facebook security best practices. Retrieved from *http://www.sophos.com/en-us/security-news-trends/best-practices/facebook.aspx*.

Weaver, S.D. and Gahegan, M. (2007) Constructing, visualizing, and analyzing a digital footprint. *Geographical Review*, 97(3): 324–50.

Webster, J. (2000 [1623]) *The Duchess of Malfi* [electronic book]. Retrieved from *http://www.gutenberg.org/catalog/world/readfile?fk_files=1448279*.

Williams, L.Y. and Neal, D.R. (2009) Disaggregated informational ownership: recommendations from the literature. Paper presented at the Cyberspace Law and Education Conference, Oxford, UK.

Social media for academic libraries

David J. Fiander

Abstract: This chapter discusses the value of the academic library engaging with its users via social media sites like Facebook and Twitter. The chapter provides some background on research into how libraries have experimented with using Facebook for outreach and how the user community has responded. It gives a brief outline of the process for creating a rich Facebook page for an academic library system, and tips for how to market a Facebook page or Twitter account and how to use social media accounts to promote the library's services. Finally, it provides some guidance for how an academic library should think about policies for posting to social sites by staff, and how to deal with user comments on social media sites.

Key words: libraries, outreach, marketing, promotion, Facebook, Twitter, YouTube.

Introduction

In 2006, Online Computer Library Center (OCLC) found that library users 'do not see a role for libraries in constructing social sites, and most would not be very likely to contribute content' (De Rosa et al., 2007). It is probably still true today that the library's users would not participate in a social community constructed by the library and hosted on the library's website, but librarians no longer think about social media as something that the library should build and provide, rather as a platform with which they should engage. Librarians are going out to the social media sites on the Internet on which the users are already active and connecting with their communities where they are: Twitter, Facebook, YouTube, and more. But using these services to connect with the community and promote the library is different from using them personally, and it is also very different from the way library administrations are accustomed to communicating with their users. Twitter isn't a PA system, and Facebook is not a monthly newsletter; they are not only immediate, they are interactive, and interacting with the users on these sites can alienate rather than attract users if the sites are viewed as 'marketing channels', rather than places where conversations take place.

Social networking sites are not broadcast media; they are places to engage in conversations with your community. Using social media like Twitter, blogs and Facebook to promote your library and engage your community is different from sending out newsletters and putting up posters and whiteboards to announce events. Social media is, first and foremost, *social*: users expect to be involved in a dialogue, and a steady stream of content (at a reasonable pace) is better than a weekly update of the 'What's new' items on the library's website (Levine et al., 2000).

Overview of social media types and sites

'Social media' is a broad term that encompasses many different services and ways of interacting. Each service has particular strengths and weaknesses, develops a particular user community and has a distinct style of interaction. Libraries beginning to look at producing a social media strategy will have to be prepared to be (almost) everywhere, but 'being everywhere' does not mean that every platform needs distinct content. Because each service is used for different types of communication, each type of content (such as videos, library news or announcements) will have a 'natural' medium; other social media platforms will usually direct users to that platform.

Blogging

In an institutional setting, blogging has two primary roles. First, it can take on the role of the traditional library newsletter and announcements board, but with neither the publication delays of the former's typical monthly schedule nor the tendency of the latter to go unnoticed. Second, it can be used by individual librarians to communicate with their constituents, deepening the relationship between the librarians and their users and personalizing 'the library' in a way that often leads to increased use of the library, especially by undergraduates (Goss, 2010).

The two most popular blog platforms are WordPress (*http://www.wordpress.com*) and Blogger (*http://www.blogger.com*). Both WordPress and Blogger provide a 'hosted' blog platform, which means that a library can quickly create a blog and begin posting content online without having to be responsible for managing a server itself. The default blog addresses for both of these services identify the platform that is hosting the blog (that is, *http://myblog.wordpress.com* and *http://myblog.blogspot.com* respectively), but it is possible to configure both systems so that the library's blog has an institutional address like *http://blog.library.school.edu*; Blogger provides this service at no charge, but WordPress charges a fee for this service. WordPress also places advertising on the pages of free blogs but those advertisements can be eliminated (for a fee, of course). If your library uses one of these platforms for blogging, then you should arrange to have appropriate institutional addresses for your blogs. Aside from the slightly unprofessional impression that having a 'blogspot.com' or 'wordpress.com' address gives, linking the blogs directly to an institutional address ensures not only that the blog is unambiguously recognized as being produced by the library, but also that if the library decides to change blog service or to start hosting the blog directly on the library's own server, then the address of the blog won't change.

If your library (or school) is managing its own website on a dedicated web server using a content management system (CMS), then it probably supports blogging directly; the IT staff responsible for managing the CMS will be able to explain what the blogging options available are. Alternatively, there are several options available for installing specialized blogging software on a local server, including WordPress. This is the most complex option, but it is also the most flexible, and gives the library the most control over how to organize the library's and librarians' blogs, and also provides options for managing user comments in keeping with Anil Dash's guidelines for managing an online community (see section 'Comment policies for libraries' social media' below). Again, the local IT staff will be able to discuss what options are available.

Microblogging/Twitter

'Microblogging' is the general term for the concept of posting very short status updates as popularized by services like Tumblr (*http://www.tumblr.com*) and Twitter (*http://www.twitter.com*). Twitter was originally conceived of by its creators as a broadcast medium: a way to share quickly where one is; and what one is doing, thinking or feeling. It is still used that way, but like any human communication channel, it has become conversational.

For libraries, Twitter should be viewed primarily as a customer service medium. Use it to announce service outages and problems with the heating on the fifth floor. It should also be used for cross-promotion: to share links to the latest news items posted on the library's home page and to new blog posts by subject librarians. Aside from such announcements, Twitter is also useful for tracking what the library's users are saying about it. If your library has a bulletin board with feedback forms on it, then you are only gathering feedback from those users who bother to come to the library to try to find that very physical feedback medium; even remote users are unlikely to go to the library's website to try to find an online feedback form. People use Twitter to rant and rave about what's going on in the moment, so library staff are more likely to find out about the heating problems on the fifth floor from Twitter than they are from any other channel, if the library is tracking what people are saying. Another advantage that Twitter has over the traditional feedback bulletin board is that Twitter is immediate and conversational: library staff can respond directly to the users at the moment of the complaint, even if only to commiserate and let them know that the facilities department is working on getting the heating working again. While the library's 'official' presence on Twitter will account for much of the interaction with users, individual staff members should also be empowered to respond to comments and questions that they see in their normal use of Twitter. The way that social media depends on the voices of individuals within an organization will be discussed further below.

Video sharing

A video sharing site is not going to create the same type of social community that might form on Facebook, nor will it be as active a communication channel as Twitter, but creating an account on a video sharing site and using it to host instructional videos makes it simpler for a library to embed videos in its own website, offloads the complications of hosting video and makes sure it is compatible with all the various browsers and operating systems out there, and gives your users a forum in which to discuss the videos. Video sharing sites like YouTube (*http:// www.youtube.com*) and Vimeo (*http://www.vimeo.com*) make it simple for a library to share video tutorials with its users. Both sites contain a rich collection of demonstrations of bibliographic tools like RefWorks and Zotero, databases like PubMed and JSTOR, and even library tours.

YouTube and Vimeo are essentially the same in terms of video sharing and community forum features. Their primary differences are related to downloading videos and video licensing options. YouTube gives video creators the option of assigning either a standard copyright 'All rights reserved' licence to their videos, or a Creative Commons 'Attribution' licence; Vimeo, however, gives creators the full range of Creative Commons licences, allowing the creators to fine-tune how they are willing to let their videos be reused (for more information about Creative Commons licences, see *http://www.creativecommons.org*). While it is unlikely that users would be interested in downloading a library's introduction to using RefWorks, Vimeo does let the video creator decide whether viewers may download it; YouTube does not allow viewers to download videos at all.

Finally, YouTube is famous for unpleasant comments (the web comic strip xkcd shows the general attitude towards YouTube comments quite clearly (Munroe, 2006)). Be prepared to remove comments or block abusive users, and keep in mind Anil Dash's guidelines for managing an online community (see pp. 206–7 below).

Facebook

Much of the library literature discusses creating a Facebook profile for the library and then adding students and faculty as 'friends' (see, for examples: Connell, 2009; Dickson and Holley, 2010; or Mack et al., 2007). Aside from the fact that research has shown that students find this practice invasive and verging on 'stalking' (Connell, 2009), it is also in violation of Facebook's terms of use which require that profiles belong to real people, and that the profile be identified by that owner's real name. Libraries that have created profiles for their organizations have found their accounts deleted without warning when Facebook has become aware of the violation. These older articles were all written prior to Facebook introducing the newer 'fan page' (already renamed by Facebook to just 'page'), which is distinct from a profile page, and which can be named after any person (real or imaginary), or organization, and which can be created by anybody. A page allows users to 'Like' the subject of the page, without giving the administrators of the page access to all the users' private information (which is another one of the disadvantages of a library 'friending' students: it exposes the students' personal information to the library in a way that neither the student nor the library is comfortable with). In order to simplify the discussion, I will refer to people who 'Like' a page as fans of that page, even though Facebook is downplaying that terminology.

Creating a Facebook page

Before you begin the page creation process, you need to gather some information. All of these settings can be changed later, but it is better if you can configure the page appropriately from the beginning. Make sure you have a suitable photo or logo that represents your library, have identified the appropriate contact email address and phone number for the library (the contact information is not necessarily for a reference service, but for *any* questions that users of the Facebook page might direct towards the library) and decided on the name you will use for the Facebook page. If your institution has several library branches, you should also consider creating a page for the library system as well as pages for each of the branches. Given the size of Facebook, think carefully about the name you're going to use so that it is simple for your users to find you: if your library is named 'Kresge' or 'Carnegie', or if you are creating the page for the music library branch, consider including the school's name in the name of the page to distinguish it from the many other Kresge, Carnegie, or music libraries in the world. Including the school's name also ensures that when people search for the school, they will also see the page(s) that belong to the library.

Facebook provides several different types of pages depending on the object of the page, and each type has different options for the information that the page administrator can provide to visitors to the page. An academic library might reasonably be an educational 'Company, organization, or institution'; a library, a 'Local business or place'; or you might even have a library 'Entertainment' page. Because of the detailed informational options available, including the library's address, phone number and opening hours, the 'Local business or place' category of page is probably the most suitable type of page to create. Providing these details enables Facebook to provide a map link on your page and indicate in real time whether the library is open when people look at your page, and will allow users accessing Facebook via their smartphones to phone the library easily.

Creating a Facebook page is a simple process, once you are logged in, and have managed to navigate to Facebook's 'Create a page' form (in fact, getting to this form might be the most difficult part of the process). The easiest way to get to the 'Create a page' link is from a pre-existing page:

- Switch to your personal profile page by clicking on your name at the top of the Facebook page, then click on the 'About' link (or 'Info' if your personal profile is not using Facebook Timeline yet) under your profile photo.
- On your profile page, click on the link for any of the pages associated with your employer, education or interests. Click on the 'Create a page' button in the upper right corner of that page. You're now ready to begin creating the Facebook page for your library.
- Select the category of page you want to create. There are options for creating 'Library' pages under both 'Local business or place' and 'Entertainment', as well as an 'Education' option under 'Company, organization, or institution'. Because 'Local business or place' provides the most detailed information, it is probably the best choice.
- Enter the name of your library. If you are creating a 'Local business or place' page, then finish the form with the library's address and telephone number (this telephone number doesn't need to be the reference desk, but should be a number that is most likely to be answered whenever the library is open).
- The next part of the process sets up some basic information about the library. First, upload a photo that is representative of your library. Use a shot of the exterior, or of your imposing reference hall, or anything that your users will recognize as being your library.
- The next step that Facebook recommends is 'Get fans', which it proposes that you do by inviting your personal friends to like the page, to like the page yourself and to post the new page on your wall. Start spreading the word about the page by liking it yourself and recommending it to library staff who are on Facebook. Promoting your page within Facebook like this is just the beginning. You will also need to spend time making your community aware of your Facebook page via other channels as well.
- The last step in the page creation process is 'Basic information'. Enter the URL for your library's website and provide a basic description of the library in the 'About' page. Consider the audience you are

Social Media for Academics

targetting on Facebook: the 'About' section of your Facebook page should be short and suitable for your users, especially the students; it is not the place for the library's vision or mission statements.

Once you've completed the 'Basic information', you will end up on your newly created page, looking at the 'Get started' section, which will remind you to complete any of the initial steps that you missed and will give you some suggestions about how to promote the page. Click on the 'Wall' link on the left side of the page, under the profile picture, to see what normal Facebook users see. You should probably post a 'Welcome to the library's page' message to the Wall to kick things off.

There are many options available to you as the administrator that give you control over how your page is displayed to users, and what users are allowed to do on the page. Click on the 'Edit page' button in the upper right corner of the screen to start exploring them. You should resist every librarian's natural tendency to very carefully control who can comment on the library's Facebook page. There will be few users initially, and the best way to encourage more users to join is by allowing free-flowing discussions to take place. Only if you start running into problems with inappropriate content should you think about placing restrictions on how your community can interact with the page.

The 'Edit page' screen also allows you to set a general contact email address that will be displayed on the page and list the library's hours. If you use Facebook's structured format for listing the library hours, then that page will automatically display whether the library is open when users visit the page. Also, make sure to indicate whether or not your library provides valet parking.

If you created pages for the library system and for each of the branches then the library system page should 'Like' all of the branches, and the branches should all 'Like' at least the system's page, in order to cross-link the different parts of the system, and to help promote the various pages. Individual branch pages may 'Like' each other if there is an obvious relationship between them (for example, the map library might 'Like' the social sciences library, which houses the geography monographs and journals).

Finally, add some additional administrators to the page. Not only does this help distribute the workload associated with keeping the page up-to-date, but it also ensures that there's always somebody available to manage the page when the creator is unavailable.

Promoting and managing the library's Facebook page

Once your library has a Facebook page, the next challenge is acquiring fans: posting news and events to your Facebook page does no good if nobody is listening. Unlike individual Facebook profiles, your library page cannot actively 'friend' users (which is for the best, since Connell (2009) concluded that users found being 'friended' by the library invasive): your page will accumulate fans organically and slowly over time. As the number of fans grows, each new user will expose your page to their friends by interacting with your page. Start by promoting the page with library staff, especially front-line service staff and instructional librarians. These staff can mention the page to users during their normal interactions and can promote it as a way to stay current with what's going on in the library. In addition, liaison librarians will often be Facebook 'friends' with faculty in the departments for which they are responsible, and this too can help spread the word about the page. Promote your library's Facebook page in the same way that you would promote any other website: with a news item on the library's homepage; by having librarians talk about it in classes they teach, and service staff mention it during interactions with users at the desk; and by putting up a poster near the library's entrance. Once you have made some fans on Facebook, then the information and links that you post to the library's Facebook page will also act as promotion: fans will share links with their friends, which will draw the friends' attention to your page, and may lead to more members of your community liking your page.

Facebook is not a medium for which the dictum 'if you build it, they will come' applies. A successful Facebook page depends not just on promotion, making your users aware of it, but also on activity on the page. Jacobson (2011, p. 88) found that 'Librarians must be aware that using Facebook as a tool requires a lot of attention, and, if a library cannot commit to updating its Facebook page at least once a week or more, it may not be a very useful or successful tool.' A static Facebook page will not attract fans, and an active Facebook page is a far better channel for communicating with your users than a 'What's new' box on the library's homepage, because many of your users, both students and faculty, will spend more time on Facebook than they do on the library's homepage.

The library's Facebook page is primarily a marketing tool: a way to connect with your user community and promote the library's facilities and services, and to advertise events. When librarians first started trying to incorporate Facebook into their outreach practices, many of them created Facebook applications that allowed users to add catalogue searching or chat reference services to their profiles. It isn't clear how many users (rather than library staff) actually took advantage of these applications, and research has shown that the users see Facebook as a social activity: it is a *break* from the academic work that the library represents (Connell, 2009). Since the library's users will be spending more time on Facebook than on the library's homepage, information about the library's services, and its stream of news announcements, need to be visible to the Facebook community. Institutional blog posts and the 'What's new' items on the library's website should also be posted to Facebook as 'notes'. Do not use Facebook just to post links back to the library's website: users are more likely to engage with the content on Facebook than they are on the library's website: they will share or 'Like' items they find interesting or of value with their friends, and they will post comments and ask questions about items that are relevant to them, but not if all they see on Facebook is a headline and a link. Unless the headline is immediately relevant, users will not bother to click through to the library's website to read the body of the message.

Facebook should also be used to advertise open workshops, tours, author readings, and any other special events taking place in, or sponsored by, the library. Don't just announce the events on the library's Facebook page like all the other news items posted there, but create 'Facebook events' for them. Facebook events have several advantages for users: as already discussed, Facebook events will be more visible to the library's fans than the announcements posted on the library's website; it is simpler for users to RSVP (although Facebook RSVPs do not necessarily translate into confirmed attendance). When users do RSVP, they automatically share the fact that they are planning to attend the event with all of their Facebook friends, thereby multiplying the exposure of the event. Facebook makes it simple for users to add events to their online calendars, which may also translate event RSVPs into attendance.

With over half a billion users, Facebook is the 800 pound gorilla of social networking sites. As such, it will inevitably be a critical, if not the central, component of the library's social media planning. To reinforce what Jacobson (2011) found, an inactive Facebook page, one that isn't being updated at least once or twice a week, is a dead Facebook page: users will not bother to become fans of a page that isn't being maintained.

However much librarians might like to think that the library's homepage is the most important way to communicate with their online and remote users, those users visit Facebook daily and only rarely look at the library's website. Make sure that your library is available where your users are.

Making social platforms work together: what goes where?

If the library has jumped into social media with both feet and created a Twitter account, Facebook page and YouTube channel, the library now must decide what information gets posted to each platform. Each platform has its own distinct culture, and each is best suited for certain types of information. But not only do you need to figure out what is the appropriate platform for each posting, you also need to determine how best to cross-promote your postings. For example, it is clear that the new RefWorks tutorial video belongs on the library's YouTube channel, but what else should the library do to promote it?

As already discussed, Twitter is a customer service platform: suitable for listening for comments from your community, and for quick announcements about short-term issues, or reminders of things that are about to happen. Facebook works well for longer 'What's new' types of information, and for posting information about upcoming events in a way that makes it easy for users to RSVP, add to their calendars and share the events with their friends. YouTube is for videos. Beyond this basic level of promotion, your social media accounts can also be used to share information about each other, which will multiply the effect of each of them, and help them all to attract more attention.

When you post a video to YouTube it should be shared on your Facebook page and announced on Twitter. You should also repost the video when it's appropriate during the academic year. For example, a few weeks before classes end and term papers are due would be a good time to remind your users about your 'How to use RefWorks to create your bibliography' video. Similarly, when you post a news item or event to Facebook you should also share that on Twitter. Not only does this get the information about the particular news item or event out to your Twitter community, but it also promotes your Facebook page to that community. In general, Twitter users are more accepting of frequent updates than Facebook users: not everything that you tweet needs to be posted on Facebook.

Twitter and Facebook are both arranged chronologically, with the newest postings appearing most prominently on their respective pages. Facebook will push what it thinks are 'interesting' items to the top of the page, but for the most part this will not affect the way that items on the library's page will appear to your users, so it shouldn't be depended on. This focus on chronology implies that when you post announcements about far-off events (interpretations of 'far off' ranging from next week to next month) or long-running events, such as special exhibits, many of your Twitter followers or Facebook fans might miss them, or might forget that they're happening. In general, Twitter and Facebook users will not mind if you repost the event every so often as a reminder that it's coming, but there is a difficult balance to be maintained: if you post the same item too often (or, in the case of Facebook, just post things too often in general), then you will be considered a spammer and will lose followers and fans.

Aside from information about the library itself, Facebook and Twitter can be used to draw the attention of fans and followers to other related events or news items that they might find interesting. For example, if the campus bookstore is having an author reading, the library Facebook page might share the event on its wall so that fans of the library will find out about it. Take care, however: too much activity on the page might be viewed by users as spam, or as clogging up their news feed with too much library and not enough real friends. Make sure that any supplementary postings are relevant to the library community (that is, they're literary or research focused in some way) and that they are spaced out in time.

Social media policies and procedures

Academic libraries tend to be highly structured organizations, with very detailed policies and procedures covering all of their day-to-day workings. If social media are going to be part of the communication process for informing your users about the library, and responding to their questions and concerns, then you will need to develop policies and procedures for doing so. The difference between a social media policy and most of the other policies developed by the library is that the social media policy needs to be flexible enough to enable staff to share information in a timely fashion, usually without a lot of internal review, and to allow staff to respond to users' comments promptly. In the world of social networks, there is no 'official spokesperson' for the library: everybody who works for the library is talking to the users. But then, that's what happens today: 'The mail clerk describes the [library's] strategy to the stranger next to him on the bus, and then provides a critique' (Levine et al., 2000, p. 107). Of course, that's not entirely true; there is still an official communication channel which the library uses for announcements about building hours and other services, new library initiatives, and documenting policies about food or off-campus access. What has changed on the modern campus is that now your users expect to be able to interact with this official channel rather than just passively receive a stream of broadcast messages. The other difference between traditional library communication practices and the social environment is that the library has less control. The community is holding conversations about the library on Facebook, Twitter and their own blogs already; all the library can do is try to join those conversations as just another participant and create a space for the library to communicate its point of view. Thus, there are two types of policies that must be developed: one covering issues related to posting to social media sites as the library, which includes not just distributing announcements, but also responding to users' comments; and one giving guidance related to moderating and managing comments that users have made on the library's own website or on the library's Facebook page.

Policies and procedures for posting as the library

The policies for posting to social media via the library's accounts will vary depending on the particular platform. Facebook updates will probably mirror the official 'What's new' news items from the library's website, but responding to comments that users make on Twitter about the library and interacting with fans of the library on Facebook require a more personal touch than that provided by standard news announcements, and they also require a much more timely response than can be afforded by the schedule of the typical library communications committee.

Specific policies must always be coloured by the local institutional environment; however, some things to keep in mind when developing policies and procedures for posting to social media as the library include:

1. Try not to be too formal in responding to comments. Even if you are only going to be pointing to a formal policy document, don't be harsh. If you are perceived to be 'slapping down' a user, then you won't get very many 'Likes'.
2. If there is a group of people who will be sharing the responsibility of responding on social media, especially on Twitter, set up a schedule so that only one person is 'on duty' for any given day (or whatever time period makes sense locally). If more than one person is monitoring and responding, users may end up confused if they get two answers from 'the library'.
3. You don't need to respond to every comment or question about the library. It is especially dangerous to be seen as trying to have the last word in a discussion. Do keep track of all the comments that you see, though, because if there's a trend in the comments then that trend might be better addressed by a news item or longer Facebook posting, or better used as evidence for a change in library policy.

Comment policies for libraries' social media

Many libraries are concerned about comments on their websites. There is a common feeling that, as supporters of free expression, any attempt to control or moderate the user discussion on blogs or Facebook pages will be considered censorship, and somewhat hypocritical. These libraries are, of course, assuming that there will be a lot of discussion and community engagement on their blogs and website. While the library's goal is to have an active community participating online, its website, blog or Facebook page will probably not get as much traffic as the staff think.

Developing comment moderation policies does not mean that the library is practising censorship; the policies ensure that the library's social media presence is respectful and (mostly) on topic. Anil Dash (2011) provides simple (but potentially labour intensive) guidelines that will ensure that your website is supportive of engaged users interested in true dialogue:

- Develop community policies about acceptable behaviour, and enforce them.
- Dedicate staff time to monitoring and interacting with your users.
- Require users to sign their comments with a 'persistent' identifier.
- 'Have the technology to easily identify and stop bad behaviour' (ibid., section 'This is a solved problem', para. 7).

Dash (in his final sentence) concludes by saying that 'if you don't [follow these guidelines], you're making the web a worse place. And it's your fault' (ibid.).

Community acceptable behaviour policies

The 'acceptable behaviour' policy that a site defines for users who are commenting on a website does not need to be as comprehensive as the typical library acceptable use policy for patrons using the library's public PCs or wifi. Dash recommends that the policy is short, written in plain language and flexible, so that 'people aren't trying to nitpick the details of the rules'. Librarians are often concerned about being seen as 'censors', or as trying to shut down free speech, when the topic of website moderation is raised, but blocking spammers and ensuring that a discussion stays on topic without *ad hominem* attacks or insults is not censorship. Just remember that disagreeing with you, or arguing with other members of the community, is not inappropriate behaviour (Niles, 2010).

Monitoring and interacting with your users

Managing a community is labour intensive but it is essential to ensure that your site can attract and maintain a community of users and isn't taken over by comment spam. When you first launch your library's Facebook page or blog it won't have very much traffic, so monitoring the comments will not take very much time, but be prepared to increase the amount of staff time devoted to working with the community as it becomes more active. As important as moderating the users on your social media is interacting with them: the point of social media is to be *social*. The staff involved in managing the library's social media presence are ambassadors for the library. Answer users' questions, help them to find what they're looking for and guide the conversations that arise. Sometimes this can lead to concerns about patron confidentiality; I recommend leaving this to the discretion of the staff involved in the conversation. It is important to remember that if a patron asked a question in public, then they probably won't mind getting an answer in public. If you would rather answer the question privately, post a follow-up comment asking for contact information so that you can send your answer to them separately.

Users must have persistent identifiers

Users do not necessarily have to provide their 'real names' (Hinkley (2011) provides a good overview of why pseudonyms are valuable online) but requiring persistent identifiers of some sort simplifies tracking patterns of inappropriate behaviour and may reduce 'drive-by' trolling.[1] Facebook, Twitter and most large social media platforms already implement persistent accounts, so this is of concern only if you will be hosting a blog on the library's website or one of the blog hosting services mentioned earlier. A simple way for academic libraries to implement this policy on locally hosted blogs would be to require users to log in with their standard campus identity. Such a policy does preclude members of the general community from engaging with the library's social media, however, so if your library is interested in outreach to the local community and enabling engagement, especially with alumni who may no longer have valid campus computer accounts, this option may not be feasible. Consult local IT staff to see what your options are for implementing persistent identifiers for locally hosted blogs.

Identifying and stopping bad behaviour

If you are lucky, your Facebook page will be awash in conversations, your blog postings will inspire heated debates about the relative merits of the authors you profile and there will be so much traffic that it will be difficult for your staff moderators to keep up. Or, more likely, the staff responsible for monitoring and participating in your various social endeavours will only be able to devote time to the task during the normal working day, among all their other responsibilities. And it is when your moderators are most distracted that somebody will make himself known and start posting unpleasant comments that are in violation of your community guidelines. Most platforms provide a way for users of the site to 'flag' comments by other users as inappropriate. This will allow you to move quickly to deal with spam and harassment even when you don't have time to be fully involved in the conversations that are taking place. Just make sure to remember that people will flag things they don't like, even if they're not inappropriate.

While setting policies for staff posting to social networks such as the library – and for dealing with users commenting on Facebook and library blogs – are important, don't attempt to cover every possible eventuality in your policies before launching your social media presence. The new social network environment requires flexibility on the part of the library administration and trust in the library staff who will be managing the library's presence. Having basic guidelines and ensuring that staff are empowered to respond promptly and helpfully will make the experience better for both the library staff and the community, and will ensure that the library's social network grows.

Conclusions

Librarians often talk about being where our users are. In academic libraries, this has translated into holding reference office hours in departmental offices, student centres and even residence halls (Rudin (2008) surveys the literature regarding reference outreach). Today, the users are on Twitter and Facebook but they're not looking for the librarian there: social networking is first and foremost *social*. Users are not expecting research help via Twitter or a catalogue search box in Facebook but they are open to finding out about library services and events via their social channels, and they may appreciate knowing that library staff are paying attention when they complain about 'service quality' problems in the library via their social networks if the library responds promptly, honestly and as a human being rather than as an institution. Do not expect your new social networking presence to gain a lot of followers quickly, but if promoted well, and used appropriately, it will become an effective way to inform your community about events and services, and to provide customer support services.

Note

1. 'In Internet slang, a troll is someone who posts inflammatory, extraneous, or off-topic messages in an online community, such as an online discussion forum, chat room, or blog, with the primary intent of provoking readers into an emotional response or of otherwise disrupting normal on-topic discussion' (Wikipedia, 2011, para. 1).

References

Connell, R.S. (2009) Academic libraries, Facebook and MySpace, and student outreach: a survey of student opinion. *portal: Libraries and the Academy*, 9(1): 25–36. DOI:10.1353/pla.0.0036.

Dash, A. (2011) If your website's full of assholes, it's your fault. A blog about making culture [blog post]. Retrieved from *http://dashes.com/anil/2011/07/if-your-websites-full-of-assholes-its-your-fault.html*.

De Rosa, C., Cantrell, J., Havens, A., Hawk, J. and Jenkins, L. (2007) Sharing, privacy and trust in our networked world [report]. Dublin, OH: OCLC. Retrieved from *http://www.oclc.org/reports/sharing/*.

Dickson, A. and Holley, R.P. (2010) Social networking in academic libraries: the possibilities and the concerns. *New Library World*, 111(11/12): 468–79. DOI:10.1108/03074801011094840.

Goss, H. (2010) Extending library instruction: using Blogger to collaborate, connect, and instruct. *Journal of Library & Information Services in Distance Learning*, 4(4): 166–84. DOI:10.1080/1533290X.2010.524831.

Hinkley, K. (2011) On pseudonymity, privacy and responsibility on Google+ [blog post]. TechnoSocial. Retrieved from *http://www.marrowbones.com/commons/technosocial/2011/07/on_pseudonymity_privacy_and_re.html*.

Jacobson, T.B. (2011) Facebook as a library tool: perceived vs. actual use. *College & Research Libraries*, 72(1): 79–90.

Levine, R., Locke, C., Searls, D. and Weinberger, D. (2000) *The Cluetrain Manifesto: The End of Business as Usual*. Cambridge, MA: Perseus Books.

Mack, D., Behler, A., Roberts, B. and Rimland, E. (2007) Reaching students with Facebook: data and best practices. *Electronic Journal of Special and Academic Librarianship*, 8(2). Retrieved from *http://southernlibrarianship.icaap.org/content/v08n02/mack_d01.html*.

Munroe, R. (2006) YouTube [cartoon]. Retrieved from *http://xkcd.com/202/*.

Niles, R. (2010) If you can't manage comments well, don't offer comments at all [blog post]. Retrieved from *http://www.ojr.org/ojr/people/robert/201003/1836/*.

Rudin, P. (2008) No fixed address: the evolution of outreach library services on university campuses. *Reference Librarian*, 49(1): 55–75.

Wikipedia (2011) Troll (Internet). Retrieved from *http://en.wikipedia.org/wiki/Troll_(Internet)*.

Learning social media: student and instructor perspectives

Robert Foster and Diane Rasmussen Neal

Abstract: What is it that students are looking for to help them engage in courses today? Social media tools, which most students in university have grown up with over the past decade, help enhance the experience and provide a relatively new way for teachers to actively engage their students. How successful these tools are, like any teaching method, very much depends on the student and on the methods employed by the teacher. This chapter reviews the teaching and learning of social media tools and the methods employed by Dr Diane Rasmussen Neal in her 'Social software and libraries' course in the Faculty of Information and Media Studies at The University of Western Ontario. Three students and the instructor provide their views, giving their perspectives on the course, including the social media tools employed in course delivery.

Key words: Edmodo, blogs, social media, teaching, student perspective, instructor perspective, distance education.

Introduction

> 'The importance of engaging students in new and emerging technologies in education cannot be overestimated.'
>
> (Tadros, 2011, p. 84)

What are the students of today really looking for when they enrol in a course at a college or university? Or perhaps a more appropriate question might be: How do teachers actually get their students tuned in and fully engaged to the topic at hand? As a student, it is my belief that through the adoption and use of modern technology, particularly social media tools, the instructors in the post-secondary academic setting can provide a much more comprehensive and, frankly, interesting programme for today's 'tech-savvy' students.

We are now living in a social media world. And the numbers are compelling. As at the end of September 2011, Facebook claimed it had over 800 million user accounts. Twitter, another mainstream social media tool, reported in the same month that they had over 100 million active users. After the failure of Google Buzz, Google has made another entry into the social networking field with Google+. YouTube and other media sharing sites such as Flickr remain popular. And other recent social media trends, such as location-based technologies like Foursquare or location-based capabilities in Twitter and Facebook, continue to grow in popularity.

Social media sites are no longer just person-to-person relationships. Both the business and political worlds have adopted and use social media tools for outreach to the world. Corporations such as Walmart, McDonald's, Best Buy and many others deliver information to customers through social media channels, providing marketing, promotional and general information for their followers. In the political field, parties and individual politicians now make heavy use of social media to get their messages out. The now-classic example of the power of social media is Barack Obama's quest for the US presidency in 2008. As was noted by David Carr (2008) in *The New York Times* just ahead of the new President's swearing-in, using social media 'was an online movement that begot offline behavior, including producing youth voter turnout that may have supplied the margin of victory' (para. 12). Even in the Canadian setting politicians are now using these technologies, with Treasury Board president Tony Clement apparently being the model to follow. Mia Pearson (2011), writing on the use of social media in the political sphere for *The Globe and Mail*, noted that '[w]ith frequent tweets and an honest, personable style, Mr. Clement has earned praise for his approach to Twitter and has built a large following' (para. 24).

The reality is that today's college and university-age generation, having grown up with these technologies, make heavy use of social media tools. While I do not have statistical proof, I can say anecdotally both watching and dealing with my own children and discussing with others of the same age that the social media tools of today are the communication methods of choice. And their use continues to expand with new and more powerful devices, a slew of new operating systems, expanded and cost-effective wireless capabilities, and the development of both fun and practical applications fuelling the use of social media. Thus, when it comes to academia, these are technologies that should be explored and adopted to meet the needs of today's students.

One of the most interesting and, in my opinion, relevant courses to my future role in the library world was taught by the editor of this book, Dr Diane Rasmussen Neal, at The University of Western Ontario (UWO) in the winter of 2011. Entitled 'Social software and libraries', this was an online course that explored a wide array of social media applications, including blogs, wikis, social bookmarking, and online social networks. Since it was an elective course for the Master of Library and Information Science degree, the course also focused on the role of social media software in the context of library service provision.

Designing and delivering a class in social media

Our 'Social software and libraries' course had been a favourite among our students even before I started teaching it in winter 2011. The previous instructor had only taught the course online. The administration asked me to teach two sections of the class in the same term and suggested that I teach one section online and one face-to-face. Since I had taught courses online since 2004 and I possess a strong interest in online education pedagogy, I requested that both sections be taught online. I felt strongly that *using* social media to teach students *about* social media made the most pedagogical sense. With this approach, the course delivery itself becomes part of the learning experience. Ultimately, we decided to combine the two sections into one large section, with 39 students enrolled in total.

At the time, the university officially supported the use of WebCT to deliver online courses. However, widespread student and instructor dissatisfaction with the system, as well as its lack of a social media 'feel', led me to decide against using it. Instead, I planned a number of delivery methods. Thanks to a friend's recommendation, I discovered *http://www.edmodo.com* for course management. Edmodo is a social learning website that 'provides teachers and students a secure place to connect and collaborate, share content and educational applications, and access homework, grades, class discussions and notifications. Our goal is to help educators harness the power of social media to customize the classroom for each and every learner' (Edmodo, 2012, para. 1). As of March 2012, the site claimed to serve over 6,500,000 students and teachers. Edmodo has a 'look and feel' that is similar to Facebook. The instructor creates a secure, private 'group' for each class, and everyone in the class can post files, links and comments. As a free, cloud-based service, the instructor has no need for financial resources or technical support. My university upholds academic freedom by stating that we can use any resource we choose for online course delivery; I admittedly felt quite liberated by making this choice. The students and I used Edmodo to communicate with each other, and every day we posted items of interest that we found in the news. Additionally, I requested that students contact me by private Edmodo message instead of email; any online instructor understands how overwhelming it can be to receive emails from students. This helped me organize my course communications and my time: when I was ready to work on the class each day, I logged into Edmodo, and everything was there.

I delivered most content through a course blog. On the same day each week, I posted a 'lesson' that contained my introduction to and thoughts about the week's topic, embedded links to readings and instructions for what the students needed to do to complete the lesson. I linked to each week's blog post in Edmodo when it was posted. The lessons consisted of the following topics.

1. Class introduction
2. Introduction to social media and libraries
3. Blogging and Really Simple Syndication (RSS)
4. Wikis and other collaboration tools
5. Mashups and 'non-text' user-generated content
6. Social media policies and assessment
7. Social networking
8. Microblogging
9. Bookmarking, tagging and folksonomies
10. Cloud computing
11. The mobile web
12. Virtual worlds and online games
13. Reflection and evaluation

In addition to text, I also provided screencasts and screenshots to explain how to complete more difficult tasks. For tasks that were slightly more technical, such as creating a mashup or subscribing to RSS feeds, these methods communicated much more effectively than text, and students indicated appreciation for them.

For each lesson, the students had to do hands-on tasks related to the lesson – set up a blog, edit a wiki, tag some items, etc. – and then discuss their experiences in their blog posts. Additionally, each student was required to start a class blog and blog about their experiences completing the lessons. I linked to all students' blogs on my blog so that students could read and comment on their peers' experiences.

I led an optional, weekly hour-long synchronous course chat in a Meebo group. Attendance at these chats was somewhat low but I posted a transcript of each week's chat in Edmodo so that students who were not able to participate in the chat could read it at their convenience.

Students' participation in the above social media interactions comprised their participation grade. In addition, they had to complete an individual report on a current social media topic of their choice, and an individually completed analysis of a library's social media offerings. The final project was a group project in which they had to create a social media plan, as well as sample sites and content, for a real or fictitious organization of their choice. I had made connections with a number of non-profit health organizations through professional connections for which some students completed their projects. Instead of creating a plan, one group led successful webinars on social media for a health organization's constituents.

The students' motivations and expectations for the course

Sara Wiseman, Samantha Thompson and I took the course on social media together. All three of us have similar student profiles in that time has lapsed between our original degree studies and our enrolment in the Master of Library and Information Science programme at UWO. At the same time, however, we brought quite different educational backgrounds and experience into Diane's course, providing a combination of views that supplied wide-ranging insights for the review of this type of class. Sara received an honours degree in religious studies, with a major in fine arts. Samantha had recently completed her Doctorate in Philosophy after switching from earlier courses in music and physics. As for me, I originally studied mathematics and computer science after high school but eventually completed my degree in political science.

The three of us took this course for somewhat different reasons. Samantha enrolled in the course to force her to engage more with social media. She was of course interested in how libraries use social media but she had a lack of knowledge about these types of tools, thus providing a strong motivation for her. Very few of her friends and acquaintances were actively present in social networks. However, of those that were, several were very active in Facebook. One of Samantha's concerns was that, once she joined, her friends would only communicate with her via this media. As she noted, 'I didn't want to be constrained to have to check a Facebook account frequently to keep in contact with one or two people.'

Samantha admitted that she had a lot of apprehension regarding social media and it very much took her out of her comfort zone:

> I was worried about being overwhelmed by these tools. I wasn't so much worried about their being difficult to use in themselves (after all, they're supposed to be user-friendly) as with their being difficult to manage (with number of accounts, number of passwords, number of people I would come into contact with, number of features and ways of communicating per tool). I felt that I was getting into the game at a late stage, and wouldn't feel comfortable or at home with these media. I was therefore hoping that Diane's course would hold my hand as I dove into this new world, and show me a way to use social media in a discerning way.

Sara came at the course very much from the library and future employment point of view. She noted that both in her library and Master's degree experience she was seeing major changes taking place in libraries. Information must be available online, and its use was growing both in public and academic libraries. Her first taste of this came when she purchased her first electronic book reader. As she noted, she suddenly found it inconvenient to make a trip to the public library to pick up a book instead of just downloading it at home in a matter of minutes; a visit to the library for many now happens in a virtual world. Sara decided to take this course realizing that library staff must be proficient in this area, and that it would be advantageous for her in gaining post-degree employment if she understood these technologies. Sara's expectation for the course was that she would learn more about the various social networking tools. As the course was geared to library and information science students, she expected to learn about the relevance of social media in libraries.

My perspective was a little different from my colleagues. I came into the class figuring that it would be a pretty easy credit for me. My background before joining the Master's programme at UWO was in information technology, having begun my career in programming and having eventually worked my way into project management. Perhaps somewhat naïvely I also felt I knew social media well, particularly having been an early adopter and an active user of Facebook. So, my expectation in taking the course was that it would be fairly simple and would provide a good overview of a variety of technologies that I had not used before.

The instructor's expectations

I like to think that my expectations for the course were fairly straightforward. First, as noted above, I expected that the students would use social media to learn about social media. The first week's activities included setting up their own blog, writing an introductory post on the blog, setting up an Edmodo account, and introducing themselves on Edmodo. Tasks varied as the course progressed, such as editing a Wikipedia entry, trying a social network new to them, and so on. Obviously, if they were not able to do the weekly activities they would not be able to complete the class. For this reason, I see my course design as opposite to other courses about social media in my faculty, in which the class discusses social media from a critical or theoretical perspective. Hands-on experience is essential to learning how to use new technologies, and complementary to these other courses.

This is not to say that the course was void of critical thinking. I expected the students to think about social media policy from an organizational perspective. For example, should libraries delete inflammatory patron posts on their official social media channels, or is that the antithesis of the spirit of social media? What are the privacy concerns involved in putting organizational data on social media and in the cloud? What are the ways to write social media content that engages and involves constituents, as opposed to using it as a one-way announcement channel? Which social media outlets are best for different sizes and types of libraries? These questions are difficult to answer; the industry does not have answers for exactly how to navigate the emerging Web 2.0 world, but my students have the opportunity to help answer them in their future careers.

I did not expect students to become programmers or high-level technical experts by taking my course. One power of social media is that users do not have to be hard-core 'techies'; there is no need for most of us to understand or implement the underlying structures. Despite this intent, it surprised me to find that some students were even reticent to work with technology on a level that matched my expectations, perhaps that of a 'power user'.

Students' views about the course

Communication, and the tools provided for doing this successfully, was a key component of the class's success. Edmodo, Diane's weekly blog post, the weekly chat, and the outline of the methods by which and times when we could contact her with questions and concerns were all important. This was a distance course so most students lived off-campus; communication with the instructor and other classmates can be a little daunting if communication modalities are not spelled out or clearly understood.

Sara liked the fact that we were expected to familiarize ourselves with the various tools and report to the class on our experiences. As she noted, Diane's lectures provided guidance for those of us using a social media tool for the first time, as well as some discussion about the use and relevance of the tool. Sara thought that this teaching method generally worked well for social software, which definitely needs to be learned hands-on. Some of the tools examined in the class, such as RSS feeds and wikis, were completely new to Sara. In these cases in particular, Diane's blog posts were really helpful. For instance, she explained step-by-step how to set up and use RSS feeds. Most social software programs are designed to be user-friendly, and they were not too difficult to learn. However, the more technical exercises, such as building a mashup and posting it online, were much more challenging to learn by distance. For Sara, the more technical assignments would have been easier to learn in a computer lab with a teacher on hand for assistance.

Samantha found that the Edmodo software was generally effective for congregating and sharing. As Samantha discovered, Edmodo's interface is like a stripped-down version of Facebook, so much so that when she finally started using Facebook it wasn't quite so daunting. As she noted, it was also interesting to observe some of the intra-student mentoring that was taking place. Some students had much more experience than others, and on this platform we were all able to share ideas with the whole class. As Samantha noted, because Edmodo is itself a social network, it's a way of showing rather than telling what social media is all about. Facebook could have been used, but Samantha's guess is that it would have lacked the educational features of Edmodo (such as places to post grades) while having a glut of other features that would have cluttered a group page.

Both Sara and I also quite enjoyed using Edmodo. We spent a lot of time during the term posting articles and comments, using the tool in much the same way as Facebook. We both agreed with Samantha that the tool's similarity to Facebook made it an easy tool to pick up and use (both of us were active on Facebook prior to taking this course).

Samantha also liked the use of the blog for Diane's course materials. She considered it effective as a teaching tool because it was naturally chronologically organized (as lectures would be) and because it allowed us to 'keep' all our instructional material in one organized place accessible from any computer.

However, there were other tools used in the course that were not so successful in the way of communication. For example, there was an optional weekly Meebo chat session for members of the class which, due to other commitments, I was unable to attend. Sara attended regularly but was generally disappointed both with the substance and the tool being used. She felt that the chats might have been more successful had they been structured differently. For example, in another distance class that Sara had taken she was required to participate in two out of five online chats. These chats were well attended by students and each chat was structured as a discussion of a specific issue or topic. While Meebo was not difficult to use, Sara would have liked to have tried a different platform for instant messaging. For example, in the course we learned about Tweet chats and Facebook group chats; it would have been interesting to have tried either of these platforms at least once.

Diane provided an interesting variety of social media tools for us to explore on a weekly basis. As Samantha pointed out, she found that actually having to log on to various social media platforms and try them out was not only valuable but the only way to get to know what they are capable of. Because we were looking at a different platform or technology each week, it was difficult to really get to know the ins and outs of the various tools. However, we learned enough about each tool so that we all got a sense of how they compared to each other.

For the class, there was a group project to design a tool suite to fit an organization's needs. Samantha's and Sara's group agreed, after reviewing the organization they had decided upon, that, in fact, less can be more, and identified a minimalist social media plan. As Samantha noted, however, the organization their group was working with did not want this as the solution, and, as a result, the organization was quite unimpressed with the result. My group, on the other hand, did the exact opposite, outlining a fairly comprehensive and multifaceted social media plan for the organization that we reviewed. However, in this case, the organization in the end wasn't interested in expanding to a full social media suite and they, too, were unimpressed with the results. I think our conclusion from this project was that one must really understand not only the tools but also the culture of an organization before embarking on a social media programme.

Students' take-aways from the course

We all came away from the course with a much better appreciation for social media than we had when we started. In particular, we have all become very aware of the role that social media plays in many of the fast-breaking current events, locally, nationally and internationally.

Sara's take-aways

> I often find myself turning to Twitter and Facebook now for information as news events unfold, like the recent Vancouver riot or Jack Layton's announcement that he was temporarily stepping down as leader of the NDP [New Democratic Party]. I find that Twitter is a particularly good source of information, because I am able to follow authors and journalists who write on topics that are of interest to me. My connections on these sites link me to articles and news stories that I would likely miss otherwise.
>
> Now that I have taken Diane's class, I often find myself critiquing the way organizations, businesses and even people use social media. I just started to volunteer with a small charitable organization that offers free meditation and yoga classes to prisoners in Canada. Unfortunately, this organization has received some unwarranted bad press lately. In recent months, a provincial politician has repeatedly cited this organization as an example of how taxpayers' dollars are being wasted, although in fact the group receives no government funding. The organization does not really have any money to use for publicity, and they have not done anything to set the record straight. I can see how they could use social media to get a message out to the public, quickly and cheaply. By using hashtags or mentions on Twitter, they

could add their voice to the ongoing discussions about provincial politics, and be heard by politicians, journalists and the public.

Sara came away from the course actively engaged with the tools. As her friend on Facebook, I've been following her posts that have looked at library issues as well as various current social and topical issues. Many of her posts are designed to stimulate conversation among her sphere of friends, making us think about our views.

Samantha's take-aways

> I came to realize that many users only scratch the surface of what certain platforms are capable of. If you want to get the most out of social media, you need to spend some time investigating all the features of each platform; above all, you need to be on them and play around with them. Unfortunately, time is what I have lacked in the last few months, so my engagement with social media is not much greater than before I took the course. However, I know that when I'm ready to jump in I'll do so with much more confidence and discernment – if only I can remember my passwords!

> Last, I should say that prior to taking the course, I had a certain amount of shame or embarrassment at being behind the times (I'm not that old!). It was heartening to find that others (including many younger than me!) were in the same position. Indeed, it's simply not true that 'everyone does it'. I think that certain personalities are more attracted by social media than others. While I'm not particularly, and so was initially somewhat dismissive of this technology as a time-waster or a threat to privacy, I now see that it presents a lot of real advantages in both work and social life. Chief among these is the possibility of collaboration between physically distant people and organizations.

Samantha came away from the course realizing that these various social media tools all have a use and they should be chosen judiciously according to the goal. It is her view that you don't need to do everything and that, in most cases, one shouldn't try. It is best to use one or two of the tools very well rather than using many half-heartedly. Samantha is looking to start a personal blog, something she would not have considered had she not taken the course.

Robert's take-aways

The course provided a greater appreciation for the tools and the technologies that are currently available and, indeed, provided some insight as to where social media is going in the future. Examining and making use of the various tools were key factors to the success of the course. In my case, from having none to now looking after six, blogs are an important communications tool for a variety of businesses and projects I am involved with. Twitter has also become an important tool which I make use of in my political role (I am an elected councillor in my home town). I have also worked with several businesses, offering insight into social media tools and providing guidance on their successful implementation.

As I mentioned earlier, Diane clearly designed the course to force students to get involved with social media at a level at which they might not normally get involved. It is always very interesting to watch the dynamics in a physical classroom, particularly in my current Master's degree programme. Everyone in the room is motivated and all have proved they can learn, given their academic accomplishments to date. Yet, there are those such as myself who tend not to get too involved in discussions in the classroom setting. The way in which Diane designed her course encouraged students to participate, to put views forward and to offer critiques on others' postings. Personally, I felt surprisingly comfortable, particularly using Edmodo and the blogs, in putting forth both views and topics of interest. In fact, having now taken some other online courses as part of my degree, it is my view that more professors should make use of at least some of these tools to enhance the online experience. Further, a strong argument can be made that professors delivering programmes in a regular classroom setting would benefit themselves and their students by making use of several of the social media tools that are readily available.

The instructor's take-aways from the course

In August 2011, my colleague, Lu Xiao, and I presented the results of an empirical study of this winter 2011 class at the Information Science and Social Media Conference in Turku, Finland. The research did not proceed as originally planned due to a lack of willing participants but in the end I performed discourse analysis on the blogs of five students who took the course, approaching the blogs 'as constructed within a community of learners who were engaged in publicly sharing their collective educational experiences' (Neal and Xiao, 2011, p. 111). The following interpretative repertoires (Potter, 1996) emerged from my analysis:

1. Definitive growth occurred in the students' understanding of social media throughout the term.
2. Past experience influenced students' experience with class activities.
3. Quasi-public informal sharing of personal learning experiences led to a sense of community among the students. (Neal and Xiao, 2011, p. 111.)

These findings, as well as my teaching evaluations, told me that the course had gone quite well. However, when instructors teach a course for the first time, a naturally resulting question is how they can improve it the next time they teach it. Very early in my teaching career, one of my mentors told me that it took her three attempts to get a course right: the first time to see what works and what doesn't work; the second time to try some changes; and the third time to make changes feel comfortable with them. Now that I have taught this course three times, I have reached that point.

Despite small tweaks here and there, I have retained most of the course structure. Since the social media world changes so rapidly my most important focus is on keeping the material up-to-date. In the past year alone, new and 'hot' sites such as Google+ and Pinterest have entered the spotlight. It is not possible to teach technology courses without staying up-to-date, a fact I have worked with since I started teaching technology courses in 2004. However, I try to remain balanced in this regard: I cannot expect myself to track every new social network, gadget or news update. Many of the topics that I cover in class are relatively constant (for now), and I can update the blog posts and supplement them with Edmodo posts as I see items in the news.

The most substantial change I've made to the course delivery is the weekly chats. I found that making them optional tended to result in irregular and low student attendance. This meant that too few students got the benefit of the synchronous interaction, and I felt that my time was not well spent on the chat sessions. Therefore, I asked the administration to list my required weekly chat times in the registration information, to begin in the winter 2012 term. This allowed the students to plan their schedules accordingly. With all the students present, the chat sessions are fun and lively, and the hour goes by before we realize it!

In addition, since Meebo discontinued their group chat rooms in late 2011, I now use different software for the chats. Most weeks, we use Skype instant messaging; this works well because the instructor can create a Skype 'group' easily and I have a separate Skype account for each class. We have tried Twitter group conversations, using a hashtag that I specify to track the discussion, with varying levels of satisfaction. (Mostly, we concluded that Twitter is not a good modality for this type of discussion!) With the help of 'guest chatters' we have participated in real-time Flickr tagging exercises, watched my fellow gamer friends play the massive multiplayer online role playing game (MMORPG), World of Warcraft, using Skype's screen sharing feature and read through Facebook's and Google's privacy policies together. We learned through experimentation that Google+ Hangouts unfortunately only accommodate ten people at once, and that Skype voice calls don't work well at all with 20 people on the call! Although I believe it is possible to create community in a course asynchronously, these synchronous interactions provide social outlets as well as learning interactions that can feel lacking in an online course.

Conclusions from the student

> 'It's not enough for a course to be accessible online, it must also be designed in a way that keys into the digital pulse of current events, trending topics and insider knowledge endemic to the web.'
>
> (Masoni, 2010, para. 7)

We live in a social media world and it is important that these tools are adapted and adopted in the academic setting to face this reality. As I work towards my Master's degree, I continue to watch how my professors are making use of social media tools to help teach and prepare our classes for our future roles in the library field. On a current course I am taking, our instructor decided a few weeks into the class to use a blog to help enhance our understanding of the topic, a move I thought was very progressive. Yet he is one of the few professors in our institution who has taken advantage of this type of inexpensive, yet effective tool.

Diane's course provided our class with a good grounding in the tools available in the social media realm. But the course also showed us that social media tools themselves are an effective way of teaching in our 'tech-savvy' world. Generally speaking, university students today have grown up over the past decade using and understanding the multitude of technologies available. And with the advent of lower-cost, high-speed networks and smartphones, making use of social media continues to get easier and easier.

Conclusions from the instructor

I have been teaching online since 2004, and teaching social media use to librarians since 2006. It is a reality, however, that not all professors have my fortunate background in a climate where online courses are increasingly viewed by university administrators as positive, revenue-generating business decisions. This can feel uncomfortable to faculty members for many reasons: we might not feel like we're trained to teach online; we might resent the fact that we don't have instructional designers ready to translate our course materials into an online format; we might believe that it takes too much time to teach online; and so on. As Maureen Henninger and I discuss in Chapter 8 of this book, we can actually leverage the ease of using social media to assist us in addressing these issues.

Therefore, I can say with experience and confidence that using social media to teach is a pleasure. It does not involve dependence on university IT staff, the tools are easy to use and you can find free options for anything you need. Using social media to teach social media is, to me, a logical connection, because it requires students to use the tools they need to learn every time they 'go to class'. Hands-on experience is essential to learning new skills. After all, medical school students don't learn how to perform surgery solely by talking in a classroom about performing surgery – or, for that matter, by talking about it in an institutionally-sanctioned, expensive, IT department-controlled proprietary course management system.

References

Carr, D. (2008, 9 November) How Obama tapped into social networks' power. *The New York Times*. Retrieved from *http://www.nytimes.com/2008/11/10/business/media/10carr.html*.

Edmodo (2012) About. Retrieved from *http://about.edmodo.com/*.

Facebook (2011) Statistics. Retrieved from *https://www.facebook.com/press/info.php?statistics*.

Felesky, L. (2008, 5 December) Social media strategy: inside Obama's online campaign. *CBC News*. Retrieved from *http://www.cbc.ca/news/technology/story/2008/12/04/felesky-rahaf.html*.

Masoni, M. (2010, 6 August) Why online education needs to get social. Retrieved from *http://mashable.com/2010/08/06/online-education-social/*.

Neal, D. and Xiao, L. (2011) 'The use of blogs in online courses: a case study', in *Proceedings of the International Conference on Information Science and Social Media*, (pp. 107–15). Åbo/Turku, Finland: Åbo Akademi University. Retrieved from *http://issome2011.library2pointoh.fi/wp-content/uploads/2011/10/ISSOME2011-proceedings.pdf*.

Pearson, M. (2011, 22 September) Party platform: take a page from politicians on social media use. *The Globe and Mail*. Retrieved from *http://www.theglobeandmail.com/report-on-business/small-business/party-platform-take-a-page-from-politicians-on-social-media-use/article2174686/*.

Potter, J. (1996) *Representing Reality: Discourse, Rhetoric, and Social Construction*. Thousand Oaks, CA: Sage.

Tadros, M. (2011) 'A social media approach to higher education', in C. Wankel (ed.). *Cutting Edge Technologies in Higher Education: Educating Educators with Social Media, Volume 1* (pp. 83–105). Bingley, UK: Emerald Group Publishing.

Twitter (2011) One hundred million voices [blog post]. Retrieved from *http://blog.twitter.com/2011/09/one-hundred-million-voices.html*.

Index

Academia.edu, 31–2
AcademiaMap, 24–6
academic bloggers, 5, 7, 14
academic blogging, 3–4
   features of, 7–8
   getting started with, 7–13
   growth of, 7
   terminating, 12–13
academic blogs
   benefits of, 5–6
   directory listing of, 5
   drawing attention to, 11–12
   improvement strategies, 6–7
   motivations for, 5
   network of, 5
   publishing of, 7–11
   terms and policies for, 9–11
   and Twitter, 119
academic libraries
   ambassadors for, 207
   definition of, 204
   for social media, 193–209
Academic Search, 69–72
academics
   social networking sites for, 21–36
   Twitter for, 107–8, 116–18
Adobe Connect, 146
Atom, as syndication format, 12

backchannel, 128
back-up, of blogs, 14

bibliographic tools
   benefits of, 90
   brief history of, 87–9
   choosing the right tool, 101–3
   CiteULike, 67, 97–100
   Connotea, 97–100
   cost of, 101–2
   EndNote, 87–9
   Mendeley, 67, 95–7
   mobile technology and, 102
   online, social, 87–100
   RefWorks, 87–9, 197
   role in research, writing and collaboration, 101
   types of, 93–100
   uses of, 90–3
   Zotero, 93–5, 197
bibliometric analysis, 62–3, 68, 71, 73, 75, 77
big data, 179–80
Blackboard
   as learning management system, 148
   in online learning, case study, 151–2
   in teaching, 113–14
   as virtual conference tool, case study, 155
blog directory listing, 5
blog platforms, 195
blog tools, 8

bloggers, 195. *See also* academic bloggers
blogging, 194–5. *See also* academic blogging
blogs, 4, 106–7, 166–7. *See also* academic blogs
   academic publishing of, 7–11
   back-up of, 14–17
   communication through, 13
   as online learning tool, 146, 219
   preservation of, 13–17

Camtasia, 145
chat, 43
citation analysis, 69
citation metrics, 92
CiteSeer, search engine, 60
CiteULike, 67, 97–100
classroom, division of, 128
co-authorship, in blog publishing, 17
co-blogs, 7
collaborative networks, in research and teaching, 39–54
collaborative work tools, for online learning, 147
communication, 39–40
community acceptable behaviour policy, 207
Connotea, 97–100
content management system (CMS), 171, 195
copyright, for academic blogs, 10
Creative Commons licence, 10, 15, 197
crowdsourcing, 111–12

data type, in real-time technologies, 50
digital footprint, 178–80, 188
digital preservation, 13–14
digital tools, 41–2, 49
Dropbox, 39, 126

Edmodo, 124, 148, 213–15, 218–19
e-learning. *See* online learning
Elluminate Live, 146
Elsevier, 73–5
EndNote, 87–9

Facebook, 22–3, 42, 79, 162–4, 166, 181, 193–4
   creating a page, 198–200
   privacy best practices, 184, 186–7
   promoting and managing the page in, 201–4
   as social networking service, case study, 149–51
   as virtual conference tool, case study, 155–6
the filter bubble, 167–8
Filttr, 120
frontchannel, 128

Generation Y, 53–4. *See also* Millennial generation
Google, 167–71
Google+, 26–8, 180
Google Alerts, 188
Google Docs, 39, 42, 44–5, 49–50, 147
   privacy issues, 183–4
Google forms, 45
Google+ Hangouts, 43–4, 49
Google PageRank, 167
Google privacy policy, 180
Google Reader, 12
Google Scholar, 63, 66–7, 170–1

hashtags, 26, 108–9
Horizon Report, 124
Hotseat, 127–9
HUBzero, 33
hyperbolic visualizations, 62–3

identity, online, 115, 176–7
  personal and professional, 180–2, 188–90
IdentityGuard, 190
InSciences.org, 33
instant messaging, 50
institutional privacy, 52
institutional repository (IR), 171–2
Internet Archive, 14

Kaywa reader, 133
KnowledgeNetwork, 33

learning management system (LMS), 113–14, 148–9
legal content, 67–8
Library of Congress' Legal Blawgs Web Archive, 14
library's Facebook page, 201–4
LifeLock, 190
LinkedIn, 164–5, 172, 187
locating scholarly papers of interest online, 59–80
LOCKSS (Lots Of Copies Keeps Stuff Safe), 15

Meebo, in online learning, 219
Mendeley, 67, 95–7
MethodSpace.com, 33
microarticle, 29
microblogging, 105, 107, 195–6
Microsoft's Academic Search, 63, 66, 69–73
Millennial generation, 53. *See also* Generation Y
Mixable, 126–7
mobile technology
  academic, uses of, 125
  applications in higher education, 123–38
  bibliographic tools and, 102
  marketing peripheral services for, 125
  teaching and learning using, 125
Moodle
  as a learning management system, 148
  in online learning, case study, 151
  in teaching, 113–14
MSN Messenger, 48

network type, in real-time technologies, 49
non-academics, social networking sites for, 21–36

Office Live, 183
one-dimensional barcode, 130
online identity, 115, 176–7, 180–2, 188–90
online learning
  communication policies for, 143
  engagement and interaction in, 141–4
  infrastructure for students in, 146–7
  management systems for, 148
  tools for, 144–9
online reference management tools. *See also* bibliographic tools
Open Access Initiative-Protocol for Metadata Harvesting (OAI-PMH), 65
Open Access movement, impact of, 63, 65
Open Source Scientific Software (OSSS), 30

patent documents, 68
policies and procedures, for social media, 204–7

privacy
    best practices for, 184–8
    data, 182–8
    definition of, 177–8
    in social networking sites, 175–91
privacy loss, 52
productivity paradox, 51
professional branding, 115–16
proprietary scholarly search services, 74–9. *See also* Scopus search interface; Web of Science
public scholarly search services, 59–74, 79. *See also* Google Scholar; Microsoft's Academic Search; Scirus service
Purdue's information technology, 126–7
push vs. pull technology, in real-time technology, 50–1

QR codes
    Boise State, use of, 135
    linkages to online content in physical space, 130–8
    potential of, 135–6
    use of, 131–2

rDmap (Research Discovery Map), 33
Really Simple Syndication (RSS), 11–12, 113, 166–7
real-time technologies, 39–54
    challenges of/detriments of, 51–3
    concept of, 41–2
    definition of, 41
    dimensions of, 49–51
    research and, 42–7
    teaching and, 48–9
RedLaser, 133
reference management. *See* bibliographic tools

reference manager software, key requirements for, 88–9
RefWorks, 87–9, 197
research
    real-time technologies and, 39–54
    Twitter and, 110–13
ResearchGate.net, 28–30
retweeting, 110
revision control, 47

Sakai
    as learning management systems, 148
    in online learning, case study, 151
scalability, in real-time technology, 49–50
scholar blogs. *See* academic blogs
scholarly communication, 5, 13, 61–2
scholarly literature, 61–2
scholarly papers
    locating online, 59–80
    search services, 60–3
scholarly sites, 28–32
Science Citation databases, 62–3
Science Exchange, 47
ScienceFeed.com, 33
Scientific WebPlus, 77
Scirus service, 65–6, 73–4
SciVerse Scopus, 65, 74–5, 77
Scopus search interface, 65, 74–5, 77
search engine optimization (SEO), 168
search engines
    functionality of, 65
    proprietary scholarly, 74–9
    public scholarly, 59–74, 79
    web-based scholarly, 59–80
semantic search, 181–2
SketchPad, 47
Skype, 39, 42–3, 49–50, 145, 224

Index

social media, 61–2, 67, 69, 79,
  161–72
  for academic libraries, 193–209
  benefits of, 22
  blogging, 194–5
  comment policies for libraries in,
    206–7
  designing and delivering classes in,
    213–15
  developing policies and procedures
    for, 205–6
  Facebook, 79, 197–204
  identifying and stopping bad
    behaviour in, 208–9
  microblogging, 195–6
  monitoring and interacting with
    users, 207
  for online learning, 146–7
  online learning course on. *See*
    Social software and libraries
    course
  persistent identifiers in, 208
  policies and procedures for, 204–7
  student and instructor's
    perspectives on, 211–25
  tools in research and teaching, 40
  Twitter, 195–6, 203–4
  types and sites of, 194–8
  video sharing site, 196–7
  YouTube, 203
Social Media Lab blog, 33
social media tools
  impact on academics, 211–13
  instructor's view on, 225
  online learning and, 149–58
social networking, 163–71
  blogs, 166–7
  Facebook, 162–4, 166
  Google, 167–71
  LinkedIn, 164–5, 172
  opportunities in, 69, 73, 75, 77
  Twitter, 162, 164, 166, 172
  YouTube, 162, 165–6, 172
social networking sites (SNSs)
  Academia.edu, 31–2
  AcademiaMap, 24–6
  academic, 21–36
  benefits of, 22
  in classroom services, case study,
    149–51
  Facebook, 22–3
  Google+, 26–8
  non-academic, for online scholarly
    communities, 21–36
  overview of, 21
  privacy settings for, 175–91
  ResearchGate.net, 28–30
  Twitter, 23–4, 105–20
social privacy, 52
Social software and libraries course
  instructor's expectations of,
    217–18
  instructor's take-aways from,
    222–4
  student's expectations of, 215–17
  student's take-aways from, 220–2
  student's view on, 218–20, 224–5
Spezify, 188

tag clouds, 92, 112
TapMedia's QRReader, 133
teaching
  and real-time technologies, 39–54
  and Twitter, 113–15
Technorati, 3–4, 106
traditional barcodes, 130
tumblelogs, 107
Tumblr, 195
TweetDeck, 112–13, 120
tweeter, 105, 107, 120

tweeting, 105, 119–20
tweetiquette, 108, 110
tweets, 105, 108–9
Twitscoop, 112
Twitter, 23–4, 162, 164, 166, 172, 193–6, 203–4
  for academics, 107–8, 116–18
  application programming interfaces in, 127
  for connection and collaboration, 118–19
  definition of, 107
  getting started, 108–10
  for news media, 107
  in online class delivery, 224
  overview, 105–7
  for politicians, 107
  privacy best practices, 187–8
  for professional engagement, 118–19
  research and, 110–13
  teaching and, 113–15

version control, 47
video sharing, 196–7
Vimeo, 196–7
viral marketing, for research, 161–72
virtual conferences, tools for, 155–8
VIVO, 33

Web 2.0, 106
Web of Science, 75, 77–9
WebCT, 148
White, Nancy, 118
wikis, 147
  in classroom services, case study, 151–5
  as virtual conference tools, case study, 155
WordPress, 195

YouTube, 162, 165–6, 172, 193, 196–7, 203

Zotero, 93–5, 197

Made in the USA
San Bernardino, CA
19 September 2016